Heike Kahlert, Waltraud Ernst (Eds.)

Reframing Demographic Change in Europe

Focus Gender

herausgegeben vom

ZIF
Zentrum für Interdisziplinäre
Frauen- und Geschlechterstudien
der HAWK FH Hildesheim/Holzminden/Göttingen
und der
Stiftung Universität Hildesheim

Band 11

LIT

Reframing Demographic Change in Europe

Perspectives on Gender and Welfare State Transformations

edited by

Heike Kahlert and Waltraud Ernst

LIT

This publication has been made possible with the support of the Ministry for Science and Culture of Lower Saxony, Germany.

Cover picture and page layout: Annika Worpenberg

Bibliographic information published by the Deutsche Nationalbibliothek
The Deutsche Nationalbibliothek lists this publication in the Deutsche Nationalbibliografie; detailed bibliographic data are available in the Internet at http://dnb.d-nb.de.

ISBN 978-3-643-10411-3

A catalogue record for this book is available from the British Library

Fresnostr. 2 D-48159 Münster
Tel. +49 (0) 2 51-620 320 Fax +49 (0) 2 51-922 60 99
e-Mail: lit@lit-verlag.de http://www.lit-verlag.de

Distribution:

In Germany: LIT Verlag Fresnostr. 2, D-48159 Münster
Tel. +49 (0) 2 51-620 32 22, Fax +49 (0) 2 51-922 60 99, e-Mail: vertrieb@lit-verlag.de

In Austria: Medienlogistik Pichler-ÖBZ GmbH & Co KG
IZ-NÖ, Süd, Straße 1, Objekt 34, A-2355 Wiener Neudorf
Tel. +43 (0) 22 36-63 53 52 90, Fax +43 (0) 22 36-63 53 52 43, e-Mail: mlo@medien-logistik.at

In Switzerland: B + M Buch- und Medienvertriebs AG
Hochstr. 357, CH-8200 Schaffhausen
Tel. +41 (0) 52-643 54 30, Fax +41 (0) 52-643 54 35, e-Mail: order@buch-medien.ch

In the UK by: Global Book Marketing, 99B Wallis Rd, London, E9 5LN
Phone: +44 (0) 20 8533 5800 – Fax: +44 (0) 1600 775 663
http://www.centralbooks.co.uk/html

In North America by:

Transaction Publishers
New Brunswick (U.S.A.) and London (U.K.)

Transaction Publishers
Rutgers University
35 Berrue Circle
Piscataway, NJ 08854

Phone: +1 (732) 445 - 2280
Fax: + 1 (732) 445 - 3138
for orders (U. S. only):
toll free (888) 999 - 6778
e-mail: orders@transactionpub.com

Contents

Heike Kahlert and Waltraud Ernst

Introduction

Demographic change in Europe has been a topic of great public and political interest since the 1990s. Most of the statistical prognoses on population development seem to indicate that the population of Europe is expected to decline and to age from the beginning of the 21st century. According to the data, however, there are many differences between the nation-states and regions of Europe. But differences do not only exist on the level of data, the debates also differ widely when it comes to the reasons and consequences of demographic change. These debates address demographic changes in fertility, ageing and migration. They address the transformation of the welfare state as well as changes in gender relations. Changes in gender relations sometimes function as a cause and sometimes as a consequence of demographic change. Do discourses on the declining and ageing population in Europe serve as a background for strategies and policies for the restructuring of the welfare state and gender relations? The discussion of these issues is only rarely linked systematically. The authors of this book make an effort to take them into account and develop their own results regarding their interrelation. In this way, this book aims to reframe demographic change in Europe by focussing on perspectives on gender and welfare state transformations.

A main aspect in these discussions is that in most countries throughout Europe the participation of women in the labour market has greatly increased since the 1960s. However, there is still gender segregation in the labour market; there are still differences in income between women and men; and there are still only few women in leadership positions in science, economy and politics.

A closer look at the division of labour in the private sphere clearly shows that here nearly nothing has changed in the traditional arrangement between women and men: Housework and care are still strong domains of women and only randomly shared equally within heterosexual partnerships. Is it possible to analyze the decreasing birth rates in the light of these gender arrangements as a birth strike? And is it possible to understand some men's open rejection to become fathers as a rejection of the traditional male gender role, being the 'breadwinners' for the family? What are the impacts of the demographic changes and the changes in gender relations on the structure and the possibilities of welfare states?

Since the 1980s, the understanding of welfare has been changing in modern welfare states under the influence of globalization and the growing weight of the economy. These changes concern the relationship between the state and the market, between the state and the family and between the market and the family.

The growing economic influence on the political can be described by increasing regimes of the market, growing support of competition, reducing the public sector in size, new instruments to reflect and optimize political practices like quality management, benchmarking and evaluation, and affirmation to values like family, community and nation. Could it be argued that the restructuring of the welfare state is ruled by masculinist standards?

An important part in the transformation of the welfare state under market conditions is a new connection between the private and the public spheres. The old model of the division of productive and reproductive work that was combined with traditional gender roles does not function anymore because the labour market currently demands mobile and flexible people. How does this affect life styles and, in particular, decisions to form a family? Which kind of family formation is supported by the state? Can it be argued that, as an effect of the new global economy, work is feminised in a double sense: as the increasing participation of women in the labour market and the decreasing security of (wages for) work traditionally done by men?

Because of the demographic change, the labour market seems to demand women to take part in it, and the welfare state seems to demand women to become mothers. Which are the new arrangements between women and men to be constructed in order to combine labour and private family life? The adult worker model is currently promoted by European politics. This model seems to enable more justice and equality between women and men and, in this respect, realizes an important socio-political demand of women's movements. However, the adult worker model only finds partial approval among feminist welfare state researchers and activists: It claims to ensure women's financial independence through employment (without equalizing the differences in wages between women and men), but fails to solve the problem of the asymmetric participation of the sexes in homemaking tasks.

One could argue that the decline in birth rates across most of Europe beginning in the 1960s corresponds to the asymmetric division of labour between women and men and the resulting social inequality. If one relates this idea to changes in demography, one could further argue that the asymmetric division of homemaking tasks between women and men seems to be a growing problem in the European welfare states, not only because of the problems of combining work and childcare, especially in conservative welfare states, but also because of the problems of combining work and care for the elderly. Seen in this light, the adult worker model produces new social inequalities, not only between women and men, but among women (and among men?) as well: In couples with two breadwinners, homemaking tasks can be delegated to other persons (mostly women), who not seldom have a precarious social and civic status as migrant workers, thereby making this new arrangement between the sexes possible. Seen in this light, does the adult worker model really solve problems of social and gender inequality? Does it also create new problems of social inequality that challenge the welfare state to act for equality?

About the contributions

The three trends just outlined – demographic change in Europe, transformation of the welfare state, simultaneity of continuity and change in gender relations – are seldom combined in international research and discussion. There is much research on each of these topics, and much research that tries to connect two of the three topics, e.g., demographic change and the transformation of the welfare state, or the restructuring of the welfare state from a perspective of gender. But there is less research on demographic change from the perspective of gender and even less research that tries to connect all three topics.

Thus, the central aim of this book is to create new questions for research by connecting the three topics in international comparison: demographic change, restructuring of the welfare state (or, better: of welfare in European societies and on the transnational European level) and change in gender relations. The articles in this book have a closer look at the interrelation of these social and political changes by highlighting different national situations as well as different theoretical and empirical aspects. And they try to reframe the 'problem' of demographic change by analyzing it in the context of gender and welfare state transformations. The authors come from different disciplines, such as sociology, political science, law, pedagogy, social work, history and philosophy. They have different methodological and theoretical approaches and highlight different national settings and comparisons. Together, the papers present a critical analysis on current political and social developments concerning the interrelatedness of gender relations, restructuring politics of the welfare state and discourses on demographic change in Europe.

The first three papers deal with *Theories and Politics of Demographic Change*. In her paper entitled "The (Missing) Welfare State in Demography – Critical Remarks on the Idea of the 'Second Demographic Transition' from a Gender Perspective", *Heike Kahlert* focuses on the question of how to analyze demographic change in a theoretical framework of wider processes of social change. Therefore, she deconstructs the concept of the 'Second Demographic Transition' and proposes to widen and deepen it from two different perspectives that she considers interrelated. Her first argument emphasizes the necessity to integrate the concept of 'gender' as a principle that organizes social and demographic change and as an analytical category. And her second argument relates to the necessity to integrate the concept of the welfare state and its politics to demographic theory. She argues that the welfare state is not only an agent in gender and demographic changes, but is also currently questioned by reforms inspired by economic rationality. Thus, in her perspective, the institution of the welfare state is not only changed in its philosophy, its structure and its tasks, but also in its power to shape demographic issues in society and politics.

In her article "Trojan Horses and the Implications of Strategic Framing: Reflections on Gender Equality Policies, Intimate Citizenship and Demographic Change", *Mieke Verloo* asks how gender equality is seen to be related to fertility and to demographic decline or growth in Europe. She investigates family policies of the European Union, ideologies of motherhood and traditional heterosexual families in rulings of the European Court of Justice. She detects a shift in articulated policy goals in policy texts of Austria, the Netherlands and Greece from 'gender equality' to 'reconciliation of work and family life', which brings with it a (re-)traditionalisation of thinking about families and the role of women in families. Verloo presents initial findings of the ongoing pan-European comparative research project on gender equality policies *QUING*. With a critical frame analysis, she shows how arguments are made that link 'gender' and 'improving the demographic balance' in governmental texts from Bulgaria, Croatia, Estonia, Germany, Hungary, Italy, Poland, Romania and Spain. She concludes that "European family policies to some extent have buried gender equality goals 'beneath' goals to strengthen the economy or the demographic balance". The author strives to identify the 'Trojan Horse' and calls for new feminist voices and positions on this issue.

In her paper "Gender Equality and Policies towards Women as Mothers in the Contemporary Norwegian Welfare State", *Nina Berven* investigates the seemingly paradoxical situation in Norway that despite extensive public policies and a high level of formal gender equality, many women are financially dependent on a spouse to form and maintain a household. Since Norway is among the states with the highest birth rate in European comparison, she has a closer look at Norwegian policy programmes for families with young children and asks how families adapt to them. Berven concludes that in Norway care is still a gender issue because a significantly higher percentage of women are employed part time than men. In addition, families reacted receptively (75 percent) to the 'Cash for Care' policy introduced by the Norwegian government in 1998, when there was not a sufficient supply of public child care. Furthermore, she states that this leads to a citizenship issue. Since many entitlements of the Norwegian welfare state are linked to employment, it is precisely because women, as mothers, perform care obligations much more frequently than men that women are deprived of the benefits of the welfare state.

The papers in the second section deal with the *Economies of Demographic Change* by relating the issue to the work of Michel Foucault. *Gabriele Michalitsch* draws on Austria as an example in her article "No Sharing, No Caring. Demographics, Gender Hierarchies and Neoliberal Restructuring". She links neoliberal labour and social policies to family policy and current demographic developments for her outline of mechanisms of reproduction of gender hierarchies within a theoretical framework of governmentality in alliance with Foucault. She shows the implicit gender rationality of neoliberalism within conservative family policy in Austria and relates it at crucial points to other European states. The author offers an interpretation of declining birth rates as an outcome of neoliberal transformation and as a de-politicised, individualized form of female resistance against discriminating societal circumstances.

In her paper "Dynamization of Gender and Generation – Shifting Orders and Ambivalent (Self-)Relations as Educational Challenges of Lifelong Learning in the Field of Social Work", *Jutta Hartmann* thoroughly investigates the concepts and strategies of lifelong learning. In doing so, she contrasts an existing need for lifelong learning processes in light of a dynamization of gender, generation and sexual identity with the implementation of lifelong learning programmes of the European Council, the UNESCO and the OECD. In her view, the latter tend to promote learning processes oriented towards self-functionalisation to adapt to a neoliberal state. Therefore, social work is challenged to reflect the ambivalent character of its educative tasks. Hartmann promotes social work to systematically expand educational spaces in order to challenge traditional arrangements of gender and generation and to enable and support dynamic shaping of a variety of ways of living.

In her paper entitled "People of Age in the Volunteer Sector and Demographic Change", *Ute Karl* discusses programmes initiated by the German government and the European Union to educate elderly people to do voluntary work as a 'seniorTrainer' from a perspective of governmentality. She shows, using the concepts of 'active ageing' or 'productive ageing' as a theoretical basis of gerontological models and in educational goals explicit in programmes such as 'self-organization', how a neoliberal, managerial rationale has entered voluntary work and civil engagement of older people. Karl concludes that, together with cutbacks in the social sector, especially in women's jobs, which are already often underpaid, this has consequences not only for older individuals but also for gender relations in the labour market.

Finally, the papers in the third section deal with *Symbolic Fields of Demographic Change*. *Mary Daly* and *Kirsten Scheiwe* present a detailed evaluation of recent developments in family law and social security in their article "Changing Gender Models in Law and Social Policy in Germany and the UK". They show that during the last ten years in both countries family policy and law has been a site of dramatic change which cannot simply be described as individualization or defamilization. Instead, it has been repositioning individuals in new relations to the family and the family towards the state and the market in rather contradictory ways. Nevertheless, they point out some cross-national trends in family law reform, such as the upgrading of child support claims over those of the ex-spouse after divorce and the extending of the fatherhood role.

Furthermore, the authors work out corresponding trends in changes in social security: the encouragement of mothers to become employed (through cutbacks of unemployment benefits), tax benefits for two-earner households and the growth in the provision of childcare services outside the home. In general, Daly and Scheiwe identify a change from marriage to parenthood as the main target of state support and control in both countries that eliminates and creates at the same time new inequalities concerning gender, class and sexuality.

In her article “Anti-Modernist Political Thoughts on Motherhood in Europe in a Historical Perspective”, *Andrea Petö* points to the contradiction that, in Hungary, there is a constant decrease in the birth rate since 1989 and in 2006, 35.6 percent of all children were born to unmarried women, while there is a growing political rhetoric on the normative motherhood of the Virgin Mary as well as a successful mobilization of women by neoconservative and extreme rightist women's movement. She draws from her empirical study on this movement and shows how the rhetoric of the Virgin Mary and her pre-Christian Hungarian sister, the ‘Woman dressed in Sun’, could become a site of resistance to the EU discourse on motherhood, which reminds too heavily of the statist feminist period and the failed leftist emancipation project in Eastern Europe, which promoted an increase in women's employment as a measure and precondition of emancipation and progress.

Waltraud Ernst explores the concept of citizenship in her article “Towards a Global Gender Democracy? Rethinking Citizenship in the Context of the Globalization of Gender Relations”. She argues that migrant workers in Europe, especially the often illegalized female care providers for the new gender arrangements, challenge the traditional concepts of citizenship on an epistemic, normative and empirical level in far reaching ways. Ernst opts for a concept of ‘democratic’ or ‘lived’ citizenship, which pushes forward the idea of citizenship that implicates democratic practises and feelings of belonging beyond formal rights and duties. She criticizes norms of homogeneity in the ideal of European citizenship and provides examples that link democratic participation on a local, national and transnational level as a step towards global gender democracy. Finally, she concludes that citizenship theory needs to reflect the empirical context of the globalization of gender relations, since it is in processes where hegemonic power structures are questioned that citizenship unfolds its democratic dimension.

Acknowledgements

The papers in this book were presented at the international conference “Demographic Change, Restructuring of the Welfare State and Gender Relations in European Comparison”. This conference was held on September 25-26, 2008 at the Centre for Interdisciplinary Women's and Gender Studies (ZIF) of the University of Applied Sciences and Arts Hildesheim/Holzminden/Göttingen and the University of Hildesheim, Germany. It was made possible through the support of the Maria-Goeppert-Mayer-Programme for International Women's and Gender Studies of the Ministry for Science and Culture of Lower Saxony, Germany. We are very grateful for their aid. We also thank the conjoint council of the ZIF for its support of our idea and the Department of Social and Organizational Pedagogy of the University of Hildesheim, namely Kirsten Scheiwe, for her advice and support in the planning process and the Department of Social Work and Health of the University of Applied Sciences and Arts for its cooperation. Furthermore, we are thankful to our colleagues at the ZIF, namely Sylke Bosse-Vahsen and Katharina Weichl, who arranged everything so pleasantly for the conference and Svenja Zimmer and Till Teske for their help. We thank Darrin Miral for the professional English language review of all the texts. And for the careful layout of the book, we thank Annika Worpenberg. Finally, we are very grateful to all the authors who agreed to discuss with us these complex topics in order to better understand ongoing social and political discourses and life transforming processes under the conditions of demographic change in Europe.

Theories and Politics of Demographic Change

Heike Kahlert

The (Missing) Welfare State in Demography – Critical Reflections on the Idea of the "Second Demographic Transition" from a Gender Perspective

1 Demographic change in Europe – a topic for critical societal analysis

At the spring summit of the European Union in Brussels in March 2007, the heads of state and government under the German council presidency agreed upon the creation of a 'European Alliance for the Family'.[1] The objective of this alliance is to give impetus to family-friendlier politics, in which ideas and experiences of the different member states are exchanged in the European Union, and co-operation as well as fruitful mutual learning is promoted. To this end, a web portal was developed.[2] The formation of this alliance is within the framework of existing activities and measures of the European Union to respond politically to the changes in population development that have had a long term effect and thus are far reaching, in particular low birth rates.

Demographic change in Europe encompasses different, but connected or not self-contained, demographic processes. These include a rise in life expectancy: Women born in 2006 in the EU-27 have an average life expectancy of 82.00 years and men of 75.84 years (cf. Eurostat 2009b). In the same year, the birth rate for the EU-27, with on average 1.53 children per woman, like previous years, lay clearly below the demographic preservation level of 2.1 children per woman (cf. Eurostat 2009a)[3]. Additionally, (EU-) Europe has shifted from

1 The article was written within the framework of the research project "Generativity and gender in welfare states – an international comparative analysis of institutions", which I held while guest professor at the Centre for Interdisciplinary Women's and Gender Studies of the HAWK University for Applied Sciences and Arts Hildesheim/Holzminden/Göttingen, and the Stiftung Universität Hildesheim between Summer Semester 2008 and Summer Semester 2009, supported by the Maria-Goeppert-Mayer-Programme for International Women's and Gender Studies of the Ministry for Science and Culture of Lower Saxony, Germany.

2 Cf. http://ec.europa.eu/employment_social/emplweb/families/index.cfm (10/07/2009).

3 Differences exist between the individual member states: in the Nordic countries, as

a continent from which people emigrated to a continent to which people (want to) immigrate. Accordingly, questions about the increasing multiculturalism in European welfare states, as well as the question of citizenship as it relates to immigration are on the political and social agenda and feed the controversial debate on the presumed need to preserve Europe's cultural legacy.

Although clearly all demographically relevant processes in Europe are in flux, the public spotlight has above all been focused on the decline in births, and the concomitant changes in family form, ways of life and gender relations. Enduring effects of the decline in births on the future of Europe are expected and feared. The demographic changes can have medium and long term effects on social and economic developments in Europe. In the light of the societal ageing process, the social systems of welfare assurance such as healthcare and pensions, which are based upon a balanced generational contract, are under pressure to be restructured. A decline in economic growth and with it a weakening of Europe's position on the global stage is feared in view of the expected process of shrinkage. The demographic data is thus also of importance for political actions in the present and future. Questions of demographic change, closely associated with changes in gender relations and the restructuring of welfare statism are consequently on the transnational political agenda of the European Union, but also on the political agenda of its member states (if taking shape in different intensities) (cf. Kahlert 2009).

In the social scientific analyses of present times, these connections in their complexity have so far been only insufficiently recognized. This is especially true of the connection between the change in gender relations and demographic change. That is first of all astounding because the closeness between gender questions and demographic developments is obvious, particularly looking at generativity. Demographic analyses also frequently refer to the gender question. However, this reference is mostly truncated, as the problematisation of demographically relevant changes is reduced to women. In contrast, gender as one of the principles of organizing society and thus as an analytical category finds here only very sporadic attention. Conversely, gender research has up to now also had difficulties comprehending the demographic change in Europe and other modern welfare societies (cf. as an exception Mason/Jensen 1995;

well as Ireland, in 2006 the birth rate stood at around 1.9 children per woman. In France it was even 2.0, whereas in the East European countries, but also in Germany and Italy the birth rate stood at around 1.4 children.

Gal/Kligman 2000a, 2000b; Berger/Kahlert 2006).[4] Particularly macro-sociological and multi-level analyses and international comparative studies on this subject are lacking (cf. Kahlert 2006a: 306-307).

The state of research regarding the connections between changes in welfare statism and demographic change is similarly in deficit. In welfare state research demographic change is necessarily considered, for example in relation to the associated challenges to the systems of social security, but also to the care and accommodation of children and older people. In this context the question of gender is also addressed (cf. for example Bauer/Gröning 2008), whereby admittedly even here gender is only sporadically considered as a principle which organizes society and thus as an analytical category. In contrast, demographic analyses seem to hardly consider the meaning of the welfare state and its developments to demographic change. In demography usually only two sides of the welfare triangle – (employment) market and family – are highlighted: the welfare state conversely receives little attention. At the same time, the construction of welfare statism in the 1960s and 1970s, and its reorganization and dismantling from the 1990s, but also socio-political attempts to influence demographic development, for example through family and gender policies, are without doubt demographically relevant.

The aim of the following socio-theoretical exposition is the development of a conceptual framework for the societal analysis diagnosing the current age, which enables one to capture the connections between demographic change, the transformation of gender relations and the transformation of welfare statism. The diagnosed gaps in demography are taken as the point of departure. In view of the necessary brevity of this article, admittedly only approximate contours of this framework can be outlined and a possible path can be drafted, could then be further developed. Empirical substantiation of these ideas, particularly regarding European comparisons, must inevitably be reserved for further studies.

A critical discussion of the concept of the Second Demographic Transition lies at the centre of this article. Although this concept is controversially discussed in the social sciences, in its analyses demography frequently harks back to this concept to describe the transformation in population develop-

4 In contrast, feminist research and discussion on demographic development in the so-called Third World looks back on a longer and wider tradition (cf., for example, Riley 1997).

ment in Europe and other industrial countries since the 1960s. In this article, I will suggest two ways of extending and consolidating the concept. The first extension and consolidation refers to the integration of gender as the societal principle which arranges social and demographic transformation. The second extension and consolidation concerns the integration of the welfare state and its policies as a significant institution for demographic change. At the same time, the welfare state is not solely viewed as an actor in the transformation of gender relations and population development. The question of how the reforms in politics currently to be observed capture the welfare state and transforms in its shape and creative power, also with regard to demographic questions will also be discussed.

In my argumentation, referring to critical sociological discussion of modernity, I will firstly highlight the concept of demographic transition, which is widespread in demography (1). In connection with that, in the second section I will look into the differentiation of two demographic transitions in the course of social change, which has been dealt with in demography since the 1980s and which, despite a constant flow of criticism of the fundamental idea of demographic transition, is widespread in demographic research (3). Then I will put forward a suggestion for how gender could be considered as a societal principle of organization and as an analytical category in the concept of the Second Demographic Transition (4). Finally, in a widening and deepening of the concept of the Second Demographic Transition, I will state that the welfare state is a central actor in demographic change and I will sketch out its ambivalent influences upon demographic development (5). The final conclusion ties up the argumentation with a view to research strategies and suggests some starting points for more in-depth and wider theoretical and empirical European comparative work with this concept (6).

At this point a note about methodology should be made: From the social scientific perspective, demographic change presents itself as a complicated phenomenon in which the interplay between individual action, institutional factors, societal processes and demographic behaviour are conveyed. For the theoretical as well as the empirical study of this complex phenomenon, it is necessary to proceed in a multi- and inter-disciplinary manner and make multilevel analyses. The following exposition is conscious of its limited disciplinary perspective, which is primarily inspired by sociological ways of thinking and those of (social scientific) gender studies. The need for multi-levelled analytical approaches in examining this phenomenon is accommodated with implicit reference to Giddens' structuration theory. This enables the conceptualization of the macro, meso and micro levels in their connections and ascribes particular attention to the institutions regarding the analysis of societal change (cf. Giddens 1984; Kahlert 2008). This theory is, as I consider it, also suitable to adequately capture the phenomenon of demographic change in its complexity, and thus consider more accurately institutions such as the family, the (employment) market, and the (welfare) state. I also owe from Giddens' work the insight that the analysis of change must always also include the analysis of stability.

2 The analysis of demographic change in the context of modernization theory

The thematisation and problematisation of demographic development are among the more relevant social science questions in the analysis of the formation of modern civil society and the modern state. To be more precise, demographic development means birth development (fertility), the development of life expectancy and morbidity (mortality) and ultimately the question of migratory movements (migration). Demographic change is thus an integral part of social change. The analysis of demographic change cannot be separated from the analysis of social change.

In research on social change concerning the question of population development, the differentiation of two opposed demographic regimes in so-called traditional – i.e. pre-industrial – and so-called modern – i.e. industrialized – societies can be found. According to this perception, presented in a somewhat simplified form due to the requested concision, pre-industrial societies are with few exceptions characterized by high birth rates and simultaneously high mortality figures (because of low life expectancy). Connected with that is said to be a stationary or slowly growing population, certainly with a very high loss of human life. The demographically contingent migration rates are low. In the transition to modern industrialized society, in Europe and other modern societies dating from the 18th century and in developing countries lasting until the present day, a demographic regime has in contrast prevailed, in which mortality figures are relatively small and the majority of the population lives long lives. In addition, relatively few children are born and the birth rate ranges between just over or under the level of 2.1 children per woman, which is necessary to maintain the population. In the long term, the population hardly grows, or it even declines, which for demographic reasons is corrected or must be corrected upwards by migration (cf. Höpflinger 1997: 32).

The long term change from high to low birth and mortality figures, which is seen as a demographically relevant component of the transition from traditional pre-industrial societies to modern industrial societies, is termed demographic transition in social scientific literature. The theory describes the different constellations of demographic balance and demographic growth in the interplay between fertility, mortality and migration. Thus, from a demographic perspective, a decline in births is seen as the crux of the far reaching social and economic changes induced by the industrial revolution.

The concept of demographic transition developed in United States demography[5] is based upon a supposedly universally applicable phase and development model, which is characterized by a supposition of social evolution that was more pertinent in the 19th century than the 20th century. This supposition experienced its heyday in the course of the dominance of the structural-functionalist paradigm of Parsonsist sociology and the associated modernization thought from the 1950s to the 1970s. This modernization thought has however to the present day not been undisputed with regard to its claimed empirical validity for different regions and historical epochs, and also due to its theoretical consistency.

The critics of modernization thought are also highly relevant for the assessment of the concept of demographic transition. Thus they will be summarized in the following section in six points referring to Hans van der Loo and Willem van Reijen (1997: 19-29).

The criticism firstly is directed against the underlying evolutionary thought, according to which reality is composed of phenomenon, which can be ordered hierarchically into 'higher' (modern) and 'lower' (traditional) ways of

5 Szreter (1993: 661) points out that the idea of demographic transition was born twice. It was firstly publicised by the leading American demographer of his time, Warren S. Thompson in 1929, but was not well received. It was published again in its classic form in two separate publications in 1945 by Frank W. Notestein and Kingsley Davis, also leading American demographers, and from that point in time onwards it was adopted and further developed. Szreter explains this active reception with reference to the post-war relevance of this idea for the development of family planning programmes for and in the so-called Third World.

life. This thought is ethnocentric. It is also questionable in this context which aspect of the claimed transition from one societal formation to another can be pin-pointed. Does one special and central point of transition really exist? When and what is the beginning of the transition, when and what is its end? Secondly, the assumption of modernization as a total development is criticized, as modernization is not an all-encompassing process, but partial and selective. Closely allied with that is the third point of criticism, which is directed against the presumption of a harmonious character. Modernization has no continuity and is not regular, but characterized by paradoxes. Fourthly, it is problematic that modernization thought appears to be based upon mono-causal explanations, as modernization is predicated on a complex conglomerate of factors, which are closely tied together. Fifthly, the idea that modernization is presented as shaped by structural dominance is criticized: Modernization is presented as a development that seems to take place beyond the control of individuals. On the contrary, individuals can not only inherit existing structures, they can also change them. Indeed, structures are what make human action possible in the first place. Finally, sixthly, the problematic relationship between distance and participation in modernization thought is mentioned. They are too abstract and too generally formulated and require an empirical examination and – if need be – modification.

Formulated as a concept for the analysis of the demographic development of the world population, the idea of demographic transition is based upon an evolutionary concept of global population development. According to this, supposedly less developed societies are characterized by relatively high birth and death rates, as well as a lower life expectancy, and supposedly more highly developed societies by comparatively low birth and death rates, as well as high life expectancy. Indeed, demography does consider social and regional differentials in its theoretical models and empirical prognoses on population development. However, despite that, it acts on the assumption of a continuity of trends and their validity for each examined country or region. A central reference parameter remains the context of the respective nation state. It is also critical that even the most subtle empirical population statistics and prognoses suggest, not least in view of the characteristic reduction of social processes to quantifiable data which can be abstracted from the acting of tangible people, that demographic developments are about the power of nature which supposedly cannot be influenced. In this, the decline in births is presented as having fallen upon people and not caused by their changed views and behaviours.

Among other criticisms, feminist academics criticize the concept of demographic transition for saying nothing about sexuality or gender roles and gender relations: According to this, fertility is the result of immaculate conception, and couples appear as a uniform and harmonious union. Power relations which influence fertility decisions and which are relevant for the explanation of differential fertility behaviour are missing in this framework (Solsona i Pairó 1997: 172). The feminist historian Alison Mackinnon (1995) presents a similar argument. In view of the supposed lack of subjects in demographic theory, she asks critically whether women were present in the demographic transition. The changes in the concrete life situations of men and women, as well as in their relationship and emotional patterns which have gone alongside the modernization process and accompanying demographic transition are hardly considered in the demographic focus of the modern population regime, according to her summary discussing research on demographic transition. This is even more astounding as demographic talk of fertility permanently makes an issue out of a particular aspect of womanhood. Mackinnon concludes:

> "In part the explanation lies in the highjacking of population studies by a policy agenda obsessed with economic and political outcomes in a post-World War II climate. In part it lies in the politically volatile nature of all fertility discourse, with its potential to slide all too easily into pro-natalist, nationalist, racist rhetoric. But, most tellingly [...], it reflects an inability to envisage women as active agents in social change." (Mackinnon 1995: 223)

In demographic expositions women were either portrayed as endued with a lack of decision-making ability, or if they were recognized as decision-makers, as responsible for wrong decisions: "In development literature they are frequently viewed as problem overproducers; in developed societies they underproduce." (Mackinnon 1995: 223) In both scenarios women are represented solely as bodies, as productive resources in the service of the nation, but not as having identities whose subjectivities are gendered and endued with motives and desires to want to have children – or not. Here, Mackinnon does not only criticize the extremely restricted perception of gender as the feminine ability to bare children, which pervades the numerous publications on demographic transition. She also demands a multi-levelled analytical examination of demographic change, in which not only birth figures in statistics would be considered, but also the subjects who act reproductively[6] and the feminist movements as a vehicle for social change. Ultimately, this discovery in social historical research is nothing new.

In sociology, modernization thought has received criticism to the present day. Over the course of time, extensive theoretical and empirical activities have been stressed that should invalidate the critical aspects described. Nevertheless, demography seems relatively untouched by the different, but very basic critical points, and its analysis of demographic change relies now just as then upon the concept of demographic transition inspired by evolution theory, even if in a somewhat different framework. Simon Szreter (1993) attributes the demographic interest in this – in itself purely descriptive – idea to its enduring attractiveness to population policies, such as for the development of family planning programmes for the so-called developing countries. In his sketch of a critical intellectual history of the idea of demographic transition, he writes:

> "The idea of demographic transition has continued to provide both a ready-made rationale for policy-activism and a convenient projection tool for forecasting demographic futures under varying assumptions as to policy effectiveness [...]. Demographic transition theory was itself a product of a particular conception of social science as at one and the same time an engine for investigation and for prediction and for guidance of social change. As a linear, evolutionary classification scheme, it was an archetypical construct for simultaneously specifying and justifying the direction that active policy should follow. [...] This was an idea originally born out of a covering laws conception of social science, and it continues to be an idea well suited to the predictive requirements of policy." (Szreter 1993: 686, 689, 692)

With this, Szreter criticizes not only the close relationship that his analysis revealed between demography and politics, which brought the concept of demographic transition, conceptualized in US demography, to prominence in the 1940s and 1950s, but also that this socio-technological understanding under-

6 Mackinnon criticizes only the lacking of women as active subjects in demography. That men also act reproductively does not come into her critical feminist view. The concept of "reproductive acting" is used in this text following Regina-Maria Dackweiler (2006: 81, 83), who criticizes the concept of demographic behaviour, which she identifies as belonging to the behaviourist paradigm of psychology and which she considers as too narrow to describe the demographically relevant action of individuals as action in social structures.

lying this relationship, according to which demographic knowledge is directly politically relevant and realizable in both political and administrative actions. This proximity to politics, also supported in other critical academic studies related to demography (cf. for example, Presser 1997; Hummel 2000), which I will return to at the end of this article, may also be a central reason for the fact that despite the serious methodological criticisms of the concept of the Second Demographic Transition since the 1980s, the distinction of two demographic transitions enriches the spectrum critiquing the present and finds great currency in demography.

3 Continuity or discontinuity in demographic transition? The concept of the Second Demographic Transition

Two demographers are the creators of the distinction between two demographic transitions and thus the discourse on the First and the Second Demographic Transition – the Dutchman Dirk J. Van de Kaa (for example 1987, 2002) and his Belgian colleague Ron Lesthaeghe (for example 1995, without year). In 1986 together they developed the idea that from the mid-1960s the countries of Western Europe and the other industrialized countries of the world had entered a new stage in their population history, again characterized by a decline in births. Demographically, they see this new stage as characterized by "very significant changes since the mid-1960s" (van de Kaa 2002: 4). The starting point of this new transition built in their view a "multifaceted revolution", the central elements of which consist of a "contraceptive revolution" with the introduction of hormonal contraceptives, a "sexual revolution" with a decreasing age of first sexual activity and a "gender revolution", which questioned the male breadwinner model and the accompanied gendered division of labour (Lesthaeghe without year: 3). These three revolutions integrated far reaching social changes into a single framework, in which authority was rejected, individual freedom was highly valued and the traditional normative structure was seen as outdated.

In their theoretical explanation for the differentiation of a new stage of demographic development, van de Kaa and Lesthaeghe hark back to different studies on changes of needs and values. The analyses of the social historian Philippe Ariés (1980), who established two successful motivations for low fertility and exemplified this with the change in adults' view of children: According to him, the predominant great emotional and financial investment in children associated with the establishment of modern society has since the 1960s been displaced by an attitude in which parenthood has become nothing more than self-realization for some adults and a lifestyle choice that stands in opposition to other lifestyles. This cultural perspective has found support from the ideas of Abraham Maslow (1954) on changes in needs and from Ronald Inglehart (for example 1977) on the gaining in importance of post-material values such as freedom and equality and their partial overlap of material values. Beside this cultural influence, which van de Kaa and Lesthaeghe believe is crucial, the concept of the Second Demographic Transition still fed by the neo-classical theories of the economist Richard Easterlin (for example 1976), according to which small birth cohorts had better chances in the employment market and thus better life chances than large birth cohorts, and Gary S. Becker (for example 1981), according to which through the increase in women's economic independence, which began in the 1960s, there were fewer advantages in marriage and the opportunity costs for women through motherhood grew. These changes were flanked by technological advances, for example in contraception, in reproductive medicine and healthcare and in social communication through the mass media.

Lesthaeghe and van de Kaa thus position the Second Demographic Transition in a whole-societal framework of social change, which, according to them, is principally based on cultural changes and accompanied by economic and technological – medical as well as informational – changes. In the Second Demographic Transition, numerous complexly intertwined transformation processes merge whose consequential effects, according to both the demographers, are particularly important for the analysis of the Second Decline in Births: the historical change in societal acceptance of sexuality; the availability of highly effective contraception and a strengthened and more simplified possibility for women to control reproductive decisions; the decline of social control by institutions; the increased emphasis of personal needs concerning cohabitation (including marriage) and the higher appreciation of a fair exchange in a relationship; the increased connection between orientation towards career and family for women, together with expectations of an egalitarian division of labour between the sexes in private; and finally, the discovery of the opportunity costs of children (cf. Lesthaeghe 1995: 57).

Van de Kaa and Lesthaeghe empirically associate the differentiation of two demographic transitions and changing constellations of factors, particularly in both of the declines in birth (cf. Lesthaeghe, without year: 1; Lesthaeghe 1995: 21). They attribute the First Demographic Transition to better living conditions and the associated increased life expectancy, as well as the growing importance of individual autonomy in the course of the socio-economic development of a society. The decline in death rates, including infants and children, is accompanied by stagnation in population growth corresponding with the level of fecundity necessary for demographic stability, which society and families effect through conscious birth control. Death and birth figures are balanced, and from a demographic point of view there is no need for immigration. This demographic transition strengthened the family as an institution and took place in silence. This version of the concept of demographic transition is already to a great extent familiar to us.

The Second Demographic Transition, however, according to van de Kaa's and Lesthaeghe's research, is apparent in all highly developed countries in essentially more open manifestations of individual autonomy, as well as publicly and loudly articulated demands for emancipation, for example, through the student movement. It is accompanied by marked changes in fertility behaviour, marriage behaviour, family structures, ways of life, but also by socialisation and contact with authority, which have been empirically proven: the frequency of birth sinks under the level of preservation, processes of starting a family change due to the increase in the age of marriage and parenthood, new individual ways of life spread, together with an increase in one-person households and children born outside of marriage, and the frequency of divorce is rising. Added to this is a further and as yet incomplete increase in life expectancy. The demographic balance has thus lost its continuity. According to Lesthaeghe and van de Kaa, it can be stabilized through immigration but not endurably corrected (cf. for example van de Kaa 2002: 3; van de Kaa 1987: 38-44; Lesthaeghe et al. 1991). In any case, the influx of immigrants would be a central factor in the population structure and in the population growth of societies in the Second Demographic Transition. Both demographers show that as a consequence of the Second Demographic Transition highly developed countries find themselves in a process of contraction.[7] They see a reversal of this trend as very unlikely (cf. for example Lesthaeghe 1995: 57-58).

The concept of the Second Demographic Transition considers some of

7 Cf. for Germany the thorough analysis by Kaufmann (2005).

the aforementioned points of criticism directed towards the American version of the concept of demographic transition according to Notestein and Davis. It addresses as a central theme the macro level of social-structural changes as well as the micro level of individual acting. Van de Kaa and Lesthaeghe relate to neo-classical economic theories and describe the Second Demographic Transition as being made by individuals and with that refer to the rational actions of individuals, particularly women, in family planning. Additionally, with reference to their empirical evidence, there is no basic contradiction in the social scientific community, as this evidence corresponds with other research findings on demographic transformation processes in Europe and other highly developed countries.

However, the thesis of the two European demographers that the empirically proven changes and the altering constellation factors are so fundamental that they justify the discourse of a new stage of the demographic development i.e. of a second demographic transition is met with scepticism and rejection. Critics of this thesis, for example Robert Cliquet (1991: 13), see the demographic changes diagnosed by Lesthaeghe and van de Kaa as fixed in the continuity of a process, which has been ongoing for hundreds of years and is linked to societal modernization. A comparable controversy can also be found in modernization debates in sociology, in which the thesis was put forward that modernity had been in the midst of a transition into the post-modern since the 1960s, or that it was passing out of a first phase of "simple" modernization into a second phase of "reflexive" modernization (cf. Beck et al. 1994). Here, just as in demography there are accurate theoretical arguments and empirical evidence that are directed against this differentiation in the modernization process, underpinned by just as accurate theoretical arguments and empirical evidence (cf. van Krieken 1997).

However, the theoretical justifications quoted by van de Kaa and Lesthaeghe for their concept have up to now hardly been criticized. Solely their prioritizing of the cultural transformation processes over the economic and technological transformation processes, which are commonly recognized as significant in demography, have met with opposition. In the following sections, I would like to draw attention to the necessary widening of the motivation around welfare state and political changes. Van de Kaa and Lesthaeghe target the analysis of demographic change in welfare societies, but their understanding of welfare statism seems to consist of solely two institutions: family and economy i.e. employment market. With this, the concept of the wide demographic transition only looks at two corners of the welfare triangle. It thematizes the third corner – the welfare state and its transformations – only very marginally. It is thus necessary to integrate the welfare state as the third welfare-social institution into the concept of the Second Demographic Transition and to value it as an actor in demographic change, for example through the employment market, the family, education, migration and gender politics. Before I take this argument further, an intermediate step, which is central to my thoughts will be discussed, which accords meaning to the transformation in gender relations in the Second Demographic Transition.

4 The transformation in gender relations in the Second Demographic Transition

In the whole-societal framework in which Lesthaeghe and van de Kaa present the Second Demographic Transition, they extract linked aspects of change in gender relations at all levels. Thus, they empirically prove increased participation of women and, above all, of mothers in employment and the competition between the sexes in the course of social change since the 1960s, point out the growing representation of women in politics, refer to changed gender-specific norms in view of intimate relationships and a growing independence of women in the course of general changes of values, and lastly, emphasize the medical-technical enabling of female self determination over their fertility. The previously mentioned "gender revolution", as referred to by Lesthaeghe, means in short "of course, a quest for far more egalitarian gender relations" (Lesthaeghe without year: 4). Changes in the balances of power between the sexes and conflicts over roles in different areas of life are examples of this (van de Kaa 1988, quoted by: Solsona i Pairó 1997: 184). For Lesthaeghe and van de Kaa, the change in gender relations, which in their analyses mainly affected women, is a component of the whole-societal changes in mentality and values which is taking place, which encourage the development of new ways of life and let parenthood become a more seldom made biographical decision of two people bound in intimacy.

Solsona i Pairó explicitly praises the fact that the concept of the Second Demographic Transition, unlike the concept of the First Demographic Transition, considers changes in gender roles:

> "For that reason, I think it is useful to speak about a *second* demographic transition in order to underline the importance of changes in relations between men and women related to demographic and family changes. Behind any decision of having or not having children, of getting or not getting married, exists a negotiation process in which personal expectations and bargaining power are very important. It seems clear to me, then, that women's emancipation has changed the negotiation capability of women in these processes, becoming the crucial factor of the process of deinstitutionalisation of the family." (Solsona i Pairó 1997: 172, italics in original)

The argument that the transformation in family composition is strongly influenced by changes in gender roles and through the emancipation of women can be found in numerous family demographic and gender studies works. The improvement in the position of women through modification of childbirth and caring behaviour are commonly seen as "key facilitators of demographic change" (McNay 2003: 2). Italian academics emphasize that in analyses it is not only gendered behaviour that must be considered, but also views and attitudes around gender roles (Di Giorgio et al. 2007). Solsona i Pairó (1997: 184) adds that the focus on women is too narrow and changes affecting men also need to be considered in the analyses:

> "Women's emancipation became a key factor in the acceleration of these changes, but at the same time, as a consequence of the redefinition of sex roles, relations between men and women were modified and masculine gender identity began a de-construction/reconstruction process, with preliminary effects in marriage and reproductive behaviour. To study gender relations changes and demographic changes it is absolutely necessary to include the male half of the population in our studies, to recognise that to get married and to have children is at least a matter involving two people."

With her examination of the concept of the Second Demographic Transition, Janet Saltzman Chafetz (1995) points to the analysis of the relationship between feminist movements and the transformation of the family. She argues that it is insufficient to see the changes in the family which occurred in the 1960s as the effect of feminist activism. Rather in the industrialized nations exists a complex relation amongst macro-structural change, changes in families, attitudes towards gender and the family, and the activism of the feminist movements. To question whether the feminist movements or the transformation of the family came first is like the chicken and egg question. Rather, both resulted from a growing need for women to participate in the employment market, which in turn was the result of macro-structural, technical, economic and legal changes. The intensity of the transformation of the family admittedly increased when the women's movements emerged and achieved a significant size and corresponding influence (Chafetz 1995: 63-64). Chafetz shows in an empirical comparison of the USA, the Netherlands, Great Britain, Norway, Japan and Portugal that the size of the women's movements in each respective country coincided with the level of industrialization and the size of the middle class. She also points to positive correlations between the size of the movement and the percentage of women who worked in the secondary sector (industry) and particularly in the tertiary sector (service). Lastly, the degree of female academic educational success was strongly and positively connected with the size of the movement.

Changing behaviour in starting a family is obvious. With widening chances for women to go to university and to invest their energies in careers, many of the better educated made a kind of rational calculation in the decision about starting a family and how many children to have, and indeed one that tried to maximize the successes both for the family and for employment. Chafetz emphasizes:

> "Women are not equal in their ability or desire to take advantage of newly expanding opportunities. Nevertheless, large numbers of younger female cohorts in advanced industrial nations continue their education and find reasonably good employment, so that national statistics come to reflect their new behavioural patterns. Thus, the average age at first marriage and at first birth increase, while the birth rate and the average completed family size decline and, conversely, the rate of cohabitation increases." (Chafetz 1995: 71)

In this statement Chafetz turns her attention to social inequalities between the sexes: the related change in educational, employment and reproductive behaviour appears, according to her research, above all amongst middle class women. They are regarded as beneficiaries of the expansion in education that began in the 1960s, and as the agents of the Second Decline in Births. At the same time, Chafetz suggests that there has been a shift in attitude regarding the expectation of (more) equality between the sexes, particularly women one should add. However, despite expanding opportunities for women, in particular on the employment market, but also in academic education, which resulted from macro-structural changes, they are not faced with equal chances compared with men.

These results are also backed by other empirical studies. It can be shown that it is not only different mindsets and reactions from men, covering a wide spectrum from agreement to open rejection, that juxtapose women's expectations of equal educational and career possibilities with equal division of labour in the family. Up until the present day in most modern countries in Europe and beyond, even if there are to some extent considerable differences between the individual countries, aside from the growing participation of women in higher education, in the employment market[8] and in politics, inequality has been continuing. This can be seen in the professional orientation of the sexes connected with a gendered segregation of the employment market, a virtually stable gender pay gap, and low proportions of women in leading positions in economy, science and politics.

Added to this, in most modern countries there is a persistent stability of the gendered division of labour in the private sphere. Housework, childcare and care of the elderly are still women's jobs. Obviously, there are also couples who split the housework equally, particularly if both partners are employed. However, as soon as the first child is born, this pattern changes in many partnerships. It seems as if amnesia regarding the claims of equality and their realization sets in: women then take over the housework and care work more or less as a matter of course, and men noticeably reduce their contribution to housework.

Based on these empirical observations, Marianne Rodenstein, Stephanie Bock and Susanne Heeg (1996) put forward the thesis that the increase in women's workload, through their increased participation in the workplace and the stability of the gendered division of labour in the private sphere, has triggered a crisis in reproduction. Ever more women reacted to the obligation to reproduce still placed upon them by changing how they chose to reproduce. These obligations should thus be rejected or be reduced. Rodenstein et al. (1996: 33) regard the "conscious reduction in the extent of the work of repro-

8 One should consider that the labour participation of women and mothers is only growing in western countries, whereas in eastern, post-socialist countries, in contrast, labour participation has sunk in comparison with the situation under socialist conditions.

duction" as a contingency of change in reproductive forms. Accordingly, the work associated with reproduction and in turn women's total workload ought to be reduced by decreasing the number of births.

The "gender revolution" declared by Lesthaeghe thus displays right up to the present day considerable rifts. The change in gender relations since the 1960s is indeed highly visible and probably also irreversible. It has, however, been accompanied by a practically unbroken stability of gender inequality, above all in private division of labour, but also in the positions connected with power and influence in education, employment and politics. Up to now, these inconsistencies and ambivalences have had inadequate consideration in the concept of the Second Demographic Transition. Feminist academics thus plead for the question of gender inequality and gender power relations to be considered more explicitly than hitherto in demographic research (cf. for example Mason 1986; Cain 1993; McDaniel 1996; Solsono i Pairó 1997; Riley 1998, 1999; McNay 2003).

Furthermore Nancy E. Riley (1998, 1999) demands epistemological and methodological changes concerning the handling of gender in demographic research, namely from the design to the analysis. She argues that there is indeed plenty in demography about women, but little about gender. Gender is more than an individual characteristic, more than just to ask whether one is male or female:

> "Its more pervasive effect is at the societal level. Gender is influential in the way that societies are organized, and it is part of all social institutions in any society – of the economy, part of the institution of the family, part of the state. [...] Using this definition of gender, it is clear that the meaning of gender (and its effects) will be different from one society to another." (Riley 1998: 522)

In this sense, gender is not often an integral part of demographic research, even if this research is focused on women.

On the consideration of social inequalities and of gender as a societal principle of organization, in Riley's view, demography would, moreover, benefit from considering the idea that gender is a social construction. Such an approach would not only give us a deeper understanding of the role of gender in demographic processes, but would also widen our knowledge of demographic behaviour overall, because it better reflects the social context in which demographic processes occur (Riley 1999: 370).

The concept of gender used by Riley includes the complete welfare triangle: economy, family and state. With Riley, one cannot only argue that the consideration of gender as a societal principle of organization and analytical category is of great importance for the awareness of possibilities of demographic research, but also that demographic processes are relevant in the whole welfare triangle. They are namely influenced through the interplay of the three institutions and they influence their interplay. The concept of the Second Demographic Transition analyzes how developments in the family and the economy interact with reference to cultural approaches to the transformation in values and mentalities and to neoclassical economic approaches, and it also considers how changes affecting women influence the interplay between the two institutions. However, the concept contains only short and scattered suggestions and hints about what meaning demographic change has for the third institution, the welfare state. These are not systematically theoretically conceived and are thus also not followed up in the empirical research connected to the concept. The aim of the following section is thus to outline some links for the systematic integration of the welfare state perspective into demographic transition research, based on the connectors for considering the perspective of the welfare state and the meaning of political actions applied in Lesthaeghe's and van de Kaa's concept. Gender is of course an important analytical category in this sketch. The concept of the Second Demographic Transition is methodologically deepened and widened with these suggestions.

5 The paradoxical relationship between state and family and its meaning for the demographic development in welfare societies

To pose the question of the meaning of the (welfare) state for demographic change seems strange, maybe even tenuous from the perspective of the discipline of demography. Conversely, from the perspective of a critical social science and of critical gender studies the proximity of demography and politics is obvious. Here, the subject of demography – population and its development – seems as deeply political, as the population question is without doubt closely associated with the question of the development of state-building (cf. for example Foucault 1983: 159-190, 2004: 87-133). This aforementioned view thus has repercussions on critical academic reflections on demography.

Despite or maybe even because of this, in its academic self-image demography appears distanced from political questions. Riley comments on the lack of self-reflexivity in the discipline:

> "Demographers have spent much less time examining the politics, background, and motivations of their work than have neighboring social science fields. […] Far from expressing interest in the examination of the political nature of demographic inquiry, demographers usually ignore those aspects of the field, and often even argue that demography must strive to be objective and apolitical. Thus, in spite of the fact that demography is often dealing with some of the most politically contentious of social issues (marriage, reproduction, immigration), the field as whole continues to present itself as one that avoids politics." (Riley 1998: 531)

This stance of awareness, endeavouring to remain distanced from politics, corresponds with the previously explained social-technological understanding of demography regarding its relationship with politics. Demographic processes are seen here as politically controllable. On this theme, the following citation from a leading French demographer speaks for itself:

> "Fertility is elastic; it can be reduced by family planning programs when it is considered too high (according to Population Inquiries conducted by the United Nations); it can also be stimulated by social policies when it is considered too low." (Chesnais 1998: 85)

According to this the task of politics is clear: it should evaluate and interpret demographic research conclusions and translate them into political strategies, instruments and measures.[9] Also, politics is often the sponsor of demographic research.

This social-technological understanding of the interrelationship between demography and politics also runs through the publications on the concept of the Second Demographic Transition. Thus, in one of the first and central texts on this concept, the Population Bulletin of the Population Reference Bureau in Washington, with the title "Europe's Second Demographic Transition" (1987), van de Kaa extensively develops not only the theoretical basis of his new idea and painstakingly places it in a comparative perspective with empiri-

9 That from the point of view of demography, politics should thus intensively promote demographic research with public funds is clear.

cal data. He also devotes much attention in this text to the public debate on demographic change in Europe, which at that time was virulent in the media and politics. In this context, he discusses in detail European migration politics in the post-war period (van de Kaa 1987: 38-46), as well as the pro-natalist family policy measures, then being considered in political discussion to handle the decline in births which was becoming apparent (van de Kaa 1987: 46-53). Similar passages can be found in other more recent texts by him and his Belgian colleague (cf. for example van de Kaa 2002; Lesthaeghe et al. 1991). Occasionally in this context the gender political dimension comes into view, in the comparative European empirical analyses when for example Lesthaeghe established that differences in birth rates are connected to women's employment. Looking at Nordic countries with their consistent gender equality politics, he diagnoses that the countries in which the gender roles had adapted earlier in the Second Demographic Transition are returning to a stable level of births, and conjectures that social measures such as social security, child benefit payments and day-care could have possibly played a role (Lesthaeghe 1995: 56).

The actions of welfare states are mostly presented here as being reactive, as, for example, reacting to demographic changes with pro-natalist family policies, supporting or correcting the changes (for example van de Kaa 1987: 45). That state and politics however could have also possibly influenced demographic development and that they are actively involved in the status quo of the demographic development, that consequences of demographic change could in turn become its cause, does not seem to be considered by the two demographers. Only very rarely can scant references to this view be found. Van de Kaa mentions, for example, that the changes in values and norms through the development of the welfare state after the Second World War, which are so important for the concept of the Second Demographic Transition, were facilitated: "Shifts in norms made possible by the development of the welfare state have allowed individuals and couples to make a choice of fertility behaviour" (van de Kaa 1987: 46). The Dutch demographer thus perceives the welfare state necessarily as an institution, but does not attribute to it any theoretically fundamental relevance for demographic development in the conceptualisation of his version of demographic transition.

That the state is a central – and necessarily also ambivalent – actor in demographic change, and that actions by the state are not only reactive but also active, is not reflected in the concept of the Second Demographic Transition.

At the same time, the connection between state action and family development, in which van de Kaa and Lesthaege and the demographic researchers around them are particularly interested, is obvious. Susan McDaniel sums this up neatly: "[...] reproduction is the essential act of continuity for the state as much as for the individual or family" (McDaniel 1996: 84; cf. Gauthier 1996). The state and the family are thus closely intertwined – but contradictorily, as Eva Kreisky and Marion Löffler (2003) show. The Viennese political scientists describe the paradoxical relationship between state and the family in modern society in three theses.

Their first thesis thematizes the family as a problem of the state, and states that the character and social system of the family serve the legitimization of the state and hence forms one of its cultural prerequisites and ideological lynchpins. Talk of the state is only possible because there is the family, talk of the public sphere only because there is a private sphere. Even more, these dichotomies are always newly reproduced in political thought and political action. The family is continuously portrayed as a broad social category and is secured in its continuance. At the same time its stability is stylized as a measure for the stability of the political order of the state.

The second thesis by Kreisky and Löffler describes the state as a family problem and indicates that the family as a real social form in any event requires state action and thus is to be regarded as a political construction. This particular social relationship only becomes a family if and because it is politically perceived as such and is legally regulated. The power of the concept, thus the designation of what family is, lies with the state (or its functional equivalents). The modern family in its civic-patriarchal form is, according to this, not a constant structure of human cohabitation, but a product of state politics and the associated legal fixation, which, with national definitions of family completely differing from each other, positions a particular family form as hegemonic. Normally this family is heterosexual, with their children by birth, who if possible grow up in a family structure legally legitimized through marriage and characterized by the gender-hierarchical division of labour.

Kreisky and Löffler's third thesis concerns the global success of the modern civil-patriarchal family model. The core of this success has been the operationability of the antagonism between the state and the family. A triumph of the character and social system of the patriarchal-civil family and the paradoxical relationship between the state and the family is connected with the triumph of modernity in the course of the globalization process. The so-called traditional family experienced a renaissance, even in the time of globalization and transnationalization. However, particularly in neoliberal ideologies, it acts as an emotional antipole to market conditions which are becoming harder, and a public climate that is embossed with the coldness of the social.

Through the protection of the family – defined differently in different countries – the state hopes to achieve its own survival, as the family policies aimed at the preservation of the population are still now, even in this time of globalization and transnationalism, predominantly organized at a national level.

The (national) state therefore has a great interest in the reproduction of the population. This interest guides the political regulation of the heterosexuality necessary for it. It relates to the biological functions of men as procreators and women as the ones bearing the children, and to their social function as breadwinner and as homemaker and caregiver. The demographic development thereupon suggests that since the 1960s neither the biological nor the social function of men and women seems to have been in line with state interests, as in most modern welfare societies ever fewer women and men are having ever fewer children. The differences between the individual welfare states are interesting here: the welfare states with the biggest degree of gender equality have comparatively high birth rates, for example Nordic countries, conversely the welfare states with a comparatively low level of gender equality, for example the southern countries, have low birth rates.

In the concept of the Second Demographic Transition, state interest in the family and its stability is not considered. The family is seen here as a supposedly private issue, particularly by women, who according to the theses of neo-classical economic theories rationally choose for or against starting a family or having a second child by considering the opportunity costs. That welfare states (can) considerably influence the general conditions of these decisions with national policies, for instance through the political regulation of the employment market segmented by gender, through legally fixed regulation of part-time work, through regulations to ensure wage equality between the sexes, through public childcare, through organizing the school system as whole- or half-day, through financially and politically regulating maternity and paternity leave, as well as through tax relief or burdens (cf. for example Esping-Andersen 2002) seems to play no role here.

And what is more: that the modern civil family with its attributions of roles – the breadwinner to the man and the homemaker and caregiver to the woman – conceived by van de Kaa, Lesthaeghe and other demographers as being in a state of change is a construct, which was historically produced and reproduced through political and legal regulations, does not appear in the analyses of the Second Demographic Transition, which seems to have befallen like a force of nature since the mid 1960s suddenly over the highly developed welfare societies. The (employment) market, so influential in demography, is understood uncritically from a gender perspective. Its prototype of the rationally economically behaving individual is implicitly male, as this individual can only exist on the market successfully because he is unburdened by the work of reproduction, and he is white and belongs to the middle class. Women enter this market because of their historical responsibility for the work of reproduction under other conditions from men.

Full participation and full success on the job market is thus not compatible with the demands of the family. To elaborate on this neo-classical idea, the entrance of women and mothers into the employment market, which occurred extensively in the 1960s and was promoted politically as well as economically, can only lead to a decline in births. A transformation of the employment and reproductive work arrangement, underlain by neo-classical approaches based on clear separation of roles between the sexes, was envisaged neither by the economy nor by demography. The benefits in insight that would be gained by an analysis of the relativity of this arrangement, which is supported by the welfare state, and an analysis of welfare state adjustments to this arrangement are squandered.

From the gender perspective which adopts gender equality as a normative goal of (welfare) social development, called "gender revolution" by Lesthaeghe, the decline in births since the 1960s turns out to be an answer to the historically outdated form of the civil-patriarchal family and the historically just as outdated gender constructs of the (male) breadwinner and the (female) homemaker and carer (cf. Kahlert 2006b), which is supported by the action of the welfare state and the economy. An explanation for the "feminist paradox", as it is referred to in demography, could lie in this perspective (Chesnais 1996: 733, 1998: 83), with which Jean-Claude Chesnais using the example of Sweden described the co-operation of feminism and welfare-state pro-natalism.[10]

10 Chesnais (1996: 733) develops what he calls the "feminist paradox" in the comparative analysis of developments in births in Italy, which is among the countries with the lowest birth rates, and in Sweden, which is among the countries with the highest birth

An essential starting point for population oriented family policy in modern welfare states lies in his opinion in the improvement in the situation and living conditions of women. According to him, it is not the civil-patriarchal form of the family and unequally organized gender relations that is securing the demographic future of welfare societies, but democratic family forms and ways of life in conjunction with gender equality. The "feminist paradox" of demography is thus not due to a paradoxical social development, as this pattern of thought suggests, but to the lack of gender authority and the lack of consideration of the welfare state in demographic research.

6 Research perspectives on the restructuring of the welfare state in demographic change and the change of gender relations

A critical debate on the concept of the Second Demographic Transition was at the centre of this article. The aim was to widen and deepen the concept around two aspects: the integration of gender as the societal principle which organizes social and demographic change and as an analytical category, and the integration of the welfare state and its policies as a significant institution for demographic change. To consider the welfare state as a (powerful) actor in the transformation of gender relations and population development, however, we cannot stop with the reconstruction of the paradoxical relationship between state and the family and its simplistic thematization in demographic research. One must also take into account how the reforms that we are currently observing politically conceive the welfare state and change its shape and power to create. To conclude, I would like to outline a few more closely related aspects that must consider the analyses diagnosing the age in this context.

A first, important aspect concerns the *analysis of the change in welfare*

---

rates: The emancipation of women and a birth rate close to the level of demographic preservation go hand in hand: "[...] in Sweden, and probably also elsewhere in Western Europe, empowerment of women ensures against a very low birth rate; it could be the essence of a future feminist paradox". Putting it bluntly, he formulates the result of his comparison of birth developments and the degree of gender equality in north and south Europe: "[...] in feminist societies like those in Scandinavia, the fertility rate is not as depressed as it is in the sexist societies of southern Europe" (Chesnais 1998: 96). The concept of feminism underlying this explanation is worthy of a separate analysis.

statism since the 1960s. The welfare state looks back on an eventful development since the 1960s, which was so significant for demography, which lasted from the development of this institution, particularly in the 1960s and 1970s until the reconstruction and dismantling from the 1980s, and is closely interrelated to economic changes in the course of escalating globalization. The strengthening of radical market ideas which tie personal wellbeing more than ever to participation in the employment market and establish individualization as a personal responsibility for this participation, is of particular importance here, if nationally to varying extents. The emerging understanding of welfare, linked with mobilization, associates welfare benefits more than ever with civic duties. The accompanying socio-political reforms are, taking into account nation-specific, path dependent distinctions, mostly carried out in the name of a bias in 'social investment', in which the welfare state is to invest as much as possible in human capital and be based upon positive individual and social welfare.

This restructuring is however not gender neutral, as it is accompanied by a rolling back of welfare benefits in the private sphere, i.e. the family. Thus the relationship between productive and reproductive work is newly defined in contradictory ways, as Birgit Sauer (1999: 232-233) shows. The removal of boundaries in employment, escalating in view of growing expectations of flexibility and mobility, is accompanied by a re-privatization of the once state-organized domains of the reproduction of the species. Traditional forms of social security und welfare such as the family – and consequently the unpaid work of women – were mobilized, as well as poorly paid women's work. Work that was once provided by the welfare state and thus remunerated was put back in the domain of the family. Associated with this is the production of new gender relations in the private, since the social responsibility for the coming generations, as well as the reproduction of present generations is more tightly linked to the female sex, without a fairer division of this work being politically intended. This redefinition of the private is gender-politically ambivalent and disregards the reproduction of the species, Sauer concludes:

> "The new normality is thus a re-establishment of family 'without' family, a re-privatization 'without' privateness, because people who once stayed within the family – i.e. women – are let outside the family, but people outside the family – i.e. men – cannot find a way into the family." (Sauer 1999: 233)

The conflict between family and paid work, which is relevant in emancipatory and demographic respects, also seems not to be solved in the emerging restructured understanding of welfare.

Secondly, the *analysis of welfare state action concerning gender relations*, which is closely linked with the current restructuring of the welfare state, is closely tied to this aspect. In its advancement and change, the state has also always been a powerful actor in the change and stabilisation of gender relations.[11] The action of welfare states concerning the coordination of equality and equity between the sexes has so far proved itself largely ambivalent. This appears not least in the handling of the political organization of the welfare state concept of the male breadwinner and the female homemaker, the so-called breadwinner model. In view of path-dependent national developments, differences in the socio-political measures can be established in international comparison, as the feminist welfare state research, somewhat critically following Gøsta Esping-Andersen, has shown in numerous studies (cf. for example O'Connor/Olsen 1998; cf. Fraser 1997).

The current restructuring of the welfare state accompany the politically stimulated change in the welfare state concept from the breadwinner model to the adult worker or two earner model (cf. Leitner et al. 2004), which is economically supported by an equalization of the male wage to the (lower) level of the female wage, which in turn makes the employment of both partners urgently necessary. This new approach seems, as is politically publicized, to enable (more) equality between the sexes and in this respect to meet an essential political demand of the women's movements. However, the two earner model only meets split approval in feminist welfare state research concerning the realization of equality and equity between the sexes. It secures the independent existence of women through employment and contributes to a deconstruction of the gender roles (cf. Daly 2004: 149-150). However, it promises no solution

11 At the same time, different varieties of gender policies in the form of the political promotion of particular actions favouring women and the strategy of gender mainstreaming were developed and implemented not least as a result of pressure from women and women's movements at the European as well as at the national level. Fundamental differences between the European welfare states are revealed in the initiatives and campaigns to promote gender politics. The Nordic countries are regarded as cutting edge in the implementation of equality policies. In contrast the southern countries, but also some countries such as Germany, for example, are if anything hesitant in the implementation of gender policies.

to the problem of the asymmetric split of housework and care work between the sexes. Also in the course of establishing the two earner model, the work of reproduction remains women's work. Viewed in this way, in the course of implementing a new gender model, stability and change in gender relations also seem to go hand in hand.

Demographically meaningful in this context is thirdly the question of the *organization of care work in shrinking and ageing welfare societies*, and indeed the care of the coming generation and for the elderly. One can state, looking at demographic change, that the house and care-work, split asymmetrically between the sexes, seems to be becoming a growing problem in the ageing European welfare societies, which in view of the two earner model being established can no longer be solved privately and unpaid through female care work as before. The solution lies in care work imparted by the market and primari-ly undertaken by women, which is now paid, if poorly. Viewed in this way, the two earner model shifts existing inequalities: in dual income households, the house and care work is mostly delegated to other women ('housemaids'). These women, who are often in a precarious social and uncertain intermediate status as 'temporary' economic migrants, enable the realization of this new egalitarian gender arrangement, which is beginning to escalate mainly amongst the middle class (cf. for example Ehrenreich/Hochschild 2004; Lutz 2006; Rerrich 2006; Metz-Göckel et al. 2008). Welfare state solutions for the looming increased needs for care, especially of elderly people, beyond private arrangements mostly to the disadvantage of women, are still rare.

One can state that the significance of welfare state restructuring processes is also demographically decisive – the political encouragement of the two earner model is primarily motivated by the highly qualified employment potential in Europe, which is becoming scarce through demographic change. Conversely, welfare state restructuring processes also have ramifications upon demographic processes – so, for example, the promotion of gender equality seems to contribute to the growth of birth rates. The institutional dynamics of the welfare state and its interrelation with the institutions of the family and the (employment) market have thus ambivalent influences upon demographic development. Transnational socio-political activities such as the establishment of a European Alliance for the Family, mentioned at the beginning of this article, are consequently definitely relevant to research into the causes and consequences of demographic change and thus also for the concept of the Second Demographic Transition, as discussed here. It remains to be seen how far demography will confront the methodological challenges to widen and deepen its theories.

Bibliography

Ariès, Philippe (1980): "Two Successive Motivations for the Declining Birth Rate in the West." In: *Population and Development Review* 6 (4), 645-650

Bauer, Annemarie/ Gröning, Katharina (eds.) (2008): *Gerechtigkeit, Geschlecht und demografischer Wandel*. Frankfurt/ M.: Mabuse

Beck, Ulrich/ Giddens, Anthony/ Lash, Scott (1994): *Reflexive Modernization. Politics, Tradition, and Aesthetics in the Modern Social Order.* Cambridge: Polity Press

Becker, Gary S. (1981): *A Treatise in the Family*. Cambridge/ Mass.: Harvard University Press

Berger, Peter A./ Kahlert, Heike (eds.) (2006): *Der demographische Wandel. Chancen für die Neuordnung der Geschlechterverhältnisse*. Frankfurt/ M., New York: Campus

Cain, Mead T. (1993): "Patriarchal Structure and Demographic Change." In: Federici, Nora/ Mason, Karen Oppenheim/ Sogner, Sølvi (eds.): *Women's Position and Demographic Change*. Oxford: Clarendon Press, 43-60

Chafetz, Janet Saltzman (1995): "Chicken or Egg? A Theory of the Relationship between Feminist Movements and Family Change." In: Mason, Karen Oppenheim/ Jensen, An-Margritt (eds.): *Gender and Family Change in Industrialized Countries*. Oxford: Clarendon Press, 63-81

Chesnais, Jean Claude (1996): "Fertility, Family, and Social Policy in Contemporary Western Europe." In: *Population and Development Review 22* (4), 729-739

Chesnais, Jean Claude (1998): "Below-Replacement Fertility in the European Union (EU-15): Facts and Policies, 1960-1997." In: *Review of Population and Social Policy* (7), 83-101

Cliquet, Robert L. (1991): *The Second Demographic Transition: Fact or Fiction?* Strasbourg: Council of Europe

Dackweiler, Regina-Maria (2006): "Reproduktives Handeln im Kontext wohlfahrtsstaatlicher Geschlechterregime." In: Berger, Peter A./ Kahlert,

Heike (eds.): *Der demographische Wandel. Chancen für die Neuordnung der Geschlechterverhältnisse.* Frankfurt/ M., New York: Campus, 81-110

Daly, Mary (2004): "Changing Conceptions of Family and Gender Relations in European Welfare States and the Third Way." In: Lewis, Jane/ Surender, Rebecca (eds.): *Welfare State Change. Towards a Third Way?* Oxford: Oxford University Press, 135-154

Di Giorgio, Ginevra/ Fiori, Francesca/ Santarelli, Elisabetta/ Vignoli, Daniele (2007): *Gender and New Family Patterns in Europe: Attitudes, Behaviours, and Opinions. Working Paper 2007/14.* Florenz: Università degli Studi di Firenze, http://www.ds.unifi.it/ricerca/pubblicazioni/working_papers/2007/wp2007_14.pdf (10/07/2009)

Easterlin, Richard (1976): "The Conflict Between Aspirations and Resources." In: *Population and Development Review* 2 (3-4), 417-425

Ehrenreich, Barbara/ Hochschild, Arlie Russell (eds.) (2004): *Global Women. Nannies, Maids, and Sex Workers in the New Economy.* New York/ N.Y.: Metropolitan/ Owl Book

Esping-Andersen, Gøsta (2002): "A New Gender Contract." In: Esping-Andersen, Gøsta with Gallie, Duncan/ Hemerijck, Anton/ Myles, John: *Why We Need a New Welfare State.* Oxford, New York: Oxford University Press, 68-95

Eurostat (2009a): *Gesamtfruchtbarkeitsrate – Anzahl der Kinder pro Frau, 1996-2007,* http://epp.eurostat.ec.europa.eu/tgm/table.do?tab=table&init=1&plugin=1&language=de&pcode=tsdde220 (10/07/2009)

Eurostat (2009b): *Lebenserwartung bei der Geburt, nach Geschlecht – (Jahre), 1996-2007,* http://epp.eurostat.ec.europa.eu/tgm/table.do?tab=table&init=1&plugin=1&language=de&pcode=tps00025 (10/07/2009)

Foucault, Michel (1983): *Der Wille zum Wissen.* Frankfurt/ M.: Suhrkamp

Foucault, Michael (2004): *Geschichte der Gouvernementalität I: Sicherheit, Territorium, Bevölkerung.* Frankfurt/ M.: Suhrkamp

Fraser, Nancy (1997): "After the Family Wage: A Postindustrial Thought Experiment." In: Fraser, Nancy: *Justice Interruptus: Critical Reflections on the "Postsocialist" Condition.* New York, London: Routledge, 41-68

Gal, Susan/ Kligman, Gail (eds.) (2000a): *Reproducing Gender. Politics, Publics, and Every Day Life after Socialism.* Princeton/ N.J.: Princeton University Press

Gal, Susan/ Kligman, Gail (2000b): *The Politics of Gender after Socialism.* Princeton/ N.J.: Princeton University Press

Gauthier, Anne Hélène (1996): *The State and the Family. A Comparative Analysis of Family Policies in Individualized Countries.* Oxford: Oxford University Press

Giddens, Anthony (1984): *The Constitution of Society. Outline of the Theory of Structuration.* Berkeley, Los Angeles: University of California Press

Höpflinger, François (1997): *Bevölkerungssoziologie. Eine Einführung in bevölkerungssoziologische Ansätze und demographische Prozesse.* Weinheim, München: Juventa

Hummel, Diana (2000): *Der Bevölkerungsdiskurs. Demographisches Wissen und politische Macht.* Opladen: Leske + Budrich

Inglehart, Ronald (1977): *The Silent Revolution. Changing Values and Political Styles Among Western Publics.* Princeton/ N.J.: Princeton University Press

Kahlert, Heike (2006a): "Der demographische Wandel im Blick der Frauen- und Geschlechterforschung." In: Berger, Peter A./ Kahlert, Heike (eds.): *Der demographische Wandel. Chancen für die Neuordnung der Geschlechterverhältnisse.* Frankfurt/ M., New York: Campus, 295-309

Kahlert, Heike (2006b): "Emanzipation in der schrumpfenden Gesellschaft." In: *Berliner Debatte Initial* 17 (3), 9-23

Kahlert, Heike (2008): "Giddens' Projekt einer Institutionenanalyse der Moderne in seiner Bedeutung für die Frauen- und Geschlechterforschung." In: *Zeitschrift für Frauenforschung & Geschlechterstudien* 26 (3-4), 7-22

Kahlert, Heike (2009): "Die Transformation von Wohlfahrtsstaatlichkeit im demographischen Wandel: Der Beitrag der Familien- und Geschlechterpolitik der Europäischen Union." In: Ehlers, Hella/ Kahlert, Heike/ Linke, Gabriele/ Raffel, Dorit/ Rudlof, Beate/ Trappe, Heike (eds.): *Geschlechterdifferenz – und kein Ende? Sozial- und geisteswissenschaftliche Beiträge zur Genderforschung.* Münster, Hamburg, Berlin, Wien, London: Lit, 274-293

Kaufmann, Franz-Xaver (2005): *Schrumpfende Gesellschaft. Vom Bevölkerungsrückgang und seinen Folgen.* Frankfurt/ M.: Suhrkamp

Kreisky, Eva/ Löffler, Marion (2003): "Staat und Familie: Ideologie und Realität eines Verhältnisses." In: *Österreichische Zeitschrift für Politikwissenschaft* 32 (4), 375-388

Leitner, Sigrid/ Ostner, Ilona/ Schratzenstaller, Margit (eds.) (2004): *Wohl-*

fahrtsstaat und Geschlechterverhältnis im Umbruch. Was kommt nach dem Ernährermodell? Wiesbaden: VS Verlag für Sozialwissenschaften

Lesthaeghe, Ron (without year): *Second Demographic Transition.* http://www.vub.ac.be/SOCO/ron/final_textSDTBasilBlackwellEncyclop.doc (10/07/2009)

Lesthaeghe, Ron (1995): "The Second Demographic Transition in Western Countries: An Interpretation." In: Mason, Karen Oppenheim/ Jensen, An-Margritt (eds.): *Gender and Family Change in Industrialized Countries.* Oxford: Clarendon Press, 17-62

Lesthaeghe, Ron/ Page, Hilary/ Surkyn, John (1991): "Sind Einwanderer ein Ersatz für Geburten?" In: *Zeitschrift für Bevölkerungswissenschaft* 17 (3), 281-314

Lutz, Helma unter Mitarbeit von Susanne Schwalgin (2006): *Vom Weltmarkt in den Privathaushalt. Die neuen Dienstmädchen im Zeitalter der Globalisierung.* Opladen: Barbara Budrich

Mackinnon, Alison (1995): "Where Women Present at the Demographic Transition? Questions from a Feminist Historian to Historical Demographers." In: *Gender & History* 7 (2), 222-240

Maslow, Abraham (1954): *Motivation and Personality.* New York/ N.Y.: Harper & Row

Mason, Karen Oppenheim (1986): "The Status of Women: Conceptual and Methodological Issues in Demographic Studies." In: *Sociological Forum* 1 (2), 284-300

Mason, Karen Oppenheim/ Jensen, An-Margritt (eds.) (1995): *Gender and Family Change in Industrialized Countries.* Oxford: Clarendon Press

McDaniel, Susan A. (1996): "Toward a Synthesis of Feminist and Demographic Perspectives on Fertility." In: *The Sociological Quarterly* 37 (1), 83-104

McNay, Kirsty (2003): *Women's Changing Roles in the Context of the Demographic Transition. Background Paper Prepared for the Education for All Global Monitoring Report 2003/4 "Gender and Education for All: The Leap to Equality".* Paris: United Nations Education, Scientific and Cultural Organization, http://unesdoc.unesco.org/images/0014/001468/146807e.pdf (10/07/2009).

Metz-Göckel, Sigrid/ Morokvasic-Müller, Mirjana/ Münst, A. Senganata (eds.) (2008): *Migration and Mobility in Enlarged Europe. A Gender Perspective.* Opladen: Barbara Budrich

O'Connor, Julia S./ Olsen, Gregg M. (eds.) (1998): *Power Resource Theory and the Welfare State. A Critical Approach.* Toronto, Buffalo, London: University of Toronto Press

Presser, Harriet B. (1997): "Demography, Feminism, and the Science-Policy Nexus." In: *Population and Development Review* 23 (2), 295-331

Rerrich, Maria S. (2006): *Die ganze Welt zu Hause. Cosmobile Putzfrauen in privaten Haushalten.* Hamburg: Hamburger Edition

Riley, Nancy E. (1997): *Gender, Power, and Population Change.* Washington/ D.C.: Population Reference Bureau

Riley, Nancy E. (1998): "Research on Gender in Demography: Limitations and Constraints." In: *Population Research and Policy Review* 17 (6), 521-538

Riley, Nancy E. (1999): "Challenging Demography: Contributions from Feminist Theory." In: *Sociological Forum* 14 (3), 369-397

Rodenstein, Marianne/ Bock, Stephanie/ Heeg, Susanne (1996): "Reproduktionsarbeitskrise und Stadtstruktur. Zur Entwicklung von Agglomerationsräumen aus feministischer Sicht." In: Akademie für Raumforschung und Landesplanung: *Agglomerationsräume in Deutschland. Ansichten, Einsichten, Aussichten.* Hannover: ARS, 26-50

Sauer, Birgit (1999): "'Es rettet uns (k)ein höh'res Wesen...'. Neoliberale Geschlechterkonstrukte in der Ära der Globalisierung." In: Stolz-Willig, Brigitte/ Veil, Mechthild (eds.): *Es rettet uns kein höh'res Wesen. Feministische Perspektiven der Arbeitsgesellschaft.* Hamburg: VSA, 215-239

Solsona i Pairó, Montserrat (1997): "The Second Demographic Transition from a Gender Perspective: The Case of Catalonia." In: Cosio-Zavala, Maria-Eugenia (ed.): *Women and Families. Evolution of the Status of Women as Factor and Consequence of Changes in Family Dynamics.* Paris: CICRED, 171-190

Szreter, Simon (1993): "The Idea of Demographic Transition and the Study of Fertility Change: A Critical Intellectual History." In: *Population and Development Review* 19 (4), 659-701

van de Kaa, Dirk J. (1987): *Europe's Second Demographic Transition.* Washington/ D.C.: Population Reference Bureau

van de Kaa, Dirk J. (2002): *The Idea of a Second Demographic Transition in Industrialized Countries. Paper presented at the Sixth Welfare Policy Seminar of the National Institute of Population and Social Security, To-*

kyo, Japan, 29 January 2002. http://www.ipss.go.jp/webj-ad/WebJournal.files/population/2003_4/Kaa.pdf (10/07/2009)

van der Loo, Hans/van Reijen, Willem ([2]1997): *Modernisierung. Projekt und Paradox.* München: dtv

van Krieken, Robert (1997): "Sociology and the Reproductive Self: Demographic Transitions and Modernity." In: *Sociology* 31 (3), 445-471

Mieke Verloo

Trojan Horses and the Implications of Strategic Framing: Reflections on Gender Equality Policies, Intimate Citizenship and Demographic Change[1]

Introduction

The current presence of demographic arguments in European societies is starting to link several debates that used to be separate. The lack of children in European societies is problematized in view of the economy or because of the financing of the welfare state, generating debates, initiatives and research on the causes of the decline in child births, changing compositions and roles of families, the consequences for society and the best strategies for the future. As women are given attention (be it sometimes implicitly) as the obvious 'producers' of children in the emerging debates, it is time to take a closer look at what happens in policy making in Europe, and how gender equality is seen to be related to fertility, demographic decline or growth. This chapter will first briefly recapitulate how feminism has framed fertility in the first and second wave, and then present research on European family policies, as these policies are one of the obvious locations of interventions and understandings of gender, family and fertility. Earlier comparative research and recent data on gender equality policies in all countries of the European Union will be used to show how the goals of demographic balance and gender equality are often interwoven, implicitly or strategically. Still, some reflections on the implications of this for gender equality will end in more questions than answers.

Earlier feminist positions on fertility

Reproductive rights were at the heart of the second wave of the women's movement in Europe, which focused on the right of women to choose whether

1 Mieke Verloo is very grateful to Waltraud Ernst and Heike Kahlert for having spurred thought on the subject of this chapter, and for being wonderful, patient and careful editors.

or not, and when, to have babies. The most urgent demand was for the right *not* to have babies, and to have access to safe and affordable contraceptive and abortion methods. In this sense, the relationship of the second wave of the women's movement to fertility and motherhood had a predominantly 'negative' accent: it framed fertility and motherhood as one of the capabilities of (most) women that was closely linked to patriarchy, oppression and exploitation, and that transferred sexual and gender inequalities in child bearing and rearing to other domains such as education, the labour market and political participation.

Not all feminists in the second wave were altogether negative about women's capacity to bear children, but some extremely negative voices were very loud. Shulamith Firestone (1970), who saw biological reproduction as one of the biggest 'causes' of gender inequality, and in whose vision true gender equality could only come about if full artificial reproduction was possible and organized, keeping the power of fertility in the hands of women without burdening them with it, is maybe the best example. This is a discourse of the 'womb as a trap for women'.

At the same time, there were also feminists who saw women's biological capacity to reproduce the species as proof of their greater virtue, or simply as a model for organizing the world differently.

At the time of the first wave of feminism, Alexandra Kollontai, an early Russian feminist, talked about the 'double contribution of women to society', meaning that women not only, like men, contribute to the production processes in society, but that they have a unique second contribution, namely to 'produce new citizens' (Kollontai 1923). In Kollontai's view, motherhood is not in itself a sufficient reason for society to support mothers, but they are entitled to extra care and special treatment from society if they also share in the work for society – in the official economy – with men. She argues that the mother's function is a highly important but complementary social obligation towards society, because she produces a healthy child, breast feeding it and raising it to be a future worker for society. Her argument was meant to show how important women were for societies, defending their value against dominant understandings of women as 'less important' human beings. Even if her position strongly leans towards motherhood as a *duty* for women, I did not find any contestation of this historical feminist position.

Looking at current debates on the greying of societies and on problems related to demographic changes in Europe, Kollontai's argument sounds strangely familiar. In this chapter, I will give some examples of European countries where the demographic argument is used to defend changes in reconciliation policies, in labour market policies or in gender equality policies. Interesting things happen in these arguments that need to be reflected upon. In particular, I would like to consider whether we can say anything at all about the question whether the current attention to demographic 'problems' is positive or negative for gender equality. I use 'gender equality' in the previous sentence as shorthand for 'a vision towards the abolishment of gender inequality'. First, I will turn to European Union family policies to see if there are trends visible there.

European Union family policies and gender equality

Recent analyses of European Union family policies by Stratigaki and Duncan have produced interesting insights on the development of issues connecting gender equality and family policy.[2] They differ in what they consider important accents and shifts in framing. In an impressive overview and analysis, Maria Stratigaki shows how a concept introduced to encourage gender equality in the labour market – what is mostly labeled 'reconciliation of work and family life' – gradually shifted meaning as it became incorporated in the European Employment Strategy of the 1990s. From an objective with a feminist potential, it became a purely market-oriented objective. What her analysis shows is that, first of all, the concept of reconciling work and family has mainly addressed the gendered division of labour, not so much the gendered organization of intimacy. The original goal was 'sharing', later shifting to the policy objective of 'reconciliation of work and family life'.

> "Sharing is a term associated with equality of women and men, defining a policy objective in the area of gender relations, whereas reconciliation is derived from labour market analysis and has a more economic orientation" (Stratigaki 2004: 2).

This accent on the organization of labour is a shift that has allowed a growing policy priority on the creation of employment.

Secondly, this shift towards the organization of labour has involved a

2 The description of Duncan and Stratigaki is taken from Verloo et al. (2005).

move away from a focus on gender equality towards a focus on reproducing and consolidating women's roles and responsibilities as primary care givers. In order to facilitate the participation of women in the labour market, new policies often mainly consist of creating possibilities for women to combine care for children and paid labour, while they involve only minor options for stimulating fathers to take care of their children. This focus reproduces the norm that it is women's responsibility to take care of children, while this is optional for fathers, and thus fails to challenge stereotyped gender relations (Stratigaki 2004: 19).

Simon Duncan's analysis of the development of EU policy on 'the reconciliation of work and family life' focuses on another policy frame that interferes with gender equality, what he calls the 'demographic time bomb discourse'. In his analysis, the policies of the European Union have never been the outcome of concerns for gender equality merely. Rather, the central theme has been demography. The main reason for higher wages for women in France, according to Duncan, ultimately was French natalism, rationalized by the (gendered) equality principles of 1789, and the importance of national gender contracts for competing national political economies (Duncan 2002: 307). Duncan argues that in the 1990s various policy problems such as ageing of the population, low fertility and the need for a flexible work force could be addressed by reconciliation. The gender (equality) discourse could then fit into and exploit this agenda, given further impetus in the mid-1990s by the accession of Finland and Sweden, who had to deliver to their home constituencies (Duncan 2002: 311). Duncan concludes that, even if the dominant theme in the EU is not gender equality but a competitive economy, the debates on the demographic time bomb and on flexible labour have moved gender equality centre stage, if only because gender equality is seen as necessary to achieve success in these fields. Duncan (2002: 310) identifies two sets of policy responses to this perceived 'demographic time bomb'. Firstly, negative and descriptive measures, such as redefining women as child bearers in traditional households; and secondly, positive and supportive policies, such as changing structures so that women and men can both have a life at work and children. The latter discourse, he claims, became prominent on the EU agenda via 'reconciling employment and family life' on the accession of Sweden and Finland in 1994, actually aiming at a redistribution of work and status between women and men, or changing the gender contract (Duncan 2002: 307).

More generally, there seem to be two opposing assumptions underneath the variety of regimes in family policy: one stating that gender equality is not only good for women, but also for families; and the opposing one presenting a traditional division of labour as good for families while gender equality is bad (Kaufman 2000). In the last type of regime, family policy is often a way of facilitating home care for children by mothers.

Ideologies of motherhood in European rulings about families

Clare McGlynn analyzed, in particular, the ideologies of motherhood and the understandings of what a family is according to the rulings of the European Court of Justice (McGlynn 2000, 2001a, 2001b). She analyzed a series of cases of the European Court of Justice where this Court has reproduced, and thereby legitimated a traditional vision of motherhood and the role of women in the family and in society in general. She argues that it is important to analyze judicial reasoning, because "once a set of ideas is embedded in a particular discourse, such as judicial reasoning, it becomes particularly difficult to dislodge" (McGlynn 2000: 30). Her understanding of the content of this dominant 'traditional' ideology of motherhood follows Ann Oakley (1974: 186): "the belief that all women need to be mothers, that all mothers need their children and that all children need their mothers" (McGlynn 2000: 31). This ideology legitimates the existing sexual division of labour and particular designated roles for fathers (as breadwinners, protectors and authority figures).

She shows how the Court's approach has developed through the European Union's 'protection of women' principle, which can override the promotion of equal treatment. This 'protection of pregnancy and maternity' has developed into a 'protection of the dominant ideology of motherhood'. She discusses cases where men wanted to take a leave after adopting a child (in Italy 1983), and were denied this right. The European Court of Justice agreed with Italy that the difference in treatment between women and men "cannot be regarded as [sex] discrimination" because of the "need of the child to bond with the mother" (McGlynn 2001a: 332). This 'sex' difference apparently exists even in the case of adoption.... In other cases, the Court repeated that it is legitimate to 'protect the special relationship of a mother with her child' to deny men access to parental leave. There is no desire to protect or encourage fathers in these rulings. This went on in cases through the 90s, where the Court prohibited discrimination on the basis of pregnancy, all the time repeating the 'need to protect the special relationship between a mother and her child'.

Similarly in cases on discrimination at work, the Court stated that 'the aim of (European) community policy was to encourage and if possible adapt working conditions to family responsibilities, and to ensure the protection of women in their family lives and in the course of their professional activities'. The crucial factor here of course, as McGlynn points out, is what constitutes a family life in need of protection. This is a conception of family life based on the dominant ideology of motherhood:

> "[...] it is policy to change working conditions to meet *existing* family responsibilities – not that family responsibilities need to change in order to liberate women" (McGlynn 2001a: 339, emphasis by the author).

This is not to say that working conditions do not need to change, but to stress that they would need to change for both women *and* men. In its understanding of family life, the Court is not protecting women, but rather the existing role of women in the family.

In another work, McGlynn (2001b) analyzes the emergence of the family in the European Charter of Fundamental Rights, because the Charter, for the first time, recognizes the impact of the European Union on families, and the role it plays in shaping, conceptualizing and regulating families. The attention of the European Union for families began with the granting of rights to the families of migrant workers, and the increasing impact of the European Union's sex equality laws on family forms and roles. At the beginning, rights were granted to the families of migrant workers to facilitate the free movement of workers, and to strengthen the European economy. The family policy was driven by demographic concerns too. In line with many international human rights texts, the family and family life need to be protected.

What then is a family in European law and policy? Which families would benefit from the Charter's provisions, and which families would continue to be excluded? This question is central for McGlynn (2001b). She concludes that the 'respect' extended to family life varies according to a hierarchy of relationships. Heterosexual marriage is at the top of the hierarchy, being a protected state and one where there is always 'family life'. In second place are cohabiting heterosexual relationships. Therefore, when a child is born outside of marriage, there may still be a 'family unit'. As long as the cohabiting relationship is closely assimilated to marriage, it may gain some respect and recognition, although the status of unmarried fathers remains quite unclear. At the bottom of the hierarchy are gay, lesbian and transsexual relationships for which there is little respect and even less protection. Homosexual unions do not fall within the right to respect for family life.

In conclusion, at the European Union level the concept of family is narrow and traditional, although there are some slight positive developments (such as recognition for cohabitation). The Court justifies its refusal to expand its understanding of what a family is with the 'lack of consensus among member states' to see same-sex relationships as equivalent to heterosexual relationships because of the 'need to protect the family'. Therefore, the family life to be protected is the traditional heterosexual family, with its designated traditional roles. Across Europe, not all countries have such an excluding definition of what a family is. While some countries, such as the Netherlands, have a different and more inclusive understanding of families – a family is defined as: one or more adults taking care of/being responsible for children (State Secretary on Public Health, Welfare and Sports 1996) –, it is also argued (e.g. Stychin 2003) that legislation on same-sex partnership and marriage does not 'radicalize' understandings of family, but re-centres the traditional family through a preference for married couples. This reinforcing of "coupledom" (Stychin 2003: 83) can be visible in the granting of benefits only to couples. This means that exclusion or inclusion in the understandings of families involves not only the definitions of families that are officially put forward, but also a 'material' inclusion of all families in any kind of family policy.

Economy, demography, fertility and gender equality: different policy goals meet

So far, I have shown that there are typical patterns of understanding at the European Union level of how 'families', 'mothers' and economic and demographic dynamics go together. This results in a picture where 'reconciliation of work and family life' is a policy goal or a set of policy actions that can be used: primarily to benefit the economy (see Knijn/Smit 2007), primarily to benefit demographic developments such as increasing fertility, or primarily to benefit gender equality.

In policy making, there are many different push and pull factors and a multitude of strategic framings in which various actors defend one goal masquerading as another. This does not make analysis any easier, but as Stratigaki and Duncan have shown, it can be done. In the context of a comparative European research project, Karin Tertinegg conducted an excellent analysis of Austrian family politics. Austria is a very fine example of a country where demographic 'concerns' (the choice of words is intentional here to stress that it is seen to be a problem) take on a nationalistic character. After 1999/2000, when the landslide in the Austrian elections placed the far-right Freedom Party (FPOE), led by the charismatic and controversial Jörg Haider, in second place, a new coalition government between this FPOE and the People's Party (OEVP) ruled Austria. Typically, a new focus on family emerged in Austria: 'domestic work' was now to be 'valued equally to wage labour'; 'reconciliation' was contrasted to the concept of 'choice (of women) between work and family life'.[3] 'Family' was de-gendered and the question of having children was politicized. In such a frame, the family is the centre of a good and prosperous Austrian society, and an ideal place to provide for a child's needs. The pre-modern, multi-child farmer's family is presented as a response to the perceived danger of 'erosion of families' caused by globalization, modernization and individualization. Financial benefits are seen as stimulants for young people to give birth to more children, and for women in particular to give up employment to care for their children themselves. A demographic aspect is stressed: Austria is presented as a 'dying nation', in need of more (Austrian) children in order to keep up the pension and welfare system. Women now constitute a homogenous group of persons who are best capable to perform caring tasks within families. The importance of 'founding' a family, for women to perform care work within that family and to value this work equally to waged labour are central to the frame which we found to have become hegemonic after 2000 (Verloo et al. 2005). Men are seen as (main) breadwinners, who, individually, should try to be more active fathers.

In contradiction to the focus on family as sanctuary, there is a simultaneous neoliberal frame of 'choice' and a dual-breadwinner model. As for 'freedom of choice', 'reconciling work and family life' in the frame of the conservative parties takes on a strong, and contradictory, value frame. Favouring –'choosing' – family and family work seems to be the normative priority,

3 The description of Austrian family policies is taken from Verloo et al. (2005: 137 et seq.).

particularly for women. In terms of the two sets of policy responses identified by Duncan, it seems that in Austria, with its visible re-traditionalization of gender relations in family policy, mostly negative measures are part of the current frame.

In Austria the findings show a similar, yet markedly different, cooptation of gender concepts as at the EU level (Stratigaki 2004). Stratigaki argues that in the EU a key concept – sharing – was conceptually transformed by its subordination to other policy priorities – e.g. the labour market –, resulting in a loss of potential for changing gender relations (Stratigaki 2004: 3). A cooptation of concepts also occurred in the Austrian frames; however, even if the key concept originally appears to be the same in both the EU and the Austrian frames – more equal sharing – the policy priorities to which this original concept was subordinated in the Austrian frames clearly differ from the EU level. In contrast to Stratigaki's findings, a clear labour-market focus was present in Austria only until 1999/2000; afterwards, a different kind of cooptation can be detected, as labour-market objectives are articulated in a more hidden, less obvious way, accompanied by the emergence of a contradictory family-as-sanctuary frame, in which gender equality has become de-articulated as a goal. In such framing, the family is a de-gendered place of important socialization and tasks for society, and there is a naturalization of women and men and a re-traditionalization of the distribution of labour. Even in the frames of the left parties after 2000, female gainful employment is not stressed as much as it was before 2000; rather, 'reconciliation' of work and family life for women is stressed. Cooptation in Austrian 'reconciliation' frames changed the original meaning of 'sharing responsibilities between men and women' to a value frame of founding a family and caring for family members, with a tendency to hold women responsible for the decline of families and birth rates where that value frame is particularly strong. A loss of potential for changing gender relations is apparent. This new frame seems to carry rather contradictory goals: women are to be both primarily responsible for family care and domestic work – and, at the same time, be available for flexible forms of labour – because of their roles as caregivers. 'Choice' between family and work then is a metaphor for market oriented flexibilization: on the one hand, the new frame identifies women's (full-time) labour-market participation as a potential danger for the family-as-sanctuary; on the other hand, it is seen as inevitable that women must contribute to family income by preferably flexible part-time work.

A comparison of Austria with the Netherlands and Greece on their family policies concludes that the diagnosis of the policy problem that should be addressed by family policies is primarily the division of paid labour, and that representations of the division of unpaid labour or care as a problem are scarce, and seem to be found mainly in the 1990s (in the Netherlands, Austria and at the EU level). Slight echoes of the importance of more paternal involvement are the only part of this that remains, but these calls are never connected to hard policy. Moreover, a second common pattern is the absence of attention for gender inequality within families as a problem in itself. In most texts, families are constructed as safe havens, and problems occurring within families are seen as linked to changes in the structure of families, or to women's participation on the labour market. The implicit reasoning is that problems in families are a new phenomenon. Because there are many problems for society in connection with families, such as low fertility and generational solidarity, and because of the absence of a gender equality perspective, this framing is easily linked to traditional thinking in which families are supposed to produce children for societies, and women are the main persons responsible within families to fulfil this role.

Moreover, it is striking that in all three countries, and even at the EU level, a traditionalization of thinking about families and the role of women in families can be detected. With the exception of Greece, this seems to be a re-traditionalization. Linked to shifts in governments to the right, the analyzed texts are gendered, but not from a gender equality perspective. The Austrian frame (since 1999/2000) is the strongest of this kind, seeing the problem to be that women are forced to choose between work and family, and arguing for a family policy that facilitates the right choice, namely the choice for the care of the family. Here, not the gendered division of labour is the problem, but rather the ungendering of the division of labour, which is described as a negative process that should be reversed. The findings of our analysis are in line with Duncan (2002), as the frame is linked to the 'demographic time bomb discourse', and especially to negative policy responses. The element of putting a higher value to care and to housework is found only in connection to this frame. In Austria, an additional problem is constructed to be the lack of rights of fathers to their children. This frame takes the element of a lack of involvement of fathers in families on board to plea for more fathers' rights. The soft policy for gender equality is then combined with hard measures supporting father's rights. In this last frame, the gender problematic seems to be exclusively represented as female domination over men in families.

The above analysis shows attempts to legitimize gender equality by linking measures originating in gender equality policies, such as child care services, part-time work and parental leave with other goals such as flexible labour, more employment, more children or better functioning families. This is a problem, as increasingly the accent seems not to be on gender equality, but on traditional gender roles within families. These re-traditionalized frames redirect measures such as reconciliation towards goals that could very well be contradictory to gender equality. The underlying assumption in such frames seems to be that gender equality is not good for families, and hence detrimental to society. The Austrian case shows this most clearly, Greece to some extent as well. In the Netherlands and at the EU level, the assumption that gender equality leads to well-functioning families seems to predominate, but elements of the opposite can be found too. In the absence of a gender equality family policy, these assumptions are not addressed explicitly. As a result, the EU and the Netherlands create a vacuum that apparently can be filled quite easily by frames that build upon the idea that gender equality is bad for families and for society, and that policies being presented as gender equality policies therefore are actually reinforcing gender inequality.

Demographic arguments and gender equality policies in European countries

In the context of an ongoing pan-European comparative research project on gender equality policies[4], data have been gathered about policies related to reconciliation, care work, tax benefit policies on non-employment, equal pay, marriage and divorce, reproductive rights and violence against women. In this project, policy texts (laws, policy reports, parliamentary debates and civil society texts) have been coded using the Critical Frame Analysis (Verloo 2007). This section takes a closer look at those policy reports that had an underlying norm of 'improving the demographic balance'.[5] This was the case for 17 texts

4 The project *QUING* studies all EU countries, plus two candidate countries – Turkey and Croatia – and the European Union itself (cf. www.quing.eu).

5 This is a preliminary analysis, for which the data from laws, parliamentary debates and civil society texts have not been used yet. I have used internal reports written

(out of 341 policy reports). Note that this is only a small number of texts, and a preliminary analysis. The analysis will mainly show *how* arguments are made in the texts that link 'gender' and 'improving the demographic balance'. The texts are from: Bulgaria, Croatia, Estonia, Germany, Hungary, Italy, Poland, Romania and Spain. The strong presence of Eastern European countries should come as no surprise, as all of the Central and Eastern European Union member states judge their population growth as insufficient, their fertility rates as too low, and, all have pro-natalist policies (UN 2008). In contrast, only six of the old EU-15 judge their population growth too low, and only three see reason for intervention (Greece, Italy, Austria) (UN 2008).

In general, in these policy plans the links between gender (in)equality problems or objectives and demographic balance problems or objectives are twofold: one link is about the well-being or chances of women as mothers, and another is about reproductive rights and reproductive health. The link can be made either in such a way that the problem of gender inequality or the objective of gender equality is put forward as most important, or so that the demographic problem or objective is put as the final, most important one. Occasionally, texts are written so that they can be read both ways, which obviously serves the strategical goal of enabling support by a wide range of actors. Also, the 'problem' of demographic decline is sometimes not presented as linked to gender (in)equality at all.

An ambivalent example is the Bulgarian National Programme *Support Maternity* from 2007 that reasons that demographic crisis and unemployment or low employment of women should be reduced by the state by encouraging measures and policy plans. The main measure that is proposed is to create employment for unemployed women in child care services so that both reconciliation problems (implicitly seen as a reason to not have children) and unemployment are tackled at the same time. The argument of improving the demographic balance is mentioned as an additional reason to 'have better benefits for mothers' (Bulgaria, Benefit Maternity Programme 2007). "In Bulgaria, the policies target 'women and men as working parents' but much more in respect to the demographic crisis than to the economic growth" (Stoykova 2009: 7). In the Bulgarian case, the reference to demographic balance has nationalistic undertones. There is

by researchers in the *QUING* project. Although these reports are not public, I have included them in the bibliography to do justice to the work of these researchers.

> "a neoconservative view of the model of the family and gender roles. According to this voice, the demographic crisis is a result of the emancipation processes and the high birth rates of the Roma minority and it is to be solved by the return to the 'traditional family values' (of the Bulgarians)" (Stoykova 2009: 12).

The German text (*Together for Germany. With Courage and Humanity. Coalition Agreement of CDU, CSU and SPD [Gemeinsam für Deutschland. Mit Mut und Menschlichkeit. Koalitionsvertrag von CDU, CSU und SPD]* 2005), argues that Germany needs more children, and that the well-being of families and children needs to be ensured in order to have a higher birth rate. This is juxtaposed with ideas of how to financially support families. More generally, this text

> "has a wider range of frames: After starting off with demographic considerations, it also argues for financial independence of each partner which points to a 'gender equality' framing. More generally, it points to the need to secure the well-being and social security of families in order that they have children ('social justice')" (Urbanek 2009: 22).

The German text is a good example in that it shows how various kinds of arguments are strongly interwoven, and also in that it remains unclear what social units are meant when the text talks about families.

For Germany, other authors have also analyzed the current reforms of German family policy, asking the question whether "demography is a push towards gender equality" (Henninger et al. 2008). They see reconciliation policies as especially important for effects on fertility, and in that sense interpret the reform as "a child-bearing activation" (Henninger et al. 2008: 304). Overall, while they assess the potential impact of the reform to be greater towards increasing the labour force participation of mothers, and towards diminishing the support for motherhood as a socially acceptable alternative to employment, they nonetheless remain critical, mostly because the reform has stronger incentives for parents with higher incomes, and as such is a 'double activation' of highly qualified women to be active in the labour market and have children, while the 'less worthy' are prevented from having a family (Henninger et al. 2008: 305). Thus they see a positive effect on gender equality in the labour market, but a negative effect on class inequality. What is presented to be about gender equality is de facto dividing women into categories that deserve to be mothers and categories that do not. They do not question the 'demographic pressure' as such but rather accept it as an economic or welfare state problem, and they do not elaborate on how gender (in)equality and fertility can be connected other than through its relationships with labour market participation.

There are also texts that frame policies about reproductive rights as linked to demographic balance. An example is the *Estonian State Reproductive Health Programme for 2000-2009*, where the low birth rate is not articulated as a problem, but an increase in births is mentioned as a positive effect of more sexual education and services. In such reasoning, a high number of abortions results in less pregnancies, while more *wanted* pregnancies are the aim. In general, in Estonia,

> "there is a strong presence of nationalism/demographic balance and family and justice frames. The emphasis on demography indicates the constant and covert worry in present Estonian politics to guarantee the survival of the nation and to achieve positive natural growth (here then by means of favourable benefit policies that would encourage people to have more children). The family and justice frame is connected with the latter frame, prioritizing the well-being of families" (Jaigma 2009: 18).

Similarly, in Poland, the theme of demographic crisis is present (but not dominant) in debates on abortion. The 2004 governmental report on the *Realization of the Act of Family Planning, Foetus Protection and the Availability of Abortion* mentions the low birth rate and the 'new model of family' as social problems. Also in the case of Poland, texts on reconciliation link gender equality and demographic balance arguments. The more difficult situation of women on the labour market is related to motherhood and problems that women have with reconciliation of work and care. However, in some documents this frame is related with a demographic balance frame, in the sense that discrimination in the labour market is presented as a factor for women for delaying decisions on motherhood (Dabrowksa 2009).

In Romania as well, demography issues are quite central in issues of non-employment. The main objective of the *Government Programme for 2005-2008: Improving the Socio-economic Balance of the Family* is to improve the socio-economic balance of the family. Special social assistance measures are aimed at increasing birth rates through the allocation of financial incentives for families, parents or mothers. The value of durable marriage is affirmed through the allocation of a specific benefit to young couples, provided that both marry for the first time.

> "Although population growth is a norm too, the measures proposed to increase birth rates give financial incentives to families, parents or mothers only for the first three children. In the Romanian context, this seems to be a measure intended to curb Roma fertility" (Popa 2009: 19).

Demography is a central issue of the 2006 Romanian *Green Book of Population*. This document sees the causes of the demographic problems in a mix of economic difficulties and the devastating economic effects of transition in Romania, with changes in values and attitudes that now orient the preferences of young couples towards one child, rather than two or three. The change in preferences for the number of children is associated with women's participation in the labour market and their emancipation. "Other factors are reviewed and considered, but this one particular factor reveals the underlying norm that women are the main caregivers" (Popa 2009: 21). Particularly highly-educated middle-class women are seen as the actors most responsible for the low fertility rates. The most important effect of falling birth rates, the document argues further, is the ageing of the population, and elderly women are most affected by the resulting care and social security deficit. In an attempt to reverse the negative demographic trends, the policy plan proposes to encourage migration to Romania from those countries that have a Romanian population. In a reasoning that resonates highly with Kollontai:

> "These policy debates (in particular, the *Green Book of Population* in Romania) seem to be informed by the notion that individuals have to be 'productive' in order to be socially useful. There are two ways of achieving a larger population of productive citizens: one is to have more citizens (increasing birth rates); the other is to make citizens active for longer time (promote so called 'active ageing'). There is a tension in these policy debates between the norms of social usefulness and productivity and those of respect for the right of individuals and couples to make choices about whether or not to have children and how many of them" (Popa 2009: 22 et seq.).

In the Croatian case,

> "the demographic decline/balance frame is mostly not gendered [...]. Women are not held responsible for demographic decline. In fact, demographic decline is seen as an economic problem, a result of general economic deprivation that is not linked to gender equality policies or family/work reconciliation" (Frank 2009: 18).

In Italy, a 'demographic crisis frame' can be found in the 2007 Minister of Family's introductory speech to the Conference aimed at drafting the National Plan for Families and in the 2006 Annual Relation on the Implementation of Law 40/2004. The Minister "signals how Law 40/2004 on assisted reproduction which should have increased the number of pregnancies and newborn babies, has actually led to a decrease of both indicators" (Del Giorgio 2009: 31). In other documents, on the contrary,

> "the very low Italian birth rate as well as the discrepancy between the average number of children per family (1.35) and the number of children averagely wished by couples (2 or more) is perceived as a grave problem. The parallel increased number of very old persons is also signalled as a grave problem" (Del Giorgio 2009: 31).

It seems that in Italy, the reasoning at least links the goal of increasing the birth rate to a goal of gender equality (in this case, helping women with fertility problems or helping women to have the number of children they want). Yet, the wording is degendered (helping couples), so maybe this is not really about gender equality…

Some countries present complex arguments linking different goals. In the Hungarian policy plan *Conception of the Governmental Programme on Demographic Policies* from 2003, gender equality is present as a goal:

> "the transformation of the division of labour frame is most fully present, gender equality is seen as an important goal towards improving the demographic balance, which in turn is argued to be important in order to improve the economy" (Dombos et al. 2009: 18).

In the context of policy on sterilization, a

> "Constitutional Court decision on voluntary sterilization, as well as the left wing MPs borrowing from the reasoning of this decision, claim that prohibition of sterilization is not a solution for demographic decline, and that rather an alternative solution of a family-friendly environment (mostly financial incentives) should be used instead to solve the demographic crisis" (Dombos et al. 2009: 29).

In Hungary, the texts on assisted reproduction mainly stress the need "to making people happy by enabling them to have children if they want to" (Dombos et al. 2009: 26). Here we see that gender equality, in a degendered way (family friendly), remains an important goal in itself, even if it is seen as more important because it contributes to other important goals such as economic growth and a good demographic balance.

The Spanish text also articulates to some extent a position on choice related to children as relevant to reconciliation policies (Peterson/Pérez Orozco, 2009). *The Integral Plan for Family Support 2001-2004* has a complex diagnosis linking problems of low birth rate, ageing of the population, reconciliation and women's incorporation in the labour market. Also, the gender care gap is seen as part of the problem. The Plan highlights that there are two categories of families that have substantial problems with reconciliation: big families and single parents (single mothers). Also, it represents the gap between the number of children that women/families want to have and the number of children they have, as part of the problem. The Plan wants to support families so that they can make their own decision (about having more children, above all), and has special measures targeting big families or single parents. The idea is that if policies result in a better economic situation of families they will have more children. While the unequal distribution of tasks within the family is part of the diagnosis, according to this Plan it is the role of families to improve sharing responsibilities and promote egalitarian values.

So it seems that in Italy, Hungary and Spain, policy reasoning on demography includes attention on how context affects people's decision to have children or not. This is presented as linked to the demographic crisis in that 'people do not have the number of children that they would like to have', representing a common interest between citizens and the state. While women are sometimes mentioned as the ones that 'want' children, the discourse is not explicitly gendered, and does not include a deep analysis.

Reflections

In this chapter, I have shown that explicit feminist positions on fertility have often been negative ones, but that explicit feminist positions of the first and second wave of the feminist movement have differed widely in articulating the meaning of motherhood for gender equality. Moreover, on the European Union level, I have shown that European family policies to some extent have buried gender equality goals 'beneath' goals to strengthen the economy or the demographic balance. Research on the rulings of the European court have shown that the background to understand reconciliation policies and their material impact is the dominant classic patriarchal understanding of what constitutes a family and what are the proper/normal/existing roles in families that are in need of protection or facilitation. I have used Austria to highlight that conservative and nationalistic tendencies can be very close to family policies that accentuate higher fertility rates.

Using data from the *QUING* project, I have tried to show how policies on reconciliation or reproductive rights include a differentiation between categories of women that are deemed worthy of reproducing: women with the Bulgarian, Estonian or Romanian nationality, highly qualified women in Germany and Romania), and women that are not (Roma women in Romania, poorly qualified women in Germany, women with the wrong nationality in Bulgaria, Estonia, Romania).

Policies on reconciliation or reproductive rights are also a very ambiguous field of policies in terms of their underlying norms and reasoning: they mix goals on economy, demography and gender equality. Looking at policies of the European Union and of European countries, I ask myself what kind of Trojan horse reconciliation policy is: Are policies on reconciliation and reproductive rights presented as a way to protect 'family values' but de facto hiding feminist demands on the ability to have children and on childcare? Or are policies on reconciliation and reproductive rights presented to be about gender equality, only to be hiding a strengthening of conventional family roles and an instrumentalization of women for the economy (much like the old Soviet model that resonates with Kollontai's ideas)? Or do they do both things at the same time, implying that the proof of the pudding will be in the eating – that is, in the specific implementation of measures proposed in specific contexts.

After having looked at some of the literature on fertility, gender equality and demographic issues, I also wonder about the absence or lack of visibility of feminist voices on this issue. There seems to be an urgent need to articulate feminist positions. More individualist feminist positions could accentuate the need for women to have a real choice about whether or not to have children. A recent article by Hobson and Olah sees the 'lack' of fertility as an expression of a lack of 'capabilities' that women have to raise children and have paid work. Implicitly, this seems to be a demand for 'the right of all women to have children'. Their concept of a 'birth strike' as a social phenomenon that reflects the disjuncture between aspirations and expectations and capabilities is a good example of this. They see economic uncertainty, inequality in families and different risk assessment by women and men when it comes to family formation (Hobson/Olah 2006). But what about more structural feminist positions? Would these imply that 'sharing' is a way to improve the demographic balance? Would these have any positions on what the role and rights of men would be? How would a cyborg think about gender equality and the demographic 'problem'? Is there any articulated feminist position on whether the demographic time bomb exists at all? Whether it is really a serious problem? Whether it needs governmental action? How to deal with it in a gender equal way?

Bibliography

Dabrowksa, Madalena (2009): *LARG Comparative Country Study Poland.* Internal QUING Report (unpublished)

Del Giorgio, Elena (2009). *Italy – EU Frame Comparison Report.* Internal QUING Report (unpublished)

Dombos, Tamás/ Kispéter, Erika/ Krizsán, Andrea (2009): *Hungary – EU Frame Comparison Report.* Internal QUING Report (unpublished)

Duncan, Simon (2002): "Policy Discourses on 'Reconciling Work and Life' in the EU." In: *Social Policy and Society* 1 (4), 305-314

Firestone, Shulamith (1970): *The Dialectic of Sex: The Case for Feminist Revolution.* New York: William Morrow

Frank, Ana (2009): *Croatia – EU Frame Comparison Report.* Internal QUING Report (unpublished)

Henninger, Annette/ Wimbauer, Christine/ Dombrowski, Rosine (2008): "Demography as a Push toward Gender Equality? Current Reforms of German Family Policy." In: *Social Politics* 15 (3), 287-314

Hobson, Barbara/ Olah, Livia Sz. (2006): "Birthstrikes? Agency and Capabilities in the Reconciliation of Employment and Family." In: *Marriage & Family Review* 39 (3), 197-227

Jaigma, Martin (2009): *LARG Comparative Country Study Estonia.* Internal QUING Report (unpublished)

Kaufman, Gayle (2000): "Do Gender Role Attitudes Matter? Family Formation and Dissolution Among Traditional and Egalitarian Men and Women." In: *Journal of Family Issues* 21 (1), 128-144

Knijn, Trudie/ Smit, Arnoud (2007): *Mixed Life Course Paradigms: Reconciliation of Work and Family Life or Reconciliation of Individualisation and Solidarity?* Paper presented at ESPAnet conference Vienna 20-22 September 2007 (unpublished)

Kollontai, Aleksandra (1923): "The Labour of Women in the Evolution of the Economy." Reprinted in: Bell, Susan Groag/ Offen, Karen (1983): *Women, the Family and Freedom. The Debate in Documents. Volume Two 1880-1950*. Stanford: Stanford University Press, 289-291 and 303-308

McGlynn, Clare (2000): "Ideologies of Motherhood in European Community Sex Equality Law." In: *European Law Journal* 6 (1), 29-44

McGlynn, Clare (2001a): "European Union Family Values: Ideologies of 'Family' and 'Motherhood' in European Union Law." In: *Social Politics* 8 (3), 325-350

McGlynn, Clare (2001b): "Families and the European Charter of Fundamental Rights: Progressive Change or Entrenching the Status Quo?" In: *European Law Review* 26 (6), 582-598

Oakley, Ann (1974): *Woman's Work: the Housewife, Past and Present.* New York: Pantheon Books.

Peterson, Elin/ Pérez Orozco, Amaia (2009): *LARG Comparative Country Study Spain.* Internal QUING Report (unpublished)

Popa, Raluca Maria (2009): *LARG Comparative Country Study Romania.* Internal QUING Report (unpublished)

State Secretary on Public Health, Welfare and Sports (1996): *Letter on Position and Function of the Family, September 16.* The Hague: Ministry of VWS

Stoykova, Elena (2009): *LARG Comparative Country Study Bulgaria.* Internal QUING Report (unpublished)

Stratigaki, Maria (2004): "The Cooptation of Gender Concepts in EU Policies: The Case of Reconciliation of Work and Family." In: *Social Politics* 11 (1), 3-56

Stychin, Carl F. (2003): *Governing Sexuality: The Changing Politics of Citizenship and Law Reform*. Oxford: Hart Publishing

UN (2008): *World Population Policies 2007*. New York: United Nations

Urbanek, Doris (2009): *LARG Comparative Country Study Germany.* Internal QUING Report (unpublished)

Verloo, Mieke (ed.) (2007): *Multiple Meanings of Gender Equality. A Critical Frame Analysis of Gender Policies in Europe*. CEU Press: Budapest

Verloo, Mieke/ Maratou-Alipranti, Laura/ Tertinegg, Karin/ Van Beveren, Jacintha (2005): "Framing the Organisation of Intimacy as a Policy Problem Across Europe." In: Verloo, Mieke/ Pantelidou Maloutas, Maro (eds.): *Differences in the Framing of Gender Inequality as a Policy Problem Across Europe. The Greek Review of Social Research, Special Issue* 117, 119-149

Nina Berven

Gender Equality and Policies towards Women as Mothers in the Contemporary Norwegian Welfare State[1]

Norway, with its 4.7 million inhabitants, is generally assumed to be among the top countries in the world when it comes to gender equality, quality of life and the scope of public policies of social provision.[2] Yet, I argue that despite its extensive public policies and high level of (formal) gender equality, a significant number of Norwegian women still depend on a spouse for a reasonable standard of living, while being unable to "form and maintain an autonomous household" (Orloff 1993: 327) on their own. I shall in this paper look at contemporary and common Norwegian policy programmes for families with young children and study empirically how families adapt to these policies. Although programmes are formally gender neutral, it is nevertheless women to a greater extent than men who respond and adapt to such programmes, and the title of my paper reflects this observation.

The paper is divided into three parts. The first part provides an overview of current demographic and employment patterns in Norway. The second part deals with concrete policy programmes towards families with young children, and relates these programmes to the more general issue of welfare state restructuring. Building on these two parts, the third and last part of the paper outlines a broader, more general discussion on implications and reflects on the overall, theoretical relevance of the study. However, demography, welfare state policies and restructuring, and gender are substantial fields of research in their own right. Therefore a paper like this necessarily implies big questions on rather few pages.

---

1 I thank Stein Kuhnle and Per Selle for helpful comments on a previous version of this text.

2 For years Norway has been among the top countries on the Index of Human Development; cf. www.nationmaster.com/country/no-norway/eco-economy (10/01/2009).

Master of Europe – and master of self-congratulation?

The paper relates directly to the keywords of this book, *demographic change, restructuring of the welfare state and gender relations* in European comparison, and starts with a positive view, but ends with a rather critical conclusion. The positive starting point is based on the choice of empirical focus on Norway. Here, the welfare state has not yet undergone any major processes of 'restructuring' and in a comparative perspective, the demographic situation, i.e. fertility rates and population composition, is fairly good. This means that the fertility rates are nearly 2.1, which is considered the rate necessary for the population to remain constant, rather than to decline (cf. for example Kautto et al. 2001; Bradshaw/Hatland 2006; Ostner/Schmitt 2008). Also, the positive starting point is based on my personal view that politics matters and that family policy can, is and should be used as an active tool to alter and improve current gender orders. However, we have to be careful and critical when examining what is to be gained and lost when applying the various – and sometimes even contradictory – policies. Caution is called for not only when we consider gender, which is the main focus here, but also more generally in terms of class relations and variations in current family lives and compositions. What can the 'Norwegian case' tell us about such issues?

Demography and employment patterns: An overview[3]

Norway is said to belong to the "social democratic welfare regime" (Esping-Andersen 1990: 28). Most family and welfare policies from the 1970s and onward have been explicitly aimed at strengthening women's employment by e.g. promoting public subsidized childcare and parental leave schemes. The result of these policies is a comparatively high and uninterrupted employment rate among women and mothers combined with a stable and relatively high fertility rate of 1.9. Seventy percent of all women of occupational age are engaged in paid employment, whereas the equivalent share of men is 80 percent.

Table 1 gives a breakdown of the Norwegian population by age groups. This table indicates the scope and sort of demographic challenges, addressed more thoroughly later, that are the basis for state policies.

---

3 If not stated otherwise, all data in this section are from Statistic Norway 2007.

Table 1: Age-based population groups in Norway 2008

Age (years)	0-19	20-39	40-64	65+
Total population (%)	25.8	26.7	32.9	14.6

Ref.: Statistic Norway (2008)

The table shows that 25.8 percent of the Norwegian population is below 20 years of age. These constitute the very *underlying group* in terms of family policies' cash and services. That is, having a child at the age of 18 is the maximum for parents in terms of being eligible for any form of child care services (see part two for further details).

The next cohort, people from the age of 20 to 39 years, makes up 26.7 percent of the current population. Due to its 'reproductive age', to a large extent this group also constitutes the *recipient group* of the various family policies, i.e. parents of young children.

Yet, since the mean age of women giving birth to their first child is 28 years, this recipient group to some extent has common characteristics with the next cohort, the part of the population from 40 to 64 years, which in turn constitutes 32.9 percent and thereby the core part of the current Norwegian population. Considered from a family policy perspective and given a relatively high commitment to paid employment, I choose to characterize these as the *payer group*. This group is mostly made up of parents of children who are too old to qualify for the various cash and services, and child care responsibility is not a core characteristic for the group as a whole.

The fourth in my table, people from the age of 65 and above, constitutes 14.6 percent of the Norwegian population. Depending on empirical focus and how one defines 'family policy' this group can also constitute a core group – because when people get older, they often have a higher need for care and services. While care for the elderly is among the core tasks of the Norwegian, and most other welfare states, it falls beyond the empirical scope of this paper, which shall only be concerned with policies towards families (mothers) with young children.

Despite the focus on family policies, we also need to take a closer look at current Norwegian employment patterns. There are several reasons for this. First, welfare state, employment, and family policies are not regarded as separated, but closely intertwined policy fields. Second, and to be elaborated below, the division of paid and unpaid work, is highly gendered, which not only affects relations between men and women – but also men and women's relations towards the welfare state.

Table 2: Current Norwegian employment 2007

	Women	Men
Employment rate (% of all in occupational age, 16-64)	70	80
Fulltime employment (% of all employed)	57	87
Part-time employment (% of all employed)	43	13
Sick leaves, all lengths (%)	7.8	4.5

Ref.: Statistic Norway (2007)

With an unemployment rate of 2.8 percent (2007), most people in Norway are connected to the labour market in one way or another. This is clearly reflected in Table 2, which shows that 70 percent of women and 80 percent of men of occupational age are gainfully employed. We also see that 57 percent of all women employed work fulltime[4] and 43 percent work part time.[5] For men, the equivalent shares are 87 percent and 13 percent, respectively.

Despite the comparatively high labour force participation of women, Norway has one of the most gender segregated labour markets in Europe.[6] The (very) general picture is one in which most women are employed in the pub-

4 Fulltime (wage-) work week in Norway is 37.5 hours per week (Statistic Norway 2007).

5 Average part-time work is 22 hours per week. Yet there are different patterns when it comes to men's and women's part-time work. With the health sector as an important exception, most of women's part-time work is chosen/voluntary. Men's part-time on the other hand, is mostly due to 'seasonal variations', for example in tourism or the fish industry. That is, among those working part-time, most men work full weeks with periodical breaks, while most women work shorter days/weeks over the year (Statistic Norway 2007).

6 Cf. for example http://genderstats.worldbank.org/home.asp (31/10/2008) for comparative data.

lic sector, while most men are employed in the private sector. Also, the sorts of occupations vary substantially with gender. While women are overrepresented in occupations related to care and human services, men dominate within engineering, finance, the oil industry, etc. Moreover, after adjustments for variations in working hours, women's wages only add up to 84 percent of men's income.

As a preliminary summarization, we can say that Norway is among the European 'masters' both when it comes to fertility, part time work among women and gender segregation in the labour market (see footnote six below). My argument is that these phenomena are closely interconnected. Moreover, I claim that welfare state policies and welfare state politics not only reflect but also contribute to both creating and maintaining these patterns.

Family policies and welfare state restructuring

Public responsibility for childcare and political commitments to facilitate the combination of parenthood and employment for both women and men are important components of the picture of Norway (and the other Scandinavian countries) as a potential "women-friendly welfare state" (Hernes 1987; Bergquist et al. 1999). Moreover, welfare policy is closely integrated with family and gender equality policies. This means that childcare and other care obligations, to a larger extent than in most other countries and welfare regimes, are interpreted not solely as a private, but also as a public concern and policy issue.

In Norway and other Scandinavian countries, most programmes are universal, not selective. This implies that social programmes like old-age pensions, health care, childcare allowances, education, health insurance and so on are not targeted to 'the poor'. Rather, they cover the whole population regardless of their ability to pay (Rothstein 2000; Esping-Andersen 1990, 1999). The welfare state enjoys broad popular support, which in turn represents the basis as well as the challenge for the future Norwegian welfare state (Kuhnle/ Alestalo 2000; Esping-Andersen 2002).

The institutional characteristics, in combination with a relatively high and egalitarian level of material well-being, are important for an understanding of the Norwegian welfare programmes and the debates surrounding them. Other important factors are comparatively low unemployment rates and high governmental revenues from the petroleum sector. First, the image of a welfare state in crisis was never that prevalent in Norway, as it was in many other countries, and the crisis was framed more as a problem of organization and effectiveness than as a matter of financing (White Paper No. 35, 1994-95). The White Paper, *Welfare towards 2030* (English version, original quotations), nevertheless points to the importance of adapting and adjusting contemporary policies in order to be prepared for future challenges:

> "The Government will not try to hide the fact that we are faced with great challenges regarding the future financing of our welfare schemes. Demographic prospects indicate a considerably increased number of pensioners after the turn of the century. [...] Economic growth is necessary in order to meet the future financial obligations of the National Insurance Scheme. The Work Approach constitutes a vital element in the Government's strategy to establish a firm basis for our welfare schemes. We must create the basis for the welfare we desire." (White Paper No. 35, 1994-95, English version: chapter 1).

Stressing the importance of employment for the individual as well as the overall society, the 'work approach' implies that as many as possible should be able to provide for themselves through their own wage work. According to the White Paper (No. 35, 1994-95: chapter 1) this will lead to:

- an enhanced and more equitable redistribution of welfare,
- reduced needs for redistribution from the occupationally active population to social security beneficiaries,
- increased number of persons in a position to contribute to the financing of social security.

In such a context, family policies become important as tools of assistance to enable parents to manage the combination of child care and wage work. Table 3 shows the basic, universal and most widespread Norwegian policy programmes towards families with young children.

Table 3: Norwegian family programmes[7]

Parental Leave	44 weeks at full wage replacement or 54 weeks at 80% replacement
MaternityLeave	9 weeks (3 weeks before, 6 weeks after birth) at full wage replacement
Paternity Leave	2 weeks (paid or unpaid decided by employer)
Father's Quota	6 weeks
Cash for Care Benefit	Kontantstøtte (€ 389 per month) for children age 1-3
Childcare	84% of children age 1-5 are in kindergarten. No legal entitlement
Child Benefit	€ 115 per month until the child is 18.

Ref.: NAV (2008)

As mentioned, the image of a welfare state in crisis was not as prevalent in Norway as in most other European countries. This is probably one of the reasons why debates on 'restructuring of the welfare state' (as a key concept of this book) are rather absent in Norwegian public and political life. But I will also argue that it is not entirely clear what 'welfare state restructuring' really means and implies. This lack of clarity in turn means that it is difficult to state, place and measure eventual restructuring efforts. Therefore, I find it useful to distinguish between four forms of 'welfare state restructuring':

1. *retrenchment* in existing programmes
2. *abolition* of existing programmes
3. *expansion* of current programmes
4. *establishment* of new programmes

In terms of Norwegian policies towards families with young children, numbers 3 and 4, i.e. expansion and establishment of new programmes, are the most relevant.[8]

7 € 1 = NOK 8.5 (28/10/2008).

8 Still there are some examples of retrenchment and abolishing. In 1998, the

Table 3 indicates that various forms of parental leave during children's first year of life make up a substantial share of family policies. Here *expansion* has been the trend since the 1980s, where the total weeks of parental leave gradually have been increased from 12 to 44/54 weeks. And at the time of writing (October 2008), there is a government proposal to increase the leave further to 46/56 weeks of full wage compensation as of July 2009 (Ministry of Children and Equality 2008).[9] Out of these, 10 weeks should be reserved for the father, i.e. expanding the current father quota by four more weeks.[10]

Introduced in 1993, the father quota is an important example of how state policies have the potential of being effective tools in shaping and changing gender relations. Explicitly aimed at increasing the role of the father in early childhood, 6 of the 44/54 weeks of parental leave were made exclusively for the father, i.e. if the father does not make use of the leave the parents loose them all together.[11] Prior to the father quota, only 1.5 percent of the fathers took any leave beyond the two weeks of paternity leave while currently nearly 90 percent make use of the current quota (Håland 2001; Brandt/Kvande 1998). Often characterized as 'soft force' *(mild tvang)*, the father quota is nevertheless an example that supports my argument that politics matters.

While the father quota can be interpreted partly as an expansion of the current parental leave scheme and partly as a new programme, the Cash for Care allowance is the most central example of the 'establishment of new programmes' category in Norwegian family politics from the last decades. Introduced in 1998, the programme aimed to offer families of children from the age of one to three improved possibilities to take care of their own children,

---

programme *Transitional allowance for single parents (Overgangsstønaden for enslige forsørgere)*underwent major restrictions in terms of the time period in which the recipient was eligible for support, while the support itself became more generous while simultaneously made contingent on educational or other wage-work related activities. Moreover in 1997, a special supplement for parents of children age one to three *(Småbarnstillegget i barnetrygden)* got 'transferred' to the Cash for Care programme (NAV 2008; Berven 2005; Fjær/Syltevik 2002).

9 Cf. www.regjeringen.no/en/dep/bld/Press-Center/Press-releases/2008/fedrekvoten-blir-utvida-fra-seks-til-ti-.html?id=531155 (07/10/2008).

10 Two more weeks will be added, while two of the 'parental weeks' (which the parents can share as they wish) are to be reserved for the father (Ministry of Children and Equality 2008).

11 When introduced in 1993, the parental leave was 42/52 weeks, and four of these weeks were reserved for the father (NOU 27, 1995).

to provide them with increased freedom of choice regarding use of different forms of childcare programmes and to increase equality in public transfers to the families regardless of how childcare is organized (St.prp.53, 1997-98; Berven 2005). In practice, the reform implies that all parents of children from one to three not making use of state subsidized kindergartens can opt for a monthly cash allowance equal to this subsidy, which in 1998 was 3000 NOK per child per month (approximately € 353).[12] Except for the criterion of not making use of subsidized childcare services when receiving the allowance, it is up to the parents to decide how to reconcile wage and care work.[13] In 2005, about 75 percent of all families with children aged one to three were paid a Cash for Care allowance, and this rate has been relatively stable since 1998 (Baklien et al. 2001). Since then, however, the rate has been decreasing and is now 47.9 percent (NAV 2008).[14]

The decrease is mostly due to the rapid increase in kindergartens over the recent years, but it is also relevant to see the decrease in light of the various, simultaneously and partly contradictory goals embedded in the reform. When introduced, the programme was heavily criticized by the left-leaning opposition parties for 'forcing women back to the kitchen'. Freedom of choice, the criticism went, is not a plausible argument as long as there are insufficient places in kindergarten for children in the eligible age group. Moreover, many saw the goal of making it easier for parents to spend more time with their own children and the goal of increased freedom of choice in organizing care and wage work as opposed to each other (cf. Berven 2005 for an extensive analysis of the Cash for Care debate).

Given such potential conflicting goals, the decrease in number of recipients may be interpreted either as a further orientation towards employment among Norwegian women, suggesting that the previous high recipient rate was basically due to lack of kindergartens or that € 400/month simply is not

---

12 The current allowance is 3303 NOK per month (approximately € 389) (NAV 2008, www.nav.no/805369180.cms [31/10/2008]).

13 In principle, parents also can choose to use part-time kindergartens and receive a partial amount of cash for care, but due to most state-sponsored kindergartens being full-time, the average percent of children age one to three being paid partial/reduced allowance is relatively low. In June 2008 it was approximately 25 percent (NAV 2008), cf. nav.no/87312.cms (10/01/2009).

14 www.nav.no/Om+NAV/Tall+og+analyse/Familie+og+omsorg/Kontantst%C3%B8tte (10/01/2009).

enough to make childcare pay, or that norms and/or preferences are rapidly changing.

What is the problem?

Comparatively high fertility rates and levels of female employment in combination with extensive family policies may at first seem like a great combination. Providing tax revenues *and* new citizens with the high employment and fertility rates not only works as a bolster for an extensive Norwegian welfare state in the future. The combination also helps to avert demographically related challenges associated with 'the ageing of the population'. Yet, as will be demonstrated below, there are important challenges related to this comparatively 'lucky situation'. And these challenges, in turn, have critical and crucially gendered consequences in terms of men's/fathers' and women's/mothers' relations to the workplace, the household and the (welfare) state – these consequences are the theme of the last section of the paper. But first, some comments on the challenges themselves.

Table 4: Time spent on paid and unpaid work (2002)

Average per day	Mothers of children age 0-6	Fathers of children age 0-6
Housework (hh:mm)	5:51	3:37
Wage work (hh:mm)	2:37	5:37

Ref.: Statistic Norway (2002)

Table 4 shows that on an average weekday in 2002, fathers spent 5 hours and 37 minutes on wage work and 3 hours and 37 minutes on housework. The equivalent figures for mothers are 2 hours and 37 minutes and 5 hours and 51 minutes, respectively. These are self-reported, average numbers, i.e. the parents themselves report to Statistic Norway how they spend their time.[15]

15 There are also other 'areas' which I excluded from the table because they go beyond the scope of this paper, for example sleep, leisure and educational activities. See www.ssb.no/samfunnsspeilet/utg/200204/03/tab-2002-10-08-01.html (31/10/2008)

That parents of children age zero to one, i.e. parents of babies, are included in the data may explain the relatively high amount of time reported spent on housework. First, because the survey also includes care work in the category 'housework', and second, because most parents in this group make use of the parental leave scheme of 44/54 weeks and therefore spend more time than they would otherwise.

Yet, what is more important to note is the considerable differences between the time mothers and fathers of children from zero to six years old spent on wage work – 2 hours and 37 minutes and 5 hours and 37 minutes, respectively. These differences matter because for the welfare state paid work is considered more important than care work, in that many entitlements towards the (welfare) state are linked to (prior) participation in the labour market. For the purpose of this paper, parental leave is the most relevant example: To stay at home with children at 80 or 100 percent wage compensation simply requires that one has a wage and job to be compensated for.[16] This is also the case when it comes to programmes like unemployment and sickness schemes, and future retirement pensions. When women as a group are less active in paid work than men as a group, the short and long term consequences of such adaptations are highly gendered.[17] This, in turn, raises questions and calls for reflection on the role of the state versus the role of the individual in the organization of wage and care work, although a thorough elaboration and discussion of these issues are beyond the scope of this paper.

for methodological details and considerations.

16 Moreover, fathers' rights to parental leave beyond the father quota depend upon mothers' employment, and the wage compensation is calculated on the basis of her income (Ministry of Children and Equality 2008, www.regjeringen.no/nb/dep/bld/tema/andre/Fodsels-_og_adopsjonspenger/Fedres-rettigheter-.html?id=414878 [31/10/2008]).

17 In 1992 "Points for Care Work" *(Omsorgspoeng)* was introduced to the National Insurance Scheme. These points are credited to persons who care for children less than 7 years of age, or who carry out unpaid work in caring for the sick, disabled or elderly. Only one of the parents can receive points for care work. These points do not represent any benefit from the National Insurance Scheme, but they can contribute to higher pensions at retirement (NAV 2008, www.nav.no/805374461.cms [31/10/2008]).

Overall implications and theoretical relevance

The discussion on gender differences in time spent on house and wage work suggests that policy and welfare state analyses still need to be sensitive to gendered differences and to how policies may contribute not only to maintaining the current 'gender order' but also to changing it.[18]

During the 1990s several feministically oriented scholars (among others Orloff 1993; Sainsbury 1999; O'Connor et al. 1999) criticized the so-called mainstream welfare state research, represented by Esping-Andersen (1990, 1996) and Korpi (1983, 1985, 1989) for not considering gender in their comparative analyses. While some of these scholars rejected the 'mainstream' framework altogether (Sainsbury 1996), others suggested taking advantage of the comparative qualities in the current frameworks (Orloff 1993). However, they had to be modified and adjusted, for example by adding gender to the preexisting dimensions and eventually adding some new dimensions.

As a spokeswoman for this latter approach, Orloff (1993) added gender to the three 'mainstream' dimensions proposed by Esping-Andersen, and simultaneously developed two new dimensions to supply that framework. Esping-Andersen's framework basically built on his book from 1990, *The Three Worlds of Welfare Capitalism*. There are three dimensions, he claims, which in various ways form the basis for all (western) welfare states. These are:

1. The dimension of state-market-household relations. Or, "how state activities are interlocked with the market's and the family's role in social provision" (Esping-Andersen 1990: 21).
2. The stratification dimension. This dimension points out that 'the welfare state' is an active force in the ordering of social provision, recognizing that some policies may increase equalities, while other policies may decrease them.
3. The dimension of social citizenship, which points to the distinctions between universal, conditional and means-tested benefits within the welfare state institution.

18 They also need to be sensitive to class, i.e. differences between 'women' as a group and 'men' as a group, although a further discussion of this is beyond the scope of this paper (cf. among others Berven 2005; Siim/Borchorst 2005).

Depending on how the various western welfare states cluster along these dimensions, they are classified as belonging to different sorts of *welfare regimes – liberal, social democratic or conservative*. These welfare regimes, Esping-Andersen claims, are to be understood as prototypes. That means that there are no countries that fit perfectly into any of them. Still, the regime typology reflects various principles, dynamics and patterns in how countries, grouped in various 'regimes', tend to approach the overall need of producing individual and societal welfare.

In short, every single state has many welfare needs to take care of, but there are several, alternative ways of handling these (common) challenges, or *'risks'*. While countries grouped in the liberal welfare regime tend to let collective risks be handled by the *market* (rather than by the state or family), it is the state that is the core actor for countries grouped in the social democratic regime. In countries placed within the conservative regime, however, the family (or 'household') is – or has been – the primary provider of these tasks. Orloff (1993) has criticized Esping-Andersen's typology for focusing more on the roles of state and market in welfare provision than on the role of the family (or 'the household'). Although formally recognized as a pillar within welfare regimes, the family institution and moreover the gendered divisions of labour (both within family and elsewhere) has been uncontested or even absent in most mainstream analyses.

Closely related to the three dimensions above is the concept of *decommodification*. The questions of how and to what extent citizens can be defined as 'decommodified' are important because these processes take different forms across the three welfare regimes. But it is also crucial as a background for the feminist critique of mainstream gender-blind research. Workers are not commodities, as for example washing machines are, Esping-Andersen claims (1990: 37). Rather, workers must survive and reproduce – and are therefore vulnerable to unemployment, falling wages, competition and other processes related to the market. In short, the logic underlying the concept of decommodification is that the more the individual has access to incomes and entitlements regardless of participation in the labour market, the more de-commodified and empowered he or she is.

For example, Esping-Andersen argues that in order to be decommodified individuals should have the ability to opt out of employment when and if they find it necessary. However, this line of argumentation is based on an implicit assumption that *individuals actually have a job to opt-out o*f (Berven 2005:

37). Yet, as shown in Table 2, even in contemporary Norway this is generally and systematically to a much lesser extent the case for women (as a group) than for men (as a group). Or, as a more general point made by Orloff:

> "By ignoring gender differences in the situations of men and women workers, particularly with reference to domestic and caring labor, and in access to the paid labor force, Esping-Andersen's concept is inadequate for understanding the effects of state social provision on all workers" (Orloff 1993: 317).

In order to better capture the effects of social provision on gender relations, two new dimensions are added (Orloff 1993: 318-319). These are:

4. access to paid work,
5. the capacity to form and maintain an autonomous household.

This addition is necessary, Orloff claims, because traditionally and generally men's and women's life courses differ in terms of child rearing, domestic responsibilities, patterns of employment and so on.

Adding the *"access to paid work"* dimension highlights how gender based divisions of paid and unpaid work result in men and women being differently affected by social benefits and entitlements aimed at creating decommodification: In short, we can say that many women first have to be commodified in order to be decommodified later on.

That women traditionally and generally have been the primary provider of unpaid care work is also reflected in the fifth dimension: *"the capacity to form and maintain an autonomous household"*. This dimension indicates the extent to which the various welfare regimes enable the primary caregivers, which mostly means 'women', to survive and support a family without depending on spouses' income – i.e. without having to marry or stay married due to 'material necessities'. In line with this, I see Orloff's fifth dimension for gendering welfare state analyses as a (gendered) parallel to the gender-blind conception of decommodification.

Applying this framework to the contemporary Norwegian context, with widespread use of part-time employment and a strongly gender segregated labour market, I will argue that many two-parent families actually are 1½-income households. In that way, mothers as a group and fathers as a group have diffe-rent relations and entitlements towards the welfare state, because of diffe-rences in care obligations. Therefore, my claim is, care is both a gender issue and a citizenship issue.

What then are the implications for mothers in two-parent families that in reality subsidize the male income while many of them simultaneously are unable to form and maintain an autonomous household on their own? As Knijn and Kremer argue, "Care is paid or unpaid as a consequence of political choices, shared cultural beliefs, and gender structures" (Knijn/Kremer 1997: 330). In my view, this statement is highly relevant yet somewhat ambiguous: Care (still) counts, the question is how.

A negative interpretation is that the Norwegian, as all (European) welfare states still relies on, yet takes for granted, the considerable amount of unpaid care work performed by mothers within the family institution. On the other hand, a positive interpretation of the statement is that not only gender but also politics matters, i.e. there are potentials for using state policies as active means towards a more gender-neutral society, in terms of the division of paid and unpaid work. This neutrality may be achieved by 'making care pay' – in the same way as many states have used politics as tools for 'making work pay' towards people on social assistance etc. – but how, at what cost and for whom?[19]

Comparatively, however, in Norway there is a high level of coincidence between feminist and gender issues on the one hand and state policy on the other. These processes are important factors for explaining a 'public commitment to gender equality' and to the acknowledgement of parents' care obligations. In other words, the story of 'reproduction going public' is a central part of the processes of turning the Nordic states into potential *women-friendly* welfare states (Hernes 1987: 9). On the one hand, it points to the way in which the states themselves, through their policies and expansion of public welfare services, have 'pulled' women into the public sphere. On the other hand, it points to how women, through labour, corporate and governmental represen-

19 A further discussion of these topics is beyond the scope of this paper, yet, a few current policy examples may be relevant. On the on hand, policies like Cash for Care, Points for Care Work (see footnote 17) and exclusively the 'Father Quota' in the parental leave schemes may be seen as steps towards 'making care pay'. On the other hand, except for the Father Quota, women are the main users of these programmes, and the programmes are (still?) relatively limited in scope, robustness and eligibility. For closer reflections on 'care' as such, cf. among others Knijn/Kremer (1997), Tronto (2001), Fraser (1994) and Wærness (1987).

tation, once they entered the public sphere have begun to 'push' developments in accordance with their own interests. These dual processes, i.e., the 'fit' between women's actions and demands on the one hand and the structure and capacities of the political system on the other, have then been interpreted as processes giving Nordic women extraordinary opportunities or maneuvering room (cf. also Bergquist et al. 1999).

Conclusion

As shown, the general picture of Norway as a gender equal society, where women and men combine breadwinning and care giving on an equal basis, is ambiguous. 'Modern' and 'traditional' elements largely coexist. Policies concerning families are (still), basically, linked to women/mothers to a much greater extent than to men/fathers. That is, it is still women as mothers who are politically and socially expected to, and who actually perform, the necessary or 'required' adaptations towards (changing) welfare state policies. Moreover, "care is paid or unpaid as a consequence of political choices, shared cultural beliefs, and gender structures" (Knijn/Kremer 1997: 330). In turn, the division of paid and unpaid work is closely linked to gender. And even more important, it is linked to citizenship because many entitlements towards the welfare state are based on participation in the labour market.

Therefore, the rediscovery of gender in contemporary welfare state research and political debates across Europe is important, yet ambivalent. As often pointed out, in a broader European context Norway and the other Scandinavian countries have the relative advantage of fairly high fertility rates combined with a high level of female employment. These factors are often regarded as main ingredients in recipes to 'save' the European welfare state from restructuring efforts and future (demographic and economic) crises. I have tried to demonstrate how gender (still) matters as an organizational principle in the division of paid and unpaid work and as a basis for entitlements vis-à-vis the welfare state. An increased awareness of such mechanisms is an important step towards a less gender biased society. However, there is also a substantial risk that the current revival of 'gender equality' becomes purely instrumental, as a means to save the welfare state, rather than as a principal value in its own right. This in turn poses new challenges and raises new questions for future research.

Bibliography

Baklien, Bergljot/ Ellingsæter, Anne Lise/ Gulbrandsen, Lars (2001): *Evaluering av kontantstøttereformen.* Oslo: Norges Forskningsråd

Bergquist, Christina/ Borchorst, Anette/ Christensen, Ann-Dorte/ Raaum, Nina C./ Ramnstedt-Silén, Viveca/ Styrkasdottir, Audur (eds.) (1999): *Equal Democracies? Gender and Politics in the Nordic Countries.* Oslo: Scandinavian University Press

Berven, Nina (2005): *National Politics and Cross-National Ideas. Welfare, Work and Legitimacy in the United States and Norway.* Bergen: Rokkancenter report 5

Bradshaw, Jonathan and Aksel Hatland (eds.) (2006): *Social Policy, Employment and Family Change in Comparative Perspective.* Cheltenham: Edward Elgar

Brandt, Berit/ Kvande, Elin (1998): *Fleksible fedre i et fleksibelt arbeids marked.* Trondheim: Allforsk Notat 6

Esping-Andersen, Gøsta (1990): *The Three Worlds of Welfare Capitalism.* Cambridge, Princeton: University Press

Esping-Andersen, Gøsta (1996): "After the Golden Age? Welfare State Dilemmas in a Global Economy." In Esping-Andersen, Gøsta (ed.): *Welfare States in Transition. National Adaptations in Global Economies.* London: Sage, 1-31

Esping-Andersen, Gøsta (1999): *Social Foundations of Postindustrial Economies.* New York, Oxford: University Press

Esping-Andersen, Gøsta with Gallie, Duncan/ Hemerijck, Anton/Myles, John: (2002): *Why We Need a New Welfare State.* New York: Oxford, University Press

Fjær, Svanaug/ Syltevik, Liv (2002): *Omsorg, tid og penger for likes tillingens frontløpere. Sluttrapport fra evalueringen av reformen for enslige forsørgere.* Rapport 2. Bergen: Rokkansenterets Publikasjonsserie

Fraser, Nancy (1994): "After the Family Wage: Gender Equity and the Welfare State." In: *Political Theory* 22 (4), 591-618

Hernes, Helga (1987): *Welfare State and Woman Power. Essays in State Feminism.* Oslo: Universitetsforlaget

Håland, Kari (2001): *Kontantstøtten – et veiskille i norsk familiepolitikk? En sammenligning av kontantstøtten til småbarnsforeldre og fødselsper-*

misjonsordningene. Trondheim: Hovedoppgave i statsvitenskap, NTNU, Institutt for sosiologi og statsvitenskap

Kautto, Mikko (ed.) (2001): *Nordic Welfare States in the European Context.* London: Routledge

Knijn, Trudie/ Kremer, Monique (1997): "Gender and the Caring Dimension of Welfare States: Toward Inclusive Citizenship." In: *Social Politics. International Studies in Gender, State and Society.*4 (3), 328-361

Korpi, Walter (1983): *The Democratic Class Struggle.* London, Boston, Melbourne: Routledge and Kegan Paul

Korpi, Walter (1985): "Power Resources Approach vs. Action and Conflict: On Causal and Intentional Explanations in the Study of Power." In: *Sociological Theory* 3 (2), 31-45

Korpi, Walter (1989): "Power, Politics, and State Autonomy in the Development of Social Citizenship." In: *American Sociological Review* 54 (3), 309-328

Kuhnle, Stein/ Alestalo, Matti (2000): "Growth, Adjustments and Survival of European Welfare States." In: Kuhnle, Stein (ed.): *Survival of the European Welfare State.* London, New York: Routledge, 3-19

O'Connor, Julia/ Orloff, Ann Shola/ Shaver, Sheila (1999): *States, Markets, Families. Gender, Liberalism and Social Policy in Australia, Canada, Great Britain and the United States.* Cambridge: Cambridge University Press

Orloff, Ann Shola (1993): "Gender and the Social Rights of Citizenship: The Comparative Analysis of Gender Relations and Welfare States." In: *American Sociological Review* 58 (3), 303-328

Ostner, Ilona/ Schmitt, Christoph (eds.) (2008): *Family Policies in the Context of Family Change: the Nordic Countries in Comparative Perspective.* Wiesbaden: VS Verlag für Sozialwissenschaften

Rothstein, Bo (2000): "The Future of the Universal Welfare State. An Institutional Approach." In: Kuhnle, Stein (ed.): *Survival of the European Welfare State.* London, New York: Routledge, 217-233

Sainsbury, Diane (1999): "Gender and Social-Democratic Welfare State." In: Sainsbury, Diane (ed.): *Gender and Welfare State Regimes.* Oxford, New York: Oxford University Press, 75-114

Siim, Birthe/ Borchorst, Annette (2005): "The Women-Friendly Welfare State Revisited." In: Kildal, Nanna/ Kuhnle, Stein (eds.): *Normative*

Foundation of the Welfare State: The Nordic Experiment. London, New York: Routledge, 97-111

Tronto, Joan (2001): "Who cares? Public and Private Caring and the Rethinking of Citizenship." In: Hirschmann, Nancy J./ Liebert, Ulrike (eds.): *Women and Welfare. Theory and Practice in the United States and Europe.* New Brunswick, New Jersey, London, Rutgers University Press, 65-83

Wærness, Kari (1987): "On the Rationality of Caring." In: Sassoon, Anne Showstack (ed.): *Women and the State: the Shifting Boundaries of Public and Private.* London, Hutchinson, 206-234

White Paper No. 35 (1994-95): *Welfare Towards 2030.* Oslo: Ministry of Health and Social Affairs

Websites

Gender Stats. Database of Gender Statistic. http://genderstats.worldbank.org/home.asp (28/10/2008)

Index of Human Development: www.nationmaster.com/country/no-norway/eco-economy (28/10/2008)

Ministry of Children and Equality (2008): www.regjeringen.no/en/dep/bld.html?id=298 (28/10/2008)

NAV (2008): www.nav.no/page?id=248 (28/10/2008)

NOU 27, 1995: www.regjeringen.no/nb/dep/bld/dok/NOUer/1995/NOU-1995-27.html?id=115764 (28/10/2008)

Statistic Norway (2002, 2007, 2008): www.ssb.no (28/10/2008)

St.prp.5,1997-98:www.regjeringen.no/nb/dep/bld/dok/regpubl/stprp/19971998/Stprp-nr-53-1997-98-.html?id=136909 (28/10/2008)

Economies of Demographic Change

Gabriele Michalitsch

No Sharing, No Caring
Demographics, Gender Hierarchies and Neoliberal Restructuring

Aiming at self-regulation in accordance with market principles, neoliberal transformation of the welfare state implies increasing subjection of all sectors of society to economic competition. Minimization of (equalizing) state intervention and deregulation of the labour markets coupled with continuous appeals to self-reliance lead to growing individualization of social risks.

The Austrian example shows how these processes of restructuring the relation between the state and the economy, the public and the private redefine gender relations: Liberalized labour markets lead to mostly women's precarious employment while – by diminishing child care, care for the elderly and for the sick – re-orientation of social policy and reductions in the public sector cause increasing pressure on the care economy, reinforcing the traditionally female ascription of unpaid care work and thus the gender-specific division of labour. Consequently, not only polarization between men and women, but also between groups of women rises.

By linking neoliberal labour and social policies to family policy and current demographic developments, this paper will identify Austria's gender regime and, in particular, mechanisms of reproduction of gender hierarchies and embed them into Foucault's theoretical framework of government and governmentality in order to reveal the gender rationality of neoliberal governmentality. In this context, this contribution finally offers an interpretation of declining birth rates as an (unintended) outcome of neoliberal transformation, as a result of women's individual strategies to cope with its implications and, more specifically, as a form of resistance against them.

1 Demographic developments

Demographic developments in Austria are characterized by the gradual spread of two-child families since World War II (Prskawetz et al. 2008: 300). In particular, the end of the 1960s' baby boom caused a relatively rapid decline in the proportion of families with four or more children, while childlessness[1] gradually increased, accompanied by progressive postponement of childbearing. Furthermore, net immigration constituted a major factor for demographic developments over the last decades. The most notable waves of immigration included the influx of immigrant workers between 1961 and 1973 and the migration movements during the 1990s that were linked to the breakdown of state-socialism in central and Eastern Europe, primarily to the civil war in former Yugoslavia. Due to family reunions of the recently naturalized Austrians in particular, immigration has been closely related to former migration movements since 2000. Immigration plays a key role in total population growth: Net immigration made up 0.41 percent of the annual increase of 0.49 percent during 1989-2004 (Prskawetz et al. 2008: 295).

Despite high rates of naturalization during the late 1990s, the proportion of foreigners[2] among the total population rose to 9.6 percent in 2004. Foreigners and Austrian citizens born abroad – the population with migration background – comprised one sixth of the total population (16.6 percent) by the end of 2004 (Prskawetz et al. 2008: 295 et seq.).

Due to progressive postponement of first births in particular, the mean age of mothers at first childbirth increased by more than three years between 1984 and 2006 to 27.5 years, while the median age rose even more rapidly. Having increased steadily over the last two decades, about one tenth of first births now occurs after age 34, while first births by teenagers have declined to less than a tenth (Prskawetz et al. 2008: 312).

Although women with only compulsory education still frequently become mothers at an early age, postponement of childbearing is only partly related to prolonged education and can be observed in all education groups. As a result, the mean age of mothers at childbearing exceeded 29, the highest level recorded since the early 1950s – despite the significant reduction in higher-order childbearing that usually occurs at late childbearing ages (Prskawetz et al. 2008: 309).

If one neglects major differences in place of residence, region of birth, religious affiliation, level of education and labour market participation, the total fertility rate[3] has dropped from 1.46 in the 1980s to 1.38 at the time of publi-

1 Childlessness refers to the share of women without children.

2 Residents not holding Austrian citizenship.

3 Fertility in general is related to women only, not to men. For feminist critiques on the concept of fertility cf. Dackweiler (2006).

cation, while completed fertility has gradually declined among women born after 1935, dropping below 1.7 among women born after 1965[4] (Prskawetz et al. 2008: 297).

Since the early 1980s, fertility rates have declined particularly among women below the age of 25 and gradually increased at older ages. Fertility differences show the usual patterns: lowest childlessness, highest progression rates to a third child and completed fertility close to replacement level among women with basic education, high childlessness and low completed fertility among women with university education.[5]

Eurobarometer 2006 data indicate clear preferences of Austrian women of reproductive age for small families and childlessness. According to Eurobarometer 2006, Austrian women aged 25 to 39 years tend towards the lowest general and ideal family sizes (1.6 and 1.7 children, respectively) as well as the lowest desired and intended family sizes among the EU-25 (Table 1).

Table 1: Eurobarometer 2006: Family size and childlessness indicators. Austria and EU-25, women aged 25-39

Number of children	Austria	EU-25	EU min	EU max
General ideal	1.63	2.23	1.63	2.91
Personal ideal	1.69	2.23	1.69	2.84
Desired at age 20	1.50	2.10	1.50	2.89
Actual	0.97	1.34	0.75	1.84
Ultimately intended	1.54	2.07	1.54	2.72
Childlessness (percent)				
Actual	37	31	15	56
Intended	48	18	5	48

Ref.: Testa (2007: 360)

4 ‘Women born after 1935’ include the mothers of the 1960s’ baby boom, while ‘women born after 1965’ refer to the following generation, women presently of reproductive age.

5 In addition, Spielauer (2005) found fertility differentials by profession. For fertility differentials according to social status cf. Skirbekk (2008).

Eleven percent of the women of this age group declare no-child-prefe-rences – the highest proportion among all EU-25 member states, whose ave-rage amounts to four percent. Furthermore, in comparison to 18 percent in the EU-25 almost half – the highest share among the EU countries – of Austrian women aged 25-39 without children intend to remain childless. Finally, actual childlessness in Austria is spread further than in most other EU countries: 37 percent of Austrian women aged 25-39 have no children. Similar or greater values are registered only for Greece (40 percent), Italy (56 percent) and Denmark (42 percent), while the average for the EU-25 is 31 percent (Testa 2007: 361).

Nevertheless, official projections, taking 2006 as the year of reference, foresee a population growth by about nine percent to nine million in 2050, characterized by a decline of the population below the age of 15 and, after 2020, of the working age population (15-59 years) in combination with a rise in the proportion of elderly people from 22 percent currently to about one third in 2050 (Prskawetz et al. 2008: 296).

Public discourse hardly questions the problematic assumptions underlying these projections[6], but predicted demographic ageing is taken as a fact and constructed as a problem that present politics has to prepare for and adapt to. Its dominant perspective is led by the issue of how to adapt the welfare system and, in particular, its financial basis to the foreseen population developments, excluding basic structural reform of the socio-economic frame. Contrarily, it focuses on how to ensure its persistence and how to adapt the population accordingly. As a result, demographic ageing serves as a powerful argument for cut-backs in the welfare system, not restricted to retirement benefits, but extending to the acceptability of the principle of public redistribution – frequently denouncing it as anti-competitive and hence unjust.

In addition, since fertility differentials are closely linked to nationality – for example, total fertility rates among Austrian and Turkish nationals differed by 1.63 between 2000 and 2004 (Table 2) – public debate on demographic developments is frequently based on a nationalist and xenophobic subtext: foreigners misusing the generous Austrian welfare system, bearing children only in order to gain access to family transfer payments, allowing them a comfortable personal life without any work and effort. Qualifying specific groups

6 For the limits and problematic assumptions of demographic projections cf. Lutz et al. (1999).

of foreigners[7] as 'social welfare freeloaders' implies the construction of an enemy: 'They' simply take what 'we' are working for. This xenophobic 'logic' is only openly articulated by the extreme right, but has affected the political mainstream and influenced the formulation of policies since the 1990s. While the right-wing freedom party warned against 'foreign infiltration' ('*Überfremdung*') during election campaigns, social democratic and conservative parties launched appeals to 'our' youth proclaiming 'less fun, more responsibility' with reference to founding a family.

Table 2: Total fertility rates

	Austrian citizens	Foreign nationals	Turkish nationals	Total
1990-94	1.41	2.21	3.09	1.49
1995-99	1.31	2.06	2.63	1.39
2000-04	1.29	2.04	2.92	1.38

Ref.: Prskawetz et al. (2008: 316)

Consequently, public discourse on demographics is closely linked to distribution of resources in society. In this way, nationalism and neoliberalism form an alliance that questions the legitimacy of the welfare system as an adequate mode of interfering in distributive market results by mechanisms of redistribution. Both link this issue to present and future injustice towards specific groups of the population: either Austrians or 'the competitive successful', who are characterized by high performance, are presented as disadvantaged or punished by the welfare system, whose restriction on the other hand is defined as a necessity with regards to its sustainability.

Gender relations, in contrast, constitute only a minor topic in political discourses on demographics.[8] Although reconciliation of family and career

7 The term 'foreigners' applies to specific groups of foreigners with regards to cultural, religious and economic background and partly linked to a differentiation of 'respectable' foreigners as opposed to those 'neither willing nor able' to adapt to 'Austrian culture', referring mostly to poor immigrants from developing countries and in particular to Turkish nationals.

8 In contrast to Austria, in Germany, which is characterized by similar population developments, demographic change not only plays a much more prominent role in public discourse, but it is also frequently linked to gender issues and constitutes a

is promoted, it is addressed primarily to women, neglecting options for increasing men's involvement in domestic care work and without questioning the basic gender order of society, which has been reaffirmed by the neoliberal transformation of labour markets and social security since the 1990s.

2 Fertility, family policy and the gender division of labour

The 'private' division of labour seems to be an influential factor with regards to fertility decisions. In Austria, gender still is the main criterion for the distribution of labour, with unpaid care work remaining primarily attributed to women, who perform about 75 percent of domestic work.

Women employed full-time work the highest number of total hours. Taking paid and unpaid labour together, they work 10.5 hours per day on average, 1.5 hours more than their partners with full-time jobs. For women employed part-time, the number of total work hours decreases to 9.75, still about 0.75 hours more than their partners with full-time jobs. Only when women do not participate in the labour market regularly, do total work hours of men and women amount rather equally to about 9 hours a day (Statistik Austria 2002: 89).

Thus, total work hours of women increase with extending labour force participation, while their partners' remain unchanged. Obviously, female labour market participation does not lead to partners' significant contributions to private care activities. Consequently, unpaid care work can still be considered a 'first duty' for women. Furthermore, gendered time patterns are already visible at early ages. Girls aged 10-15 spend 57 minutes a day on household tasks, while boys only 48. These differences increase with age: Daughters aged 15-20 are involved in household tasks for 1.5 hours a day, while sons only 0.75 hours (Statistik Austria 2002: 90).

In this context, it does not seem surprising that according to Buber (2002) the division of household chores between partners and its perception by women with one child do not affect their desire for a second child. In contrast, supporting similar findings for Sweden and Hungary, sharing childrearing duties

growing field of academic interest (cf. Berger/Kahlert 2006; Barlösius/Schiek 2007; Auth/Holland-Cunz 2007) also reflecting the impact of demographics on women's and gender studies (cf. Kahlert 2006).

among couples positively influences women's plans for a further child (Buber 2002: 19; Andersson/Scott 2007; Bernhardt/Goldscheider 2006).

Austrian family policy supports the traditional ascription of unpaid care work. According to Gauthier's (2002) typology of family-policy regimes[9], which differentiates between a social-democratic, conservative, liberal and a southern European regime, Austria's family policy can be classified as 'conservative', characterized by medium to high public cash support for families in relation to parents' employment status and long parental and childcare leaves in contrast to limited childcare facilities, which reinforces traditional gender roles, whereas its intended pro-natalist impact remains questionable (cf. van de Kaa 2006; McDonald 2006).

In 2001, the parental leave allowance, designed as an income substitute for employees, was replaced by a general childcare benefit (€ 14.53 per day) to every mother or father independent of his/her employment status, but linked to an income threshold of € 14,500 per year[10]. At the same time, the period of entitlement was extended from 1.5 to 2.5 years if only one parent received the childcare payment. Discriminating against single parents, the entitlement period increased to three years, in case the second parent drew it for at least six months. Nevertheless, in 2006 only 3.6 percent of the persons drawing the childcare benefit were men, about 6,000 men compared to about 164,000 women (Statistik Austria 2007: 99).

Additionally, the leave period is included for pension entitlement as well as the amount of pension received, and parents have a right to part-time employment and job security until the child reaches the age of six. Since January 2008, the reformed system of childcare benefits offers parents three options regarding the maximum duration of entitlement related to different levels of monthly allowance. Parents may choose a period of 18 months (if the second parent draws it for at least 3 months) with a monthly allowance of € 800, 2 years (if the second parent draws it for at least 4 months) with a monthly allowance of € 624 or 3 years (if the second parent draws it for at least 6 months) with a monthly allowance of € 436.

Furthermore, family allowances are paid for children below the age of 18, prolonged to age 26 for children who pursue vocational training or university

9 Gauthier's typology is based on a comparative analysis of family policies in industrialized countries during the 20th century.

10 This amount generally excludes full-time employment.

studies.[11] Family benefits also include tax allowances for children for single earner households and additional cash transfers for families in need.

Austrian family policy is primarily focused on direct transfers that provide generous financial incentives to increase fertility, which finally seem to be rather ineffective. For instance, public expenditures on maternity and parental leave payments considerably exceed those on childcare services (OECD 2003: 131), but increases in family income tend to reduce the probability of mothers' employment (Mahringer 2005: 28).

In particular, the 2001 regulation of childcare benefits had a clearly negative impact on female labour market participation, since it encouraged mothers[12] to provide full-time childcare during the child's first years: The ratio of women with children aged below 2¼ re-entering into the labour market declined from 54 percent to 35 percent, while the prolonged duration of leave increasing from 65 to 110 weeks on average made the return of mothers to the labour market more difficult (Lutz 2003). Due to the lack of childcare facilities – in particular for children below the age of three – and comparatively high childcare costs, the number and the age of children have a strong impact on the re-entry of mothers into the labour force and thereby on female employment rates (OECD 2003).

As a result of the ascription of unpaid care work, women's opportunity costs for childbearing rise and lead especially highly educated women to postponement of childbearing and high preferences for childlessness (Buber 2002). Therefore, Austrian family policy offers not only few structural incentives to reduce the incompatibilities of childrearing and employment, it reinforces the traditional gender division of labour and adds barriers that impede women's access to the labour force. In combination with neoliberal restructuring of the labour market, it enhances gender-specific segmentations of the labour market thereby promoting gender hierarchies, as will be discussed in the following section.

11 The family allowance increases according to the age and the number of children from € 105.4 for children below the age of three to € 152.7 from age 19 onwards; for three or more children an additional transfer of € 25.5 per child and month is paid.

12 Because of traditional gender roles, but also because of gender-specific income disparities in the labour market, the share of fathers that receive the childcare benefit is negligible.

3 Deregulation of the labour market

The currently prominent role of demographics hints at the state taking over human resources management in accordance with economic claims that focus on the needs of a knowledge-based economy whose starting point is the human being and its capacities to think, create, develop. Attributing the state the role of human resources management, processes of labour market restructuring were characterized by deregulation as outlined by the EU commission's 1993 white book on *Growth, Competition and Employment*. Policies of deregulation finally led to an erosion of standard fulltime employment, new forms of gender-specific segmentation and social polarization (cf. Schunter-Kleemann 2001).

Female labour force participation in Austria hovers around the average level for all EU members, for young women it is among the highest, for elderly women among the lowest. Since the 1970s, women's employment ratio (age 15-64) increased continuously to 64 percent, whereas men's dropped slightly to 77 percent (Statistik Austria 2007: 18). However, female full-time equivalents remained more or less constant since the end of the 1980s: The increase in female labour market participation went along with a decrease in the average number of weekly hours worked from about 40 in 1987 to 36 in 1999, dropping to 35 among married women.[13] Thus, the increase of female labour market participation did not imply redistribution of paid work between men and women, but between different groups of women.

Furthermore, female employment rates remain markedly differed by education. Whereas only 48 percent of women aged 15-64 (62 percent for men) with compulsory education participated in the labour force, this proportion was 85 percent for women (92 percent for men) with tertiary education in 2006 (Statistik Austria 2007: 73).

Additionally, the traditional ascription of unpaid care work becomes particularly visible, when relating women's labour force participation to the number and age of children. 'Family duties' generally reduce women's continuity, mobility and flexibility in the labour market and prevent women from exclusively dedicating their time to paid labour. Furthermore, women frequently fulfil positions below their qualification level. Given the same educational

13 In 2006, only 9 percent of the total female population and 0.02 percent of the male population were classified as 'housewives' (Statistik Austria 2007: 18).

level as men, men are attributed tasks of higher qualification, firms' vocational training programmes and career opportunities are more open to men than to women.

As a result, the Austrian labour market is characterized by high vertical segregation, segregation related to the professional hierarchy. For example women made up 55.7 percent of white-collar employees ('*Angestellte*'), but only 24 percent in leading positions of high qualification, among blue-collar workers 30 percent are females, but only 4.5 percent in leading positions (Statistik Austria 2002: 161).

In addition, the Austrian labour market is segregated horizontally with women's shares varying considerably according to industry. Income levels in typically female sectors like the textile and clothing industries or health and social services lie far below those in typically male ones like construction or transport.

Besides these forms of segregation, observable since the 1970s, deregulation of the labour market has led to a tremendous increase in 'atypical' forms of employment since the mid 1990s. Not only part-time jobs, but particular forms of part-time work, temporary employment and new forms of self-employment characterized by missing or only partial integration in the social insurance system. These forms of atypical – and mostly – precarious employment are predominantly female. While the share of women in the labour force amounts to about 46 percent, women account for about 90 percent of part-time workers. About half of the female labour force is employed on an 'atypical' basis (Statistik Austria 2007: 18).

Besides direct wage discrimination and implicitly discriminating valuation of labour, these phenomena of segregation – further expressions of specific practices of discrimination – lead to high gender-related income disparities. In 2005, women's gross mean income reached 60 percent of men's (Statistik Austria 2007: 38), while the gender pay gap[14], slightly above the EU-average, amounted to 18 percent (Statistik Austria 2007: 42). Gender-specific income differentials decreased slightly until the mid 1990s, but since then increased again, especially among low income-groups (BMSG 2004: 270 et seq.).

14 The gender pay gap is defined as the percentage women earn less per hour than men, on average.

As a consequence, wage differentials reinforce the female ascription of the private care economy. Since most households cannot afford a loss of the higher male income, primarily women interrupt their professional careers in order to take over unpaid care work. Furthermore, employment frequently does not secure an independent livelihood, particularly for women. In combination with cut-backs in the welfare system, meeting one's basic needs has become more and more difficult for many women, as will be shown in the following section.

4 Restrictions of social security

The Austrian system of social security is primarily based on labour market participation. Duration of employment and amount of income decide entitlement to and amount of transfers like pensions or unemployment benefits (Rosenberger 1995). Part-time employment for instance implies not only low wages, but in general leads to transfer payments too low for securing an independent livelihood. Gender-specific inequalities in the labour market are thereby reinforced by the welfare system, especially owing to measures of reform like extension of years of employment for pension entitlement, reductions of pensions in case of early retirement ('Frühpension') and increase of the retirement age during the last decade, which for instance implied cut-backs in retirement benefits. Consequently, female pensioners' yearly gross mean income reached only 56 percent of male pensioners in 2005 (Statistik Austria 2007: 44). Additionally, mostly female precarious employment at least partially lacks integration in the social insurance system.

The reorganization of retirement based on a 'three-column-model', which combines public, private and firm provisions, will lead to further inequalities and polarization among the elderly, since access to costly private provision is limited by women's generally low income levels. Women therefore also take less advantage of tax reductions related to private retirement insurance established in 2000, whereas firms' pension provisions are mostly limited to predominantly male full-time employees (cf. Stelzer-Orthofer 2001; Michalitsch 2004).

As a consequence, securing one's livelihood becomes more and more individualized and leads to growing gender disparities with the feminization of poverty as one of its results. In 2003, 12.3 percent of the male, but 14 percent of the female Austrian population and about a quarter of single female pensioners were in danger of dropping below the poverty line[15] (BMSG 2004: 213). The poverty risk amounts to 6 percent for full-time employees, but to 18 percent for part-time employees (BMSG 2004: 217). About 6 percent of the Austrian population live in poverty, about half of them as 'working poor' (BMSG 2004: 213, Tálos 2001).

By re-orienting labour market and social policies towards individual responsibility, neoliberal restructuring led to individualization of social risks, thereby affirming gender hierarchies. Individualization also characterizes reforms of public services. The neoliberal postulate of a 'slim state' led not only to privatizing public enterprises and reducing state bureaucracy by outsourcing public activities, but also to cut-backs – or at least the lack of extension despite growing demand – of public services. Partly, public services are replaced by monetary transfers to individuals, based on the argument of offering individuals more freedom of choice.

Nevertheless, introducing a general childcare benefit instead of extending the availability of professional childcare had quite the opposite effect. In principle, the childcare benefit allows a transfer of care work to the market sector, but in practice the very limited availability of care for children below the age of three leads to transfers to the informal sector of the economy, which implies an increase of mostly female low wage labour without social security. But mostly, the introduction of the childcare benefit, together with prevailing gender stereotypes in society and gender-specific income differentials in the labour market, leads to a renewal of the female ascription of family work and thereby to the re-traditionalization of gender relations. Therefore, it remains questionable whether women's options to choose have been increased (Hammer/Österle 2001: 67 et seq.).

Similarly, the reorganization of care for the elderly in 1993 included the substitution of public services by individual transfer payments, which are primarily used for care services offered by the informal sector, whereas more expensive supply by the formal market sector plays only a "marginal role" (Hammer/Österle 2001: 66). In parallel, most care for the elderly is performed by female relatives (Statistik Austria 2002: 91 et seq.).

In this way, neoliberal policies secure private care activities and increase pressure on the unpaid care economy, thereby reducing women's opportuni-

15 The poverty line is defined by an income level below 60 percent of the mean income.

ties to participate in the labour force, reinforcing gender segmentation of the labour market and increasing economic gender inequalities.

5 Redefinition of the public and the private

During the last decade, neoliberal policies led to a transfer of state activities to the private sector – market and/or household.[16] Processes of privatization therefore are not limited to a change of property from public to privately owned enterprises, but include the restructuring of the state administration by out-sourcing executive tasks to the market and 'slimming' bureaucracies. The state is increasingly redefined as an economic agent, subject to market principles, whose activities are measured by efficiency and even profit-orientation. As a consequence, public management gains importance when compared with the ideals of political leadership. At the same time, state activities are increasingly restricted to 'key issues' and public responsibilities replaced by private ones, which also leads to a redefinition of societal conflicts as private problems to be solved individually, beyond the public realm. Therefore, privatization can be regarded as a core strategy of neoliberal transformation based on a redefinition of the public and the private, characterized by narrowing the political sphere as the realm of democratic negotiation and control (cf. Sauer 2001; Weber 2001; Michalitsch 2004).

Closely linked to de-nationalization and de-democratization, privatization also constitutes the guiding principle of neoliberal policies with regards to labour markets and welfare systems implying 'activation' of the individual in order to establish a new social model that enforces self-reliance and personal initiative (Kocyba 2004: 20). Economic governance is linked to individual self-management guided by principles of achievement, merit, competition and economic success to transform the individual into an 'active agent' of his/her own existence. Thus, the individual is not regarded as a product of society, but of its own efforts, that must prove its quality among competitive circumstances (cf. Hondrich 2001). Decoupled from economic and societal preconditions, economic success seems to be a function of personal entrepreneurship, capabilities, flexibility and creativity (Rose 2000: 92 et seq.).

16 For the dichotomy of the public and the private as a core topic of now 'classical' feminist critique cf. Elshtain (1993), Pateman (1994), Kerchner/Wilde (1997).

Since motivation and initiative are not limited, the whole way of life becomes a matter of improvement and optimization, while instable employment relations, reduction of social security and postulated self-reliance produce not only precarious living conditions combined with a lack of biographic predictability, but also generate fears and establish "cultures of 'rigidity'", stressing the need to survive instead of good life (Fach 2000: 121).

Thereby, new forms of contradictions emerge, which express themselves primarily in an individualized form as self-alienation, resignation and indifference without disturbing the pseudo-harmonic surface of society (Gerlach 2001: 176 et seq.).

6 Neoliberal gender regime

With regards to gender relations, neoliberal restructuring produces rising economic inequalities. On the one hand, neoliberal transformation processes increase pressure on the care economy by reducing public services, which affects women's labour market participation negatively and leads to a growing segment of primarily female labour in the informal sector. On the other hand, deregulation of the labour market leads to increasing marginalization of women in the labour force and to growing income differentials. Finally, due to the reductions in the welfare system, the only partial integration of "atypical" employment in social security systems and the promotion of private forms of provision, earning differentials have been less and less diminished. Lack of economic independence of women, feminization of poverty and polarization between men and women, but also between different groups of women are the results of these developments, which make the implicitly masculine neoliberal subject model visible (cf. Kreisky 2001; Michalitsch 2006).

This masculine model is closely linked to the neoliberal focus on market activities and principles, which neglect not only the unpaid care economy, typically female life contexts or gender hierarchies, but also the logic of social relations in general, while permanent availability for market activities and equal opportunities are assumed, far from being realized.

In contrast, postulating equal opportunities and self-reliance covers gender hierarchies, which are increasingly redefined as individual problems due to (wrong) individual choice. Structural forms of discrimination are re-interpreted as individualized disadvantages and society's gender hierarchies as individual gender arrangements, while feminism and emancipatory women's policies are regarded as out-dated – but to recognize gender relations as public constitutes a precondition and means of emancipation (Demirović 2001: 23). Instead, neoliberal reforms affirm gender asymmetries of power in all segments of society.

Therefore, neoliberal restructuring and conservative family policy, as combined in Austria, prove not to be contradictory, but to form an alliance that results in policies and public discourses oriented towards gender stereotypes. Motivated also by demographic goals and population policy, primarily women are confronted with claims for higher valuation of family, children and care for others instead of 'egoistic self-realization'. Public discourses promoting the happiness of motherhood and family life as attractive alternatives to professional careers, stressing the unity of mother and child and presenting education by the mother as the 'natural' and hence best solution for the child – whereas childcare institutions might cause 'irreparable damage' – gain influence (cf. Lang 2001).

Aiming at securing reproduction and cohesion in society, the family obviously has to compensate for polarization and the loss of solidarity in society and shall fulfil emotional needs for personal warmth, closeness and affiliation. It shall constitute a protected counterpart to a cold, competitive, hostile world full of conflicts (cf. Michalitsch 2005).

Quite in contrast to constructions of 'career women', marginal integration of women in the labour market, affiliation to the unpaid care economy and public discourses reaffirm traditional concepts of motherhood and direct the promotion of reconciliation of family and profession primarily towards women. As a result, gender hierarchies are reinforced, gender relations retraditionalized.

7 Gender government, governmentality and female resistance

Neoliberal transformation shows how gender is re-regulated by state and economic practices. Abstracting these practices from their specific context and embedding them into the analytical framework of Foucault's concepts of government and governmentality reveal how political and economic practices form mechanisms to (re-)produce gender and thus how political economy reproduces gender.

According to Foucault, government means the whole complex of institutions and practices to guide human beings, as well as all procedures, techniques and methods to secure the guidance of human beings among themselves (Foucault 1996: 119). Government is not restricted to the political realm, but includes all forms of social guidance, it refers to 'the conduct of conduct', to the way individuals are formed and produced as subjects. Government therefore does not mean the suppression or subjection of individuals, but refers to their emergence as subjects (cf. Lemke 1997; Bröckling et al. 2000). Foucault's analysis of government focuses on the level of reflection on government practices. In this context, Foucault develops the term governmentality, which in general means the specific rationality immanent to each form of government. More specifically, it refers to the techniques of government underpinning the modern state. In the context of the modern state, Foucault also defines governmentality with regards to the specific historical horizon from the 18th century to the present as

> "the ensemble formed by the institutions, procedures, analyses and reflections, the calculations and tactics that allow the exercise of this very specific albeit complex form of power, which has as its target population, as its principal form of knowledge political economy, and as its essential technical means apparatuses of security" (Foucault 2004: 162).

The political figure of population emerging in the 18th century does not refer to the quantity of subjects ruled by the will of the sovereign, but the entire processes in society to be administered in accordance with their 'nature'. The political economy reveals these 'natural processes' as consequences and effects of mechanisms and conducts research on the 'nature of population' as the object of government and on government practices. The analysis offered by the political economy makes this nature of the population accessible to forces and techniques of transformation. Therefore, political economy not only means the analysis of production and the circulation of goods, but also a method of government capable of securing the wealth of a nation. Security apparatuses serve as technical instruments of government directed towards the population, whose 'natural phenomena' have to be respected. Consequently, its administration cannot be based on orders or prohibitions, but on inducement, interference and regulation of these 'natural' processes (Foucault 2004: 506).

In contrast to law and discipline as technologies of government, security apparatuses primarily register developments and regulate them by accelerating, limiting or slowing them – without prescription or prohibition. Whereas a system of law permits what is not determined, a system of discipline prescribes what has to be done, the undetermined is forbidden. Security apparatuses do not replace systems of law or discipline, but complement them.

Taking into account that gender constitutes a basic structural element of modern societies, government can be interpreted as always producing subjects as gendered subjects. In this sense, the modern state's security apparatuses, aiming at the administration of the population, also imply elements of maintaining the modern construction of gender and its hierarchic order. Therefore, apparatuses of security also aim at stabilizing the existing gender order and constitute a means of its reproduction, while tolerating a certain degree of deviation. In this respect, law and discipline lose, while apparatuses of security gain importance during the 20th century.

Interpreted as elements of the current apparatus of security, specific mechanisms with regards to gender hierarchies, their current forms, functions and effects will be specified in the following. This brief sketch of political-economic mechanisms (re-)producing gender focuses on their structural dimension and offers a starting point of analysis to be extended to manifold connections to other economic and societal fields as well as institutions. It makes visible how gender is embedded in the frame of political economy and how this frame is structured by gender. At the same time, these mechanisms, linked to each other, characterize the formation of gender.

- Attribution of labour: The differentiation of public and private as a pattern regulating social relations implies processes of social standardization of gender that accompany the exclusion of the reproductive sector from the economic and its female ascription. This fundamental exclusion forms the basis for further gender-specific economic differentiation like disparities of employment status or income level, which ensure it at the same time.
  This relation constitutes the economic core mechanism of the reproduction of gender. Unpaid care work restricts female availability to and continuity in the labour market. Thus, it can be regarded as a priority in relation to paid labour. Atypical employment dominated by women expresses this priority of reproduction. Unpaid care work at the same time forms the standard for valuation and attribution of paid work. Closeness

to reproductive activities lead to a feminization of jobs and low income, which shows that reproduction also constitutes a symbolic marker of femininity.

- Attribution of paid labour: The labour market is hierarchically structured in segments that to a great extent correlate with gender. Compared to the primary labour market, the secondary market, dominated by women, is characterized by atypical forms of employment, low job security, low wages, marginal career opportunities, bad work conditions and low social security. Transfer from the secondary to the primary labour market is restricted, and even the primary labour market is vertically and horizontally segregated by gender as shown by the over-representation of women in single industries or service sectors and in low professional positions. The recognition and valuation of qualification as defined by society correspond to these gendered segregation patterns, so the gendered structure of the labour market affirms the female ascription of unpaid care work.
- Attribution of income: Gender-specific income disparities result from direct forms of discrimination against women, but also from the above mentioned mechanisms of gender-specific attribution and valuation of paid labour.

  With regards to household income, income differentials affirm restrictions in female labour force participation for private need and thereby strengthen the female ascription of unpaid care work.[17] Income determines the access to resources and thus directly influences life conditions like housing or consumption possibilities. Furthermore, it acts as a criterion of social status and, in general, of personal independence. As such, income affects power relations in private households and consequently the distribution of unpaid care work to the disadvantage of women. Besides that, income also serves as a basis for the formation of wealth, which is closely linked to access to capital and chances of founding an enterprise. In this sense, gender-specific income disparities stabilize the dependent status of women as employed.

17 This effect of income disparities as a market result is affirmed by systems of taxation based on household income or income splitting among couples. Progressive individual taxation in contrast decreases net income differentials and therefore tends to support a more equal distribution of unpaid care work.

- Attribution of social security: Linking social security primarily to the status of employment and secondarily to the duration of employment and income level reinforces gender inequalities. Feminization of poverty and poverty risks are consequences of this relationship.
- Attribution of decision-making: Professional position and income level imply different kinds of decision-making, which becomes manifest as the private capability to shape one's life. Professional hierarchies furthermore determine decisions referring directly to other employees, but also to broader societal environments. They thereby play an essential role in the shaping of society.

The whole structure of these mechanisms forms an essential part of the political and economic frame producing subjects as gendered subjects. Each of these mechanisms is related to the others and affects further societal contexts.

These political-economic mechanisms characterize not only the specific conditions for the supply of female labour, but female labour supply expresses processes of formation based on these mechanisms. To further explore them, broader political, economic and societal contexts have to be submitted to analysis in order to shed light on the whole complex and comprising systematic character of the reproduction of gender.

Nevertheless, this brief sketch shows the multiple interrelations of political and economic mechanisms reproducing gender and gender hierarchies as well as how political and economic practices are linked to each other and form gendered apparatuses of security, which serve government as gender government shaping gendered subjects. Gender government is embedded in the state and the market with a multitude of enterprises, households and individuals making decisions within the structural frame of the mechanisms outlined above. This frame is produced by gender government and serves as its precondition. Gender government constitutes a decentralized form of government tending to restrict women's access to labour markets or social security without forbidding it. Mechanisms of security restrict women to lower levels of professional hierarchies and 'atypical' employment linked to lower income, higher social risks and low access to processes of decision-making. These mechanisms play a key role in maintaining gender hierarchies under conditions of political and economic restructuring and thus ensure the persistence of gender inequality.

Consequently, gender is inherent to neoliberal governmentality. Discourses and practices (with respect to family issues, for example) that seem contradictory to neoliberal principles at first sight become logical and consistent when linking them to the implicit gender rationality of neoliberalism, the 'hidden' gender dimensions of its governmentality.

In this context, declining birth rates and increasing childlessness may not be interpreted as signs of resignation (cf. Burkart 2006), but of individual female resistance against gender government and its manifold implications. Since, for women, childbearing in practice involves not only a high degree of incompatibility with a professional career, but exposure to a societal conception of motherhood with far-reaching consequences and, compared to men, disadvantages in daily life, 'fertility' indicates women's conscious decisions regarding their way of life. Therefore, restricting or denying childbirth expresses women's preferences for a concept of life that opposes societal propositions, indicating a silent protest against the current gender regime. Far from parents' equally sharing the burdens of child-rearing, limiting the number of children seems an individual solution to escape at least some of its repercussions and to offer more chances for autonomy, independence and personal freedom. In this sense, declining birth rates and increasing childlessness might be read as indicators of a 'baby strike' ('*Gebärstreik*')[18] which, as a consequence of neoliberal governmentality, reflects a de-politicized, individualized form of female resistance against discriminating societal circumstances. Still, it expresses an attitude of critique by denying acceptance of a certain attributed mode of life: refusing to be governed in this way (Foucault 1992: 12).

Bibliography

Andersson, Gunnar/ Scott, Kirk (2007): "Childbearing Dynamics of Couples in a Universalistic Welfare State: The Role of Labor-Market Status, Country of Origin, and Gender." In: *Demographic Research* 17/30, 897-938, www.demographic-research.org/volumes/vol17/30/ (25/01/2009)

Auth, Diana/ Holland-Cunz, Barbara (eds.) (2007): *Grenzen der Bevölkerungspolitik. Strategien und Diskurse demographischer Steuerung.* Opladen: Barbara Budrich

18 In Germany, high childlessness, in particular among women with academic education, led to broad public debates on a 'baby strike', while there is no comparable discourse in Austria.

Barlösius, Eva/ Schiek, Daniela (eds.) (2007): *Demographisierung des Gesellschaftlichen. Analysen und Debatten zur demographischen Zukunft Deutschlands.* Wiesbaden: VS Verlag für Sozialwissenschaften

Berger, Peter A./ Kahlert, Heike (eds.) (2006): *Der demographische Wandel. Chancen für die Neuordnung der Geschlechterverhältnisse.* Frankfurt/ M., New York: Campus

Bernhardt, Eva/ Goldscheider, Frances (2006): "Gender Equality, Parenthood Attitudes, and First Births in Sweden." In: *Vienna Yearbook of Population Research 2006,* 19-39

BMSG (Bundesministerium für soziale Sicherheit, Generationen und Konsumentenschutz) (ed.) (2004): *Bericht zur sozialen Lage 2003-2004.* Wien: Bundesministerium für soziale Sicherheit, Generationen und Konsumentenschutz

Bröckling, Ulrich/ Krasmann, Susanne/ Lemke, Thomas (2000): "Gouvernementalität, Neoliberalismus und Selbsttechnologien. Eine Einleitung." In: Bröckling, Ulrich/ Krasmann, Susanne/ Lemke, Thomas (eds.): *Gouvernementalität der Gegenwart. Studien zur Ökonomisierung des Sozialen.* Frankfurt/ M.: Suhrkamp, 7-40

Buber, Isabella (2002): *The Influence of the Distribution of Household and Child-rearing Tasks between Men and Women on Childbearing Intentions in Austria.* Rostock: Max Planck Institute for Demographic Research (Working Paper 2002/004), www.demogr.mpg.de/papers/working/wp-2002-004 (25/01/2009)

Burkart, Günter (2006): "Kinderlosigkeit, Kinderwunsch und politische Steuerung. Zaudernde Männer, zweifelnde Frauen, zögernde Paare: Wer ist Schuld an der Kinderlosigkeit?" In: Berger, Peter A./ Kahlert, Heike (eds.): *Der demographische Wandel. Chancen für die Neuordnung der Geschlechterverhältnisse.* Frankfurt/ M., New York: Campus, 111-136

Dackweiler, Regina-Maria (2006): "Reproduktives Handeln im Kontext wohlfahrtsstaatlicher Geschlechterregime." In: Berger, Peter A./ Kahlert, Heike (eds.): *Der demographische Wandel. Chancen für die Neuordnung der Geschlechterverhältnisse.* Frankfurt/ M., New York: Campus, 81-110

Demirović, Alex (2001): "Hegemonie und das Paradox von Privat und Öffentlich." In: *Kurswechsel. Zeitschrift für gesellschafts-, wirtschafts- und umweltpolitische Alternativen* (4), 12-23

Elshtain, Jean Bethke (1993): *Public Man, Private Woman. Women in Social and Political Thought.* Princeton: Princeton University Press

European Commission (1993): *"Growth, Competitiveness, Employment: The Challenges and Ways Forward into the 21st Century – White Paper"*, (COM(93) 700). Bruxelles: European Commission

Fach, Wolfgang (2000): "Staatskörperkultur. Ein Traktat über den 'schlanken Staat'." In: Bröckling, Ulrich/Krasmann, Susanne/Lemke, Thomas (eds.): *Gouvernementalität der Gegenwart. Studien zur Ökonomisierung des Sozialen.* Frankfurt/ M.: Suhrkamp, 110-130

Foucault, Michel (1992): *Was ist Kritik?* Berlin: Merve

Foucault, Michel (1996): *Der Mensch ist ein Erfahrungstier. Gespräch mit Ducio Trombadori*, Frankfurt/ M.: Suhrkamp

Foucault, Michel (2004): *Geschichte der Gouvernementalität I. Sicherheit, Territorium, Bevölkerung.* Frankfurt/ M.: Suhrkamp

Gauthier, Anne (2002): "Family Policies in Industrialized Countries. Is There Convergence?" In: *Population* 57 (3), 447-474.

Gerlach, Thomas (2001): *Denkgifte. Psychologischer Gehalt neoliberaler Wirtschaftstheorie und gesellschaftspolitischer Diskurse.* Bremen: University of Bremen (Dissertation)

Hammer, Elisabeth/ Österle, August (2001): "Neoliberale Gouvernementalität im österreichischen Wohlfahrtsstaat. Von der Reform der Pflegevorsorge 1993 zum Kinderbetreuungsgeld 2002." In: *Kurswechsel. Zeitschrift für gesellschafts-, wirtschafts- und umweltpolitische Alternativen* (4), 60-69

Hondrich, Karl Otto (2001): *Der Neue Mensch.* Frankfurt/ M.: Suhrkamp

Kahlert, Heike (2006): "Der demographische Wandel im Blick der Frauen- und Geschlechterforschung." In: Berger, Peter A./ Kahlert, Heike (eds.): *Der demographische Wandel. Chancen für die Neuordnung der Geschlechterverhältnisse.* Frankfurt/ M., New York: Campus, 295-310

Kerchner, Brigitte/ Wilde, Gabriele (eds.) (1997): *Staat und Privatheit. Aktuelle Studien zu einem schwierigen Verhältnis.* Opladen: Leske + Budrich

Kocyba, Hermann (2004): „Aktivierung." In: Bröckling, Ulrich/ Krasmann, Susanne/ Lemke, Thomas (ed.): *Glossar der Gegenwart.* Frankfurt/ M.: Suhrkamp, 17-22

Kreisky, Eva (2001): "Ver- und Neuformungen des politischen und kulturellen Systems. Die maskuline Ethik des Neoliberalismus." In: *Kurswechsel. Zeitschrift für gesellschafts-, wirtschafts- und umweltpolitische Alternativen* (4), 38-50

Lang, Sabine (2001): „Reprivatisierungen im neoliberalen Geschlechterregime." In: *femina politica. Zeitschrift für feministische Politik-Wissenschaft* 10 (2), 91-104

Lemke, Thomas (1997): *Eine Kritik der politischen Vernunft. Foucaults Analyse der modernen Gouvernementalität.* Berlin, Hamburg: Argument

Lutz, Hedwig (2003): "Auswirkungen der Kindergeldregelung auf die Beschäftigung von Frauen mit Kleinkindern. Erste Ergebnisse." In: *WIFO Monatsberichte* (3), 213-227

Lutz, Wolfgang/ Vaupel, James W./ Ahlburg, Dennis A. (eds.) (1999): *Frontiers of Population Forecasting.* A Supplement to Vol. 24, 1998, *Population and Development Review.* New York: The Population Council

Mahringer, Helmut (2005): *Essays on Child Care Costs and Mother's Employment Rates and on Trends in Job Stability.* Linz: University of Linz (Dissertation)

McDonald, Peter (2006): "An Assessment of Policies that Support Having Children from the Perspectives of Equity, Efficiency and Efficacy." In: *Vienna Yearbook of Population Research* 2006, 213-234

Michalitsch, Gabriele (2004): "Private Liebe statt öffentliche Leistung. Geschlechterimplikationen von Privatisierung." In: *Kurswechsel. Zeitschrift für gesellschafts-, wirtschafts- und umweltpolitische Alternativen* (3), 75-84

Michalitsch, Gabriele (2005): "Familien-Frauen-Männerpolitik. Zurückstellung von Gleichstellung." In: Dimmel, Nikolaus/ Schmee, Josef (eds.): *Politische Kultur in Österreich 2000-2005.* Wien: Promedia, 243-254

Michalitsch, Gabriele (2006): *Die neoliberale Domestizierung des Subjekts. Von den Leidenschaften zum Kalkül.* Frankfurt/ M., New York: Campus

OECD (2003): *Babies and Bosses. Reconciling Work and Family Life.* Vol. 2: Austria, Ireland and Japan. Paris: OECD

Pateman, Carole (1994): "Feminist Critiques of the Public/Private Dichotomy." In: Moller Okin, Susan/ Mansbridge, Jane (eds.): *Feminism.* Vol. 1. Aldershot: Elgar, 327-349

Prskawetz, Alexia/ Sobotka, Tomáš/ Buber, Isabella/ Engelhardt, Henriette/ Gisser, Richard (2008): "Austria: Persistent Low Fertility since the mid-1980s." In: *Demographic Research* 19/12, 293-360, www.demographic-research.org/Volumes/Vol19/12/ (25/01/2009)

Rose, Nikolas (2000): "Tod des Sozialen? Eine Neubestimmung der Grenzen des Regierens." In: Bröckling, Ulrich/ Krasmann Susanne/ Lemke, Thomas (eds.): *Gouvernementalität der Gegenwart. Studien zur Ökonomisierung des Sozialen.* Frankfurt/ M.: Suhrkamp, 72-109

Rosenberger, Sieglinde (1995): "Auswirkungen sozialpolitischer Maßnahmen auf die Gestaltung der Geschlechterverhältnisse." In: Bundesministerin für Frauenangelegenheiten/Bundeskanzleramt (ed.): *Bericht über die Situation der Frauen in Österreich. Frauenbericht 1995.* Wien: Bundesministerium für Frauenangelegenheiten, 387-397

Sauer, Birgit (2001): "Öffentlichkeit und Privatheit revisited. Grenzneuziehungen im Neoliberalismus und die Konsequenzen für Geschlechterpolitik." In: *Kurswechsel. Zeitschrift für gesellschafts-, wirtschafts- und umweltpolitische Alternativen* (4), 5-11

Schunter-Kleemann, Susanne (2001): "Zwischen Welfare und Workfare – Sozialpolitische Strategien gegen die Feminisierung der Armut." In: Stelzer-Orthofer, Christine (ed.): *Zwischen Welfare und Workfare. Soziale Leistungen in der Diskussion.* Linz: Sozialwissenschaftliche Vereinigung, 21-45

Skirbekk, Vegard (2008): "Fertility Trends by Social Status." In: *Demographic Research* 18/5, 145-180, www.demographic-research.org/Volumes/Vol18/5/ (25/01/2009)

Spielauer, Martin (2005): "Concentration of Reproduction in Austria: General Trends and Differentials by Educational Attainment and Urban-Rural Setting." In: *Vienna Yearbook of Population Research* 2005, 171-195

Statistik Austria (2002): *Geschlechtsspezifische Disparitäten.* Wien: Bundesministerium für Soziale Sicherheit und Generationen/Bundesministerium für Bildung, Wissenschaft und Kultur

Statistik Austria (2007): *Frauen und Männer in Österreich. Statistische Analysen zu geschlechtsspezifischen Unterschieden.* Wien: Statistik Austria

Stelzer-Orthofer, Christine (2001): "Auf dem Weg zu einem 'schlanken' Sozialstaat? Zur Privatisierung sozialer Risiken im österreichischen sozialen Sicherungssystem." In: *Kurswechsel. Zeitschrift für gesellschafts-, wirtschafts- und umweltpolitische Alternativen* (4), 51-59

van de Kaa, Dirk J. (2006): "Temporarily New: On Low Fertility and the Prospect of Pronatal Policies." In: *Vienna Yearbook of Population Research 2006*, 193-211

Tálos, Emmerich (2001): "Armut und atypische Beschäftigung als sozialpolitische Herausforderung." In: Stelzer-Orthofer, Christine (ed.): *Zwischen*

Welfare und Workfare. Soziale Leistungen in der Diskussion. Linz: Sozialwissenschaftliche Vereinigung, 73-90

Testa, Maria Rita (2007): "Childbearing Preferences and Family Issues in Europe: Evidence from the Eurobarometer 2006 Survey." In: *Vienna Yearbook of Population Research* 2007, 357-379

Weber, Beat (2001): "Öffentlich/Privat – neue Grenzziehungen im Übergang zum Postfordismus." In: *Kurswechsel. Zeitschrift für gesellschafts-, wirtschafts- und umweltpolitische Alternativen* (4), 24-37

Jutta Hartmann

Dynamization of Gender and Generation – Shifting Orders and Ambivalent (Self-)Relations as the Educational Challenges of Lifelong Learning in the Field of Social Work

Presently in Europe education seems to be in great demand. Aside from demographic change, the development of the knowledge society is regarded as a central cause for the increasing need to invest in education in terms of lifelong learning. Not only is it intended to meet the decline in the working population and lack of skilled workers, which is predicted to accompany the demographic changes, but also – more importantly – keep up with the changes in demand of the employment market. Thus, measures of the Commission of the European Community for example, envisage an investment in educational opportunities and employability "stronger labour participation, in particular, by women and older workers" (Kommission der Europäischen Gemeinschaften 2005: 5).

It is beyond doubt that modernization processes and demographic changes are accompanied by educational challenges for individuals and society. However, in Germany the financial problems of the social state originally connected to the demographic change were also discussed and changes were undertaken, which did not necessarily have to be bound in this form to the numerical development of the population composition (cf. Helfferich 2008: 34). Holger Ziegler (2008: 173) describes with the concept of the "post-social statehood" the new formation of the social in Germany, partly legitimized by the demographic change, in the course of which and following the core idea of the activating social state, a new civil society is fostered and a "moral agenda of the activating of a self responsibility which is compatible with common welfare" is followed. The prioritized responsibility for problems in life is pushed from the social state polity to the subject and its social surroundings. Thus a demographization of societal or social problems is often spoken of (e.g. Berger/Kahlert 2006: 10; Buchen/Maier 2008: 8).

Education also represents a social investment of the state. In my article I follow the thesis that the unexpected enhanced prestige of education and social work in view of complex educational challenges through the increased debate concerning education, would be important, yet is only feigned and does not stand in contradiction with the diagnosed post-social statehood.

Both education and social work take as their starting point the subject and aim to responsibly change it. Additionally, the principally employment-market oriented framing of education, as it is particularly fostered in the concept of lifelong learning, makes it doubtful that education in the sense of the German-speaking differentiation between upbringing (*Erziehung*) as personality-forming and education (*Bildung*) as a programme of emancipation is intended with the debate (Kessl/Richter 2006: 306) – education therefore understood as a basic creative power for dealing with the world, which follows the ambivalence of adaption and resistance as characteristics of modern education processes, and due to "the ubiquitous conformism" tries to keep in view, and even to "strengthen resistance" (Adorno 1989 [1971]: 110). A creative power understood thus would comprise a self-reflective momentum in the sense of keeping distance from the norms constituting the subject – a fixation on the employment market or normative models alongside categories of differentiation, as they are given, for example, in the form of heterosexual binary gender order and age concepts of gender and generation as social structuring and identity creating categories, and are, from the point of view of modernization and emancipation processes, moving in contradictory ways.

In order to obtain a view of the contemporary educational challenges in the background of this categorizing system, in my article I will firstly sketch out the dynamization processes alongside the categories of differentiation generation and gender, and look at family as a category at their point of intersection (1). With the term dynamization I envisage power relations as changing relations and categories which define "becoming and not being" (Adorno 1989 [1971]: 144) and which challenge the creative power of the subject in light of contradictory tendencies. As a next step I examine the concept of lifelong learning, which is highly regarded in current education policy discourse, to establish whether it seems appropriate to follow the complex educational challenges (2). In light of its employment market focused bias and selective value, the concept of lifelong learning appears to me a useful contribution of post-social statehood governmental practices. I will take its functional focus on the aptitude of the subject for the independent management of social risks as a starting point in order to further discuss how the inevitability of lifelong learning can also be constructed as a virtue in the sense of "not becoming governed to such an extent" (Foucault 1992: 12) (3). The thesis forms the basis, that given an increasing enmeshment of new educational discourses and the post-social state (increase in) responsibility, we can observe a 'didactization of social problems' (cf. Galuske 2008), from which in contrast, an education and social work orientated towards education as a programme of emancipation with critical-deconstructive educational interventions, can dissociate itself. In an envisaged critical-deconstructive educational project, the term 'dynamization' should stand for enabling experience-orientated educational areas for all and to stimulate new power agencies through (social) pedagogic educational interventions alongside social categories of differentiation, such as generation and gender, which enable changes in ways that break down more hierarchical orders and are more open, and de-emphasize firm concepts of age, as well as heterosexual binary gender order. My understanding of dynamization, seen in this way, goes beyond processes of change and transformation and emphasizes the endorsing and promotion of gender and age-related self-relations as an educational challenge.

1 Dynamized orders – processes of pluralization and normalization in generation and gender relationships

The central reference point of the concept of generation is age, understood as the duration of life spent so far. In generational relationships demographic change develops dynamic effect. Purely quantitatively, a striking change in the relationship between 'the old and the young' can be noticed,[1] which is already clearly reflected in the field of education and social work.[2] Furthermore, qualitative changes in the proportion of different generations can be observed. According to the pedagogic-anthropologic concept of generation, which has

1 According to the calculations of the Federal Office for Statistics, in 2030 "approximately every third person in Germany will be aged 60 years or older and only a sixth of the population will be under 20 years old" – and this "virtually independent of immigration developments" (BMFSFJ 2005: 73). From this one can act on the assumption of a double societal ageing: on the one hand the number of people who are over 60 years old is growing in real terms, and on the other hand the relative proportion of the younger compared to the older people is growing (Wieners 2005).

2 In Germany, the current trend for the workforce to become homogenously older is obvious in social, educational and self-improving spheres. Additionally quantitative changes in the target groups can be observed: a decrease in children and youths and an increase in persons in the so-called fourth life phase (cf. Meyer 2008).

influenced the self-image of many people, older and younger people are in a learning relationship whereby the different age-groups are characterized by different tasks and competencies. A differentiation in knowledge, experience and power is thereby implied in the form of a 'more' in the older generations. However, as this understanding, learning and education are sequentially tied to the life phases of childhood and youth, professional and family life to adulthood, as well as so-called retirement to the older generation, the implied chronology of the life cycle with its normative expectations over age-appropriate tasks and behaviours and with the "always too crude intergenerational roles and division of functions" (Winkler/Zander 2007: 140) has long begun to waver. Therefore, today many students, for example, find themselves in their education and family phases at the same time, adults complete their school leaving certificates, and pensioners begin to study (cf. Lange/Lettke 2007: 31). Additionally, transitions between education and employment, as well as between employment and retirement are becoming increasingly uncertain and fragile (cf. Meyer 2008). In contrast to established assumptions, short-termism and flexibility also characterize the stage of life of adulthood, which Rolf Arnold (2003: 12 et seq.) describes not as a state of being, "but [as] a continuous endeavour to reach maturity, a successful life, a strong identity and adequate competency for shaping one's life". Challenges that were formerly regarded exclusively as missions for the youth stage of life remain virulent in adulthood, as well as the forms of gender or sexual identity and the constant further development of life plans.

Projects and experiences at different stages of life – youth, adulthood and old age – change and multiply. There is no one type of youth, nor one type of adult, nor one type of elderly person. It is becoming less and less appropriate to attach age to one of the generations associated with the phases of life described above. Thus, age is proving to be less of a biological process than a historically changeable socio-cultural process. The concept of generation is becoming indistinct in respect to the assumption that a generation could represent a more or less uniform social group. Within a generation there are completely different social groupings whose identity-forming reference points do not have to be primarily age. Age is individualizing and duplicating itself and is at the same time accompanied by big changes. At present poverty in old age is assumed for many women, although a statistically verifiable high quality of life exists for the over-65s in comparison to younger age groups (Helfferich 2008: 33). Similarly, we see that West German men of 70 years or older are "top ranking with regards to income and property" (Buchen 2008: 95). Further social differences thus cross the age groups, so that these are repeatedly destroyed as a possible identity.

Family represents a discursive intersection of the categories generation and gender. As a fundamental educational relationship, the father-mother-child relationship is as a rule regarded as biologically-naturally established, and it is widely regarded as undisputed "that the relationship between husband and wife through the generativity leads to the relationship between parent and child, to generations" (Reinhart Kosselleck 2000, cited in Merten 2002: 22). Thus, heterosexual binary gender order is written into the family. In contrast to these positions, Michael Wimmer (1998: 81) problematizes the "basis, which has up to now been naturally assumed". According to his argument based on discourse theory, generation, together with all the living conditions associated with generational discourse, can be understood as completely generated by society. This opens up the possibility of questioning the normative expectations attached to the concept of generation – as, for example, has been happening for a long time through same-sex parenthood.

Family is not just family. Transformation processes in the intra-familial gender and generational relationships – such as the transformations in gender-based divisions of labour or the "loosening of the absolute link between heterosexuality, marriage and reproduction" (Knecht 2003: 58) – have in the last 20 to 30 years led to a multitude of adult-child combinations which are a feature of family life and brings into question formerly self-evident issues of how life is conducted. Rüdiger Peukert (2007) reports in his essay *On the Current Condition of the Family* of, among other things, unmarried cohabitation with children 'of lesbian or gay parentage', lone parent families, second families, adoptive families, and three- and more generation households. The historical process of the liberation of the individual from traditional ties and norms means taking leave of unquestioned and idealized life expectations, which among other things was accelerated through the emancipatory endeavours of the women's movement:

> "'private life' and the family, sexuality and sexual relations became agitated, in individual everyday lives as well as in public discourse, because women wanted more from life than to settle for the [latest] striped wallpaper pattern" (Schmauch 2008: 304).

However, ways of life are not simply individually changeable realities. The slogan of the development from the normal biography to the choice biography, which became popular in social scientific discussion with the individualization thesis (Beck 1986), has been repeatedly criticized as abbreviated (cf. Hartmann 2002: 37-46). Choices and forms of lifestyles are structured along relationships of societal balances of power and authority and the associated norms, and many aspects of life are not voluntarily available because of complex psychosocial processes. Monika Wohlrab-Sahr's (1997) criticism of the individualization thesis led her to the questions of how societal changes modify the inner life of the people, how external norms are even reduced, but can be found again in inner constraints. She proposes an understanding of individual identity, which is formed from institutionalized differences. Individualization, then, "does not mean freedom from dependency" (Wohlrab-Sahr 1997: 29) but points to a relationship of the individual with his/herself, which conveys itself through social and scientific discourse. If societal categories of difference, such as gender and generation as meaningful reference points for the constitution of characteristics are no longer seen as natural, but as continually developed individual and social identities, then this also leads to a questioning of the self-evidence of the heterosexuality assumption lying at the basis of the concept of family.

Deconstructive gender theories, as have been initiated among German-speaking academics and above all in the writings of Judith Butler (1991, 1995), research into how positions of identity, such as 'woman' or 'man', 'homosexual' or 'heterosexual', emerge over power relations. The concept of heteronormativity (Warner 1991; Butler 1995; Hartmann et al. 2007) emphasizes thereby the finding, that in the predominant gender discourse we are dealing with a heterosexual discourse in a double sense: it is based on the assumption on the one hand of two genders being clearly differentiated from each other and mutually exclusive, and on the other hand, of heterosexuality being natural and normal. The prevalent gender order, which, for example, links a body classified as female with female personality characteristics and patterns of behaviour, as well as a desire inevitably focused on men, receives here a fundamental criticism. This criticism is based on the observation that a multitude of social genders as well as diverse modes of desire can be discerned and also that 'biological gender' is a product of socio-cultural creation.

Thus heteronormativity appears not only in the naturalness with which heterosexual coupling underlies debates about upbringing or the family. Heteronormative thought also appears, for example where fear of homosexuality in men is depicted as a fear of becoming feminine, or where transgendered people, i.e. people who in a variety of ways experience a discrepancy between their biological and social gender, do not appear in the dominant discourse. In view of mothers living as lesbians as an example of diverse lifestyles, Ulrike Schmauch (2008: 304) points out that as a rule in terms of their concrete day-to-day life these mothers show more similarities than differences to other modern family forms. At the same time one should not underestimate what it means to choose and live such a plan against heterosexual expectations of normality. Although the pluralization of lifestyles is undisputed, one cannot speak of 'anything goes'. The real possibilities of being able to live a variety of lifestyles equally and with equal rights differ considerably along societal dimensions of inequality and in different (sub)cultural milieus (cf. Butler 2004).

Additionally, there are huge differences between life plans and life realities, especially for women. Numerous empirical studies in the past decade make clear that today it is natural for young women to complete professional training and leave themselves open to an economically independent future. Young women develop a variety of ideas in order to reconcile work and family, and expect ever more obviously in cohabitation with men a more equal split of housework and childcare. It is the socio-political reforms in the course of demographic change and the therewith suggested concessions in the negotiation process with the partner that hinder a simple practicability of these life plans.[3] Conversely, in the course of current political strategies for mobilizing employment reserves and increasing productivity, the pressure on women and men to earn will increase and the curriculum vita of women and men will in this respect be brought more into line. However, this will not dissolve the gender restriction of lifestyle. In view of the increased importance of support and care roles accompanying demographic change Gabriele Winker (2008: 56-59) points out by means of family models typed by their financial power,

3 Solutions in reconciling career and family on the political level thus continue to be directed primarily towards women and thus reproduce gender based divisions of labour and the restricted engagement of (potential) mothers on the employment market. Additionally, the „privatization of parental responsibility", as it is pursued in Germany through the family policy of "extension of financial incentives directed at parents instead of [through the; JH] extension of structural relief" (Helfferich 2008: 38 et seq.) may be decisive for the divergence of life plans and their realization.

how the concrete arrangement of care work with paid employment develop differently according to the family model, but will still be in every case principally dealt with by women.[4] Correspondingly, Cornelia Helfferich (2008: 42) sees a "next generation of women who are structurally over-stretched", who will be able to manage the tasks imposed upon them only with career breaks – which will then have a negative impact upon their pensions – or with multiple responsibilities. In view of the fact that still 70 percent of the younger generation have passed through professional training that can be characterized as gender-typical, it can be assumed that despite a high level of general education, younger women have a lower employment status with a "lower salary and fewer promotion prospects" than men (Krüger/Born 2000: 217). When heterosexual couples plan their future together, then

> "family management [slides] into gender different tracks and into new old inequalities between men and women because of these gender-different educational resources in the course of the evaluation of career patterns and the resulting time commitments" (Krüger/Born 2000: 217).

Starting a family remains in the heterosexual setting in most cases, bound to a re-traditionalizing of relations between the sexes.

The plans and experiences of gender-related lifestyles change and multiply, however they do not just take on new scopes of creativity, but also primarily structures and supposed practical constraints, which are tied back with a hierarchizing and restrictive effect to old patterns of order. The dominant gender and generational arrangements of 'young and old' as well as those of 'women and men' as they are admitted into society currently both seem to operate further, as well as shifting themselves dynamically parallel, and, in breaking the prevailing dual structure, generate new relationships and mean-

4 From this Gabriele Winker (2008: 57) assumes that in an "economized" family model, which is characterized by two adults on a good salary, care work is delegated to servants and commercialized. Thus the demands of women and men are the same in this model, however this is on the basis of an "often ethnitized separation of labour to the disadvantage of illegal female migrants" (Winker 2008: 57). In contrast women in "precarious" family models appear to be doubly burdened. As there are no financial margins to outsource care work, it is brought back into the family. The "subsistance oriented" model refers to families without paid employment, who are dependent on state benefits and must make themselves available on the employment market. Here too women predominantly undertake the care work.

ings. In order to shape one's own life in these contradictory and complex relationships recurring processes of reflection are necessary, which examine the pluralization and normalization of ways of livelihood and life, the increasingly open transitions in life, as well as the age- and gender based self relations of the subjects.

If it is a duty of social work to guide people in their life plans and the accompanying processes of learning and accomplishing, then this duty is given new meaning in the face of accelerated transformation processes and the accompanying promotion of lifelong learning processes. If social work is oriented towards the fulfilment of this duty, as established at the outset of this paper in the understanding of education as a programme which contains momentums of adaption and resistance, then it is challenged to support the target groups in their reflection on the many ways of livelihood and life as options for their own lives and hold them in equal esteem. Keeping in mind the element of resistance in education, it would be about demanding a de-essentialization of the categories gender and generation as well as critiquing encrusted polarizations, hierarchizations and exclusions, and distancing itself from normative patterns and structural constraints (cf. Hartmann 2009).

2 Imperative lifelong learning: which education for whom?

Demographic change, the restructuring of the welfare state, pluralization of ways of life and the dynamization of social categories such as gender and generation are accompanied by educational challenges, which after the first educational phase do not end upon entering adulthood or employment. Thus Christiane Schiersmann (2007: 9) assumes that further education is advancing "as the key resource for the individual and society" and will become an integral component of biographies. Constant change in private and professional life presents a permanent challenge. The erosion processes – of becoming adult, of working relations, of gender identities – launch the necessity of lifelong learning and goals oriented equally towards personality development, participation in the employment market, and participation in society. However, against this background, how is the concept of lifelong learning, which is currently being launched as a central theme in education policy at EU-level to be evaluated?

The development of the concept of lifelong learning has been moulded by international bodies such as the European Council, UNESCO and the OECD. It emphasizes the need to create learning opportunities for all age-groups – from childhood to old age. Lifelong learning is considered a precondition to enable societal and employment market participation and the extension and preservation of one's own self-determination and independence. The life-long learner with respect to his education and qualifications is the focus of this concept of education policy. The debates primarily target changes to the enhancement of the employability of individuals and the competitiveness of businesses. The clear emphasis lies on specialist and trade knowledge, which must be continually acquired, reflected and widened. The main aims of the lifelong learning proposals are to retain work capacity for as long as possible and to ensure independence into old age. The advancement of democracy and world openness, which as a rule is also an explicit aspiration, is increasingly given a back seat role (cf. Schiersmann 2007: 59-72; Gatzke 2007; Galuske 2008; BMBF 2008a, 2008b; Zeuner 2006).

The implementation of lifelong learning is also characterized by striking social inequality. In view of the participation in further education, it can be said today, just as in the 1960s and 1970s, that there is "a double selectivity [...] the likelihood to participate in further education grows with higher education, a higher income and regional contextualisation" (Faulstich/Zeuner 2006: 106). The accompanying production of inequality grows in the light of growing commercialization processes and the dismantling of publically subsidized learning opportunities (Kessl/Richter 2006: 315). An age-differentiated consideration of the participation quota of professional further education reveals that people between the ages of 50 and 64 participate the least. Also gender is proven in this field as a relevant category of differentiation. For one thing because of the 'feminizing of age' more women are affected by the exclusion mechanisms described above. For another, fewer women take part in professional further education than men, even if these numbers have aligned in recent years. Women have their further education financed by their employers less often than men, and furthermore their life circumstances play a central role for women: a survey by the Expert Commission for the Financing of Lifelong Learning showed that

> "women who live together with their partner and children participate less in professional further education. Conversely, for men, whether children live in the household plays no role in their participation in further education" (Schiersmann 2007: 133).

The political-economic orientation of lifelong learning proves explosive, for example if the close link between education and health, or rather life expectation is considered. Kolland (2008: 15) emphasizes that lifelong learning is a central prerequisite for an active life, particularly in old age. Looking at current numbers he claims that older people in particular do not feel catered for by the contents, few take part in suitable programmes and that it is leading to the social exclusion of the elderly. Exclusion from such a central area of life as education leads to poverty in the sense of weakened social integration, exclusion from life chances and the experience of failing societal demands.

At the same time a strong simulative nature and societal pressure is tied to the discourse surrounding lifelong learning, for example for one to make something socially useful out of the post-employment phase. Earlier the older generation would be released through retirement. Today, in contrast, a public rhetoric of responsibility operates, in which accordingly older people should carry out outside help in the sense of civic engagement, and self help in the sense of health-related prevention. Thus the primary orientation of the education of older people along parameters such as involvement in societal missions, as they are given through voluntary engagement, is to be evaluated as thoroughly questionable and was critized as "human capitalization of the elderly" (van den Berg 2007: 48):

> "If the need for 'activating the potential of older people' through education is emphasized in the fifth report on the elderly, these considerations are based on a concept of education which is aimed at the acquisition of skills according to their usefulness and not (self) reflexivity in terms of modernity theory discourse" (Buchen 2008: 96).

Correspondingly educational offers that are gender-based are more orientated towards bringing more women into gainful employment and thus promoting them in a functionally useful way, than dealing with the challenges of women's lives, reflecting normative expectations and demanding social equality. In addition, those who do not (successfully) take advantage of educational opportunities – which can be associated with high costs, and those who do not get actively engaged become in danger of being defamed as "educationally deprived" or "unwilling to learn" or of not being "up to date" (Siebert 2005: 54).

Therefore, lifelong learning does not present a concept of education in terms of content, but can be read as a programme for economic policy, which redefines problems across society specified by the employment market into individual learning exercises, promotes a de-institutionalization of education, and makes people themselves responsible for investment in their education. In doing so it reinforces rather than torpedoes accompanying social inequalities through categories of differentiation. With the term 'governmentality', in which he semantically binds governance and mindsets, Foucault (2000) was interested in how power is shifted into the self, i.e. how ways of subjectification are promoted, which are suitable for being associated with aims of governance. The education policy concept of lifelong learning can, following this idea, be read as a project which invites people to take responsibility for all levels of their own biography themselves and to develop competencies that equip them to manage their labour and health, thus managing social risk. Lifelong learning, seen in this way, promotes learning processes orientated towards self functionalisation, which shows a high compatibility with neoliberal post-social statehood. A learning arrangement which is aimed at creating a person who can be "flexible in the (employment) market" is becoming a "supplier of economic demand, not aimed at [creating] educated people, reflection or even wisdom, but at strengthening the subject of the market in the battle for survival" (Galuske 2008: 17). Michael Galuske speaks thus of a societal change from "welfare to workfare", which centres upon not "aid to help oneself" but upon "aid to compete", and is characterized by behavioural rather than relationship-oriented strategies:

> "The activating state contains at the heart of its philosophy an 'educational programme', i.e. the shaping of people according to the needs of the economy through prevention, education, qualification, advice, caring, pressure and sanctions" (Galuske 2008: 18).

Learning, presented in such a way, stands in contradiction to the emancipatory impetus of education.[5] Principally aimed at specialized and trade knowledge, and above all emphasizing efficiency and "future viability" (Rauschenbach 2005: 7), it results in the educational momentum of adaptability.

The educationalization of social problems – currently the economic cri-

5 This discussion of the predominant discourse concerning of lifelong learning does not consider that in concrete educational environments other aims can by all means also be realized.

sis, reflected particularly in high unemployment figures – which is exemplified in the concept of lifelong learning, applies a new mindset towards the subject, who feels or should feel responsible for all challenges and risks in his life. Galuske (2008: 25) demonstrates the counter-productiveness of market integration pursued with educational initiatives in an illustration:

> "If one imagines the magnitude of workers in a society as a queue at the gate of an employment market, motivation, qualification and educational attainment decide one's place in the queue. Whether the place allows one to enter is however dependent only on how many people from the queue in total are let in, how many workers the economy needs".

Seen in this way, educational provision in the context of lifelong learning cannot change anything in the overall economic crisis –"but solely mixes up the order of the queue, which is globally seen a zero sum game" (Galuske 2008: 25). In contrast it can, however, displace attention and responsibilities, so that people (should) no longer accept social risks to be carried collectively, but individually. The orientation of the concept of lifelong learning, in which "the social is aligned in and to the market economy" confirms the "substantial challenge so far as validly considered logic of thought, action and problematisation of social state arrangements" (Ziegler 2008: 161) implied in the thesis of post-social statehood. It follows a shifting from social state orientation towards social justice and material security to the individualized delegation of social security to the subjects, including their increasing private financing.

Seen in this way, only the functional part of education and social work, which secures adaption to economic demands and the employment market, as well as potential loss elimination effects for the social security systems, is reassessed through the lifelong learning education debate. Education as a critical corrective of a society, which does not educate blindly for market demands, but which rather stimulates critical reflective processes and accompanies coping processes, and which creates realms of experience for the challenges accompanying modernization processes and emancipation movements, as well as for the transitional self-relationships of the subjects; education, which makes an active contribution towards enabling manifold ways of life to live equally, in contrast, remains marginalized. On the other hand, a real assessment of education, its enabling pedagogy, and social work would mean guaranteeing this in a way that embraces the idea for all and securing the time and patience, spaces and capacities necessary for education. Social work is thus challenged to reflect the ambivalent character of its educative tasks. Even if it is unable to act beyond its power, it can however still frame "alternative possibilities of order", thought and being (Butler 2001: 3).

3 Ambivalent (self-)relations: critical-deconstructive perspectives of a diversity-orientated education

Referring to Gaston Bachelard, Fabian Kessl and Martina Richter presented an alternative to the prevalent thematization of the concept of education. In classifying the prevalent economy of knowledge focus of the lifelong learning education policy programme, they apply a "space of uninterrupted education", in which, following Bachelard, "not validation, but error, and not concluding appreciation of specific qualities, but permanent relationizing of the experienced stand in the centre" of the concept (Kessl/Richter 2006: 318). For them it is about opening educational spaces, where skills from experience can be taught in mutual exchange. Such spaces are to be formulated "along the concepts of criticism, experience and public security" (Kessl/Richter 2006: 319).

Picking up the concept of spaces of uninterrupted learning, it is about guaranteeing public educational spaces for all, i.e. developing strategies to break down the social exclusion in lifelong learning, to make available necessary resources for educational participation, and as a concrete example,

> "stimulating educative processes based on world experience, which place at the centre the living conditions in the neighbourhood and amongst friendship groups and thus enhance the third social space" (Kolland 2008: 17).

Horst Siebert (2005) showed in a study on the history of learning and the learning methods of adults, how adults accrue learning interests from their biographies and environment, and are to be understood from these. The logic of the need to learn, however, hardly affects the social imperative to learn, as it is transported into the concepts of lifelong learning (Siebert 2005: 64). Spaces of experience for education also require moments of inefficiency and leisure, but a successful life in the sense of a fulfilled life cannot in itself be efficient (cf. Reichenbach 2005). To understand life as a work of art, in the sense of Foucault (1987), furthermore points to art "not being so controlled".

Criticism appears there as a virtue, which Foucault contrasts with obedience, the uncritical submission to an authority. Following Butler (2001: 3) the virtue of Foucault is found in "gambling with the established order".

Consciousness-building and self-reflexive approaches, as are formulated in many gender education articles, are directed at the existing gender order. They intend to critically reflect societal power structures, expectations of men and women, gender constructions and the standardization of ways of life, and thus to dynamically intervene in these. 'Spaces of uninterrupted learning' are also about discussing "how categories come into play, how the field of knowledge is ordered, and how the thing that categories suppress, reoccurs quasi as their own constitutive occlusion" (Butler 2001: 1). The deconstructive impetus expressed here transcends the questioning of existing mechanisms of order and the accompanying normative model around the reflection of the subjective relationships to the norms. For

> "the relationship is 'critical' in the sense that it follows no given category, but rather constitutes a questioning relationship to the field of categorization itself and thus refers at least implicitly to the border of the epistemological horizon, within which methods are formed" (Butler 2001: 5).

Here Butler follows Foucault's understanding of subjectification according to which the subjects create discourses and thus constitute themselves as concurrently subordinated and free – as subordinated because subjectification includes "that which ties the individual to himself and submits him to others in this way" (Foucault 1987: 247), and free because subjectification enables one to act formatively in the field of possible ways of existence and living. As subjectification creates identity, Foucault sees a central mechanism of modern power, whereby the effects of this subjectification often appear as nature, its constructive character remains hidden. Therefore, there is educational importance in the debate over the way in which subjects understand themselves in relation to age and gender. New, controversial knowledge about reflecting dominant and alternative category-related discourses, about becoming acquainted with a variety of gender and age-related self perceptions, about the distribution of related reflections may exist and the process of dynamization of generation and gender relations may thus be promoted from the sides of the subjective self-relations. If a learning challenge was located in leaving open one's understanding of femininity or masculinity, of youth or age, and in increasing one's understanding of life, then the aim of education from a deconstructive perception turns out to be thus less securing an identity, rather recurrently questioning it, and less in locating it and rather in forming and communicating it. Here criticism as a possibility of freedom turns to its own subjectivity and existence. It can develop into a behaviour in which "the criticism of who we are is also the historical analysis of the boundaries given to us and an experiment into the possibility of crossing them" (Foucault 1990: 53).[6]

It is thus a challenge for education and social work to work with the categories *and* to challenge them, to attach to them and to shift them. Generation/ age and gender are readable as two central categories of diversity-oriented articles in education and social work. Thus, approaches to Diversity Education, as they have been discussed for a long time in the USA and are also increasingly being taken up in the German-speaking world, distinguish themselves by working with reference to different categories of differentiation, relations of power and discrimination, assumptions of normality and methods of identity. Diversity-oriented essays, which follow such qualities, aim on sensitizing and reflecting the construction and effect of social differentiations, and through the corresponding enabling of an appropriate diversity competency by dynamizing the categories of differentiation, the dismantling of discrimination and social inequality as well as the easing of the accompanying harm (cf. e.g. Fuchs 2007; Maurer 2008).

Aside from the experience of the increasing being dependent on oneself, the norms, hierarchizations and discriminations associated with ways of life are generally accompanied by uncertainties and excessive demands. Learning processes which serve the coping with life decisions and crises, are becoming of central importance in current society. In relation to the possibilities of shaping their lives, people need space to reflect and learn their whole life long. Changed generation and gender relations and the pluralization of ways of life point to the need for a knowledge of identity and orientation, which may take a lifetime to realize. Educationally viewed, lifelong learning represents a human and historical inevitability. Events and demands in life have always had

6 Whilst it is a definite duty of social work as a discipline and profession to interfere politically and demand structural changes, the educative changes initiated by and/ or accompanying it are always attached to the subject – in order to refer to society again. The argument here, principally focused on the education of the subjects, should not relieve society from its educative responsibility – on the contrary.

to be coped with, it has always been about "educational processes in an intangible life" (Reichenbach 2005: 7). Thus, educational processes do not also aim at aspects of hazard, failure and defeat in the context of social work as they increasingly occur, for example, in the case of the "strengthening of the obsolescence process of the once skilled person" and may lead to a feeling of incompleteness and an interrelated "chronic threat to self-esteem and personal safety" (Baltes 2001: 28 et seq.).

Through increasing challenge management of a life that is becoming more complex increasingly diverse educational opportunities are required for the adult generation. Learning throughout one's life, which has become necessary in a new form, and with the changes accompanying the changing age structure and explosion of knowledge on the employment market challenge not only the individual subjects. The recommendations of the Further Education Innovation Group focus explicitly on the state, which is to provide the appropriate framework, as well as "businesses, social partners, associations, educational institutions and public employers" (BMBF 2008b: 7). The developments challenge institutions of employment and education in particular to open up the possibilities of older employees being able to keep up professionally with modern developments through further education provision, and to generally direct personal development "towards needs-orientated, continued building of skills across the whole working life" (BMBF 2008b: 9). At the same time institutions of employment are also required to broaden their knowledge as they carry out active equality policies in recruitment and promotions and open up possibilities of compatibility for women and men. Furthermore, institutions of employment are challenged to learn to value more strongly and use the established ability, competencies and experience gained through the years of their older employees – for example, by establishing mixed ages working teams.

Thus demographic change does not only have repercussions on the numerical proportion, but also on the immediate relations within and between the generations. These are characterized by a considerably longer shared lifespan and thus greater potential for egalitarian mutual learning, whereby advancements in knowledge, for example new media and technology displace the traditional concepts of ageing. Against this background intergenerational concepts of learning, which follow the vision of a common mutual learning practice and want to equip young and old people with new forms of cooperation, are finding new interest in shaping social changes together. Appropriate learning processes are, for example, being tried out in multigenerational households or family centres and in the future will be increasingly extended in the content of general concepts in education and social work (cf. e.g. Franz 2006; Meyer 2008; Steinhoff 2008).

Creating meaning and stability may find subjects in contacts and relationships, which are based on respect and appreciation, as well as, so far as possible, mutual give and take. A starting-point lies in the building and nurturing of networks and the examination of manifold ways of life. Thus to recognize dynamizations of the categories generation and gender implicates the challenge of learning to think of ways of life and also family in a way which reflects the constitutional character of previous perceptions, picks up transformations of social realities and follows an understanding of malleability, which decentralizes heterosexual binary gender order. Michi Knecht (2003: 54) suggests developing for this purpose a "modified matrix to generate subjectivities, relationships and togetherness". Instead of norms this places practices as notable moments of constitution at the centre, practices of care, of belonging and of "'temporality' – i.e. the facticity of long term reciprocal care and intimacy which is not self-evidently rooted in ‚naturalized differences'" (Knecht 2003: 62).

If social work aims at supporting people to realize their basic rights and to advocate social justice (Thiersch 1993; Thole 2002; Staub-Bernasconi 2007), then it is challenged to take on and further advance dynamizations of the categories gender and generation just as much as the need for lifelong learning in the sense of spaces of uninterrupted learning, as well as to empower and support people to reflect complex orders and relationships and if necessary to develop ways of resistance. This would aim to advocate alternative orders, which make a fulfilled life possible. This can clearly only successfully happen in the knowledge that one's own alternative suggestions always remain bound to those that they seek to escape and thus that there will be no going ‚beyond power'. Thus transformations will be strived for, which for all good intentions cannot be assured *a priori*, and in each case are to newly reflect their intended and unintended, functional and non-functional effects of power. If a mark of quality for diversity-oriented approaches lies in not solely postulating difference, but rather in raising these power relations which reproduce, hierarchize, constrain or hinder them, then it challenges education and social work to look critically at their own agencies of power and systematically expand educational spaces which support and enable a dynamic shaping of a variety of ways of living.

Bibliography

Adorno, Theodor W. (1989 [1971]): *Erziehung zur Mündigkeit.* Frankfurt/ M.: Suhrkamp

Arnold, Rolf (2003): "Berufspädagogik ist Erwachsenenpädagogik und umgekehrt." In: Arnold, Rolf (ed.): *Berufs- und Erwachsenenpädagogik.* Hohengehren: Schneider, 4-41

Baltes, Paul B. (2001): "Das Zeitalter des permanent unfertigen Menschen: Lebenslanges Lernen nonstop?" In: *Aus Politik und Zeitgeschehen* B 36, 24-32

Beck, Ulrich (1986): *Risikogesellschaft. Auf dem Weg in eine andere Moderne.* Frankfurt/ M.: Suhrkamp

Berger, Peter A./ Kahlert, Heike (2006): "Das 'Problem' des demographischen Wandels." In: Berger, Peter A./ Kahlert, Heike (eds.): *Der demographische Wandel. Chancen für die Neuordnung der Geschlechterverhältnisse.* Frankfurt/ M., New York: Campus, 9-24

BMBF (ed.) (2008a): *Aufstieg durch Bildung – Qualifizierungsinitiative der Bundesregierung.* Berlin: BMBF. www.bmbf.de/pub/qualifizierungsinitiative_breg.pdf (18/05/2009)

BMBF (ed.) (2008b): *Empfehlungen des Innovationskreises Weiterbildung für eine Strategie zur Gestaltung des Lernens im Lebenslauf.* Berlin: BMBF. www.bmbf.de/pub/empfehlungen_innovationskreis_weiterbildung.pdf (18/05/2009)

BMFSFJ (2005): 12. *Kinder- und Jugendbericht. Bericht über die Lebenssituation junger Menschen und die Leistungen der Kinder- und Jugend-hilfe in Deutschland.* Berlin: BMFSFJ. www.bmfsfj.de/RedaktionBMFSFJ/Abteilung5/Pdf-Anlagen/zwoelfter-kjb,property=pdf.pdf (18/05/2009)

Buchen, Sylvia (2008): "Bildung in der dritten Lebensphase zwischen 'lebenslangem Lernen' und lernen loszulassen." In: Buchen, Sylvia/ Maier, Maja S. (eds.): *Älterwerden neu denken. Interdisziplinäre Perspektiven auf den demografischen Wandel.* Wiesbaden: VS Verlag für Sozialwissenschaften, 95-112

Buchen Sylvia/ Maier, Maja S. (2008): "Älterwerden neu denken. Interdisziplinäre Perspektiven auf den demografischen Wandel. Eine Einleitung." In: Buchen, Sylvia/ Maier, Maja S. (eds.): *Älterwerden neu denken. Interdisziplinäre Perspektiven auf den demografischen Wandel.* Wiesbaden: VS Verlag für Sozialwissenschaften, 7-27

Butler, Judith (1991): *Das Unbehagen der Geschlechter.* Frankfurt/ M.: Suhrkamp

Butler, Judith (1995): *Körper von Gewicht. Die diskursiven Grenzen des Geschlechts.* Berlin: Berlin Verlag

Butler, Judith (2001): *Was ist Kritik? Ein Essay über Foucaults Tugend.* http://transform.eipcp.net/transversal/0806/butler/de (18/05/2009)

Butler, Judith (2004): *Undoing Gender.* New York, London: Routledge

Faulstich, Peter/ Zeuner, Christine (2006): *Erwachsenenbildung. Eine handlungsorientierte Einführung in Theorie, Didaktik und Adressaten.* 2., aktualisierte Auflage. Weinheim, München: Juventa

Foucault, Michel (1987): "Genealogie der Ethik: Ein Überblick über laufende Arbeiten. Ein Interview mit Michel Foucault." In: Dreyfus, Hubert, L./ Rabinow, Paul: *Michel Foucault: Jenseits von Strukturalismus und Hermeneutik.* Mit einem Nachwort von und einem Interview mit Michel Foucault. Weinheim: Beltz, 265-292

Foucault, Michel (1990): "Was ist Aufklärung?" In: Erdmann, Eva/ Forst, Rainer/ Honneth, Axel (eds.): *Ethos der Moderne. Foucaults Kritik der Aufklärung.* Frankfurt/ M., New York: Campus, 35-54

Foucault, Michel (1992): *Was ist Kritik?* Berlin: Merve

Foucault, Michel (2000): "Die Gouvernementalität. Vorlesung am Collége de France vom 1. Februar 1978." In: Bröckling, Ulrich/ Krasmann, Susanne/ Lemke, Thomas (eds.): *Gouvernementalität der Gegenwart. Studien zur Ökonomisierung des Sozialen.* Frankfurt/ M.: Suhrkamp, 41-67

Franz, Julia (2006): "Die ältere Generation als Mentorengeneration – Intergenerationelles Lernen und intergenerationelles Engagement." In: *Bildungsforschung* 3 (2), www.bildungsforschung.org/Archiv/2006-02/intergenerationelles/ (18/05/2009)

Fuchs, Martin (2007): "Diversity und Differenz – Konzeptionelle Überlegungen." In: Krell, Gertraude/ Riedmüller, Barbara/ Sieben, Barbara/ Vinz, Dagmar (eds.): *Diversity Studies. Grundlagen und disziplinäre Ansätze.* Frankfurt/ M., New York: Campus, 18-34

Galuske, Michael (2008): "Fürsorgliche Aktivierung – Anmerkungen zu Gegenwart und Zukunft Sozialer Arbeit im aktivierenden Staat." In: Bütow, Birgit/ Chassé, Karl August/ Hirt, Rainer (eds.): *Soziale Arbeit nach dem Sozialpädagogischen Jahrhundert. Positionsbestimmungen Sozialer Arbeit im Post-Wohlfahrtsstaat.* Opladen, Farmington Hills: Barbara Budrich, 9-28

Gatzke, Nicolas (2007): *Lebenslanges Lernen in einer alternden Gesellschaft.* Berlin: Friedrich-Ebert-Stiftung

Hartmann, Jutta (2002): *Vielfältige Lebensweisen. Dynamisierungen in der Triade Geschlecht – Sexualität – Lebensform. Kritisch-dekonstruktive Perspektiven für die Pädagogik.* Opladen: Leske + Budrich

Hartmann, Jutta (2009): „Familie weiter denken – Perspektiven vielfältiger Lebensweisen für eine diversity-orientierte Theorie und Praxis Sozialer Arbeit." In: *neue praxis. Zeitschrift für Sozialarbeit, Sozialpädagogik und Sozialpolitik Sonderheft* (9), 65-75

Hartmann, Jutta/ Klesse, Christian/ Wagenknecht, Peter/ Fritzsche, Bettina/ Hackmann, Kristina (eds.) (2007): *Heteronormativität. Empirische Studien zu Geschlecht, Sexualität und Macht.* Wiesbaden: VS Verlag für Sozialwissenschaften

Helfferich, Cornelia (2008): "Alles beim Alten? Wie der demografische Wandel Lebenslaufmuster von Frauen und Männern morgen und das Alter übermorgen beeinflusst." In: Buchen, Sylvia/ Maier, Maja S. (eds.): *Älterwerden neu denken. Interdisziplinäre Perspektiven auf den demografischen Wandel.* Wiesbaden: VS Verlag für Sozialwissenschaften, 31-45

Kessl, Fabian/ Richter, Martina (2006): "Lebenslanges Lernen oder ununterbrochene Bildung? Eine symptomale Lektüre aktueller Bildungsprogrammatiken." In: *neue praxis. Zeitschrift für Sozialarbeit, Sozialpädagogik und Sozialpolitik* 36 (3), 308-323

Knecht, Michi (2003): "Die Politik der Verwandtschaft neu denken. Perspektiven der Kultur- und Sozialanthropologie." In: Zentrum für transdisziplinäre Geschlechterstudien (ed.): *Bulletin Texte Nr. 26*, 52-70

Kolland, Franz (2008): "Lebenslanges Lernen und soziale Ausgrenzung. Bildungsarmut im Alter." In: *Sozial Extra. Zeitschrift für Soziale Arbeit* 32 (5/6), 15-17

Kommission der Europäischen Gemeinschaften (2005): *Grünbuch: Angesichts des demografischen Wandels – eine neue Solidarität zwischen den Generationen.* Brüssel: Kommission der Europäischen Gemeinschaften, http://ec.europa.eu/employment_social/news/2005/mar/comm2005-94_de.pdf (18/05/2009)

Krüger, Helga/ Born, Claudia (2000): "Vom patriarchalen Diktat zur Aushandlung – Facetten des Wandels der Geschlechterrollen im familialen Generationenverbund." In: Kohli, Martin/ Szydlik, Marc (eds.): *Generationen in Familie und Gesellschaft.* Opladen: Leske + Budrich, 203-221

Lange, Andreas/ Lettke, Frank (2007): "Schrumpfung, Erweiterung, Diversität. Konzepte zur Analyse von Familie und Generationen." In: Lettke, Frank/ Lange, Andreas (eds.): *Generationen und Familien*. Frankfurt/ M.: Suhrkamp, 14-43

Maurer, Susanne (2008): "Sich verlieren im unendlich Verschiedenen? Ungleichheit – Differenz – Diversity." In: *Sozial Extra. Zeitschrift für Soziale Arbeit* 33 (11/12), 13-14

Merten, Roland (2002): "Über Möglichkeiten und Grenzen des Generationenbegriffs für die (sozial-)pädagogische Theoriebildung." In: Schweppe, Cornelia (eds.): *Generation und Sozialpädagogik. Theoriebildung, öffentliche und familiale Generationenverhältnisse, Arbeitsfelder*. Weinheim, München: Juventa, 21-39

Meyer, Christine (2008): "Mit der Zeit kommt das Alter(n) in die Soziale Arbeit. Demografischer Wandel und die Auswirkungen auf Soziale Arbeit." In: *neue praxis. Zeitschrift für Sozialarbeit, Sozialpädagogik und Sozialpolitik* 38 (3), 268-286

Peukert, Rüdiger (2007): "Zur aktuellen Lage der Familie." In: Ecarius, Jutta (ed.): *Handbuch Familie*. Wiesbaden: VS Verlag für Sozialwissenschaften, 36-56

Reichenbach, Roland (2005): "Triple L: Zur Dramaturgie ‚Lebenslangen Lernens'." In: *TOOLS*. Österreichische Fachzeitschrift für Erwachsenenbildung 1 (2), 7-10

Schiersmann, Christiane (2007): *Berufliche Weiterbildung*. Wiesbaden: VS Verlag für Sozialwissenschaften

Schmauch, Ulrike (2008): "Lesbische Familien." In: *Familiendynamik* 33 (3), 289-307

Siebert, Horst (2005): "Nachgefragt: Die Konstruktion lebenslangen Lernens." In: Voß, Reinhard (ed.): *LernLust und EigenSinn. Systemisch-konstruktivistische Lernwelten*. Heidelberg: Auer, 54-64

Staub-Bernasconi, Silvia (2007): *Soziale Arbeit als Handlungswissenschaft. Ein Lehrbuch*. Bern, Stuttgart, Wien: UTB/ Haupt

Steinhoff, Bernd (2008): "Intergenerationelles Lernen. Zur Entwicklung einer altersintegrativen Lernkultur." In: Buchen, Sylvia/ Maier, Maja S. (eds.): *Älterwerden neu denken. Interdisziplinäre Perspektiven auf den demografischen Wandel*. Wiesbaden: VS Verlag für Sozialwissenschaften, 131-144

Thiersch, Hans (1993) *Lebensweltorientierte Soziale Arbeit. Aufgaben der Praxis im sozialen Wandel.* Weinheim, München: Juventa

Thole, Werner (ed.) (2002): *Grundriss Soziale Arbeit. Ein einführendes Handbuch.* Opladen: Leske + Budrich

van den Berg, Karen (2007): "Semantiken des Alters. Diskursinterventionen und Bildlektüren von Giorgione, Auguts Sander und On Kawara." In: Pasero, Ursula/ Backes, Gertrud M./ Schroeter, Klaus R. (eds.): *Altern in Gesellschaft. Ageing – Diversity – Inclusion.* Wiesbaden: VS Verlag für Sozialwissenschaften, 43-76

Warner, Michael (1991): "Introduction." In: *Fear of a Queer Planet. Social Text* 9 (4), 3-17

Wieners, Tanja (2005): *Miteinander von Kindern und alten Menschen. Perspektiven für Familien und öffentliche Einrichtungen.* Wiesbaden: VS Verlag für Sozialwissenschaften

Wimmer, Michael (1998): "Fremdheit zwischen den Generationen. Generative Differenz, Generationsdifferenz, Kulturdifferenz." In: Ecarius, Jutta (ed.): *Was will die jüngere mit der älteren Generation? Generationsbeziehungen und Generationenverhältnisse in der Erziehungswissenschaft.* Opladen: Leske + Budrich, 81-113

Winker, Gabriele (2008): "Neoliberale Regulierung von Care Work und deren demografische Mystifikationen." In: Buchen, Sylvia/ Maier, Maja S. (eds.): *Älterwerden neu denken. Interdisziplinäre Perspektiven auf den demografischen Wandel.* Wiesbaden: VS Verlag für Sozialwissenschaften, 47-62

Winkler, Michael/ Zander, Margherita (2007 [2003]): "Demographischer Wandel – das verdrängte Problem." In: Hering, Sabine (ed.): *Bürgerschaftlichkeit und Professionalität. Wirklichkeit und Zukunftsperspektiven Sozialer Arbeit. Sozial Extra. Sonderheft* (1), 135-143

Wohlrab-Sahr, Monika (1997): "Individualisierung: Differenzierungsprozess und Zurechnungsmodus." In: Beck, Ulrich/ Sopp, Peter (eds.): *Individualisierung und Integration. Neue Konfliktlinien und neuer Integrationsmodus?* Opladen: Leske + Budrich, 23-36

Zeuner, Christine (2006): "Erwachsenenbildung zwischen Inklusion und Exklusion." In: Fatke, Reinhard/ Merkens, Hans (eds.): *Bildung über die Lebenszeit.* Wiesbaden: VS Verlag für Sozialwissenschaften, 303-314

Ziegler, Holger (2008): "Sozialpädagogik nach dem Neo-Liberalismus: Skizzen einer post-sozialstaatlichen Formierung Sozialer Arbeit." In: Bütow, Birgit/ Chassé, Karl August/ Hirt, Rainer (eds.): *Soziale Arbeit nach dem Sozialpädagogischen Jahrhundert. Positionsbestimmungen Sozialer Arbeit im Post-Wohlfahrtsstaat.* Opladen, Farmington Hills: Barbara Budrich, 159-176

Ute Karl

People of Age in the Volunteer Sector and Demographic Change[1]

In 2005, almost 25 percent of Germany's population are older than 60 years. The 11th coordinated population projection assumes that this rate will rise to 31 percent in 2020 and to 39 percent in 2040 (cf. Engels 2008; Statistisches Bundesamt 2006). Beside all incentive programmes to raise birth rates and thus influence demographic change, one big question for all governments in Western societies is: how can demographic change be actively and vitally shaped to bring generations together? One strategy is to show that older generations do contribute to society. Another is to stress the potentials they have and to support the use of these potentials for society. These potentials could consist of supporting intergenerational exchange and justice. For this reason, the *5th Report on Old Age by the Federal Government of Germany* (BMFSFJ 2005) focuses on the potentials of the elderly in economy and society and the contribution of people of age to the relationship between solidarity among different generations. One aim of this report is to find answers to the following questions: What are the genuine capacities of people of age and how can these capacities be made useful for new social roles in a changing society? What are the necessary societal prerequisites for an increased readiness to nurture and to realize the potentials of the elderly?[2] What educational programmes should be offered? One should recognize, however, that the expert commission's report explicitly mentions the danger a biased, purpose-related, one-dimensional misuse of the debate would present for a reconstruction of the social state and fairness among generations:

> "The language reveals socio-economic, utilitarian positions – e.g. to perceive people of age as 'human resources', whose potentials must be used by society, thus neglecting their self-will and self-determination" (BMFSFJ 2005: 373).

Thus, over recent years, on the one hand the federal government of Germany

1 Some of the following research results are also published in: Karl (2006, 2009).

2 Cf. also: Newsletter Potenziale des Alters (www.bmfsfj.de/Politikbereiche/aeltere-menschen,did=65316.html [28/11/2008]).

has supported pilot projects and initiatives to strengthen the realization of these potentials in the volunteer sector, and most of the recent educational programmes for people of age focus on their potential to contribute to society. On the other hand, these programmes emphasize the self-will and self-directedness of the elderly. So the question is how do they work without coercion or general laws?

A perspective derived from the theory of governmentality brings into focus the specific measures of leading and steering these parts of the population (cf. Foucault 1991: 102). The measures are directed at the subjectivity of individuals and influence the technologies of self-regulation, of self-government, and of the conduct of life.

> "The term governmentality sought to draw attention to a certain way of thinking and acting embodied in all those attempts to know and govern the wealth, health and happiness of populations" (Miller/Rose 1992: 174).

The general meaning of 'governing' according to Foucault is "to structure the possible field of action of others" (Foucault 1982: 221). 'Governmentality' is closely related with the concept of power as developed by Foucault in his later years. According to Foucault, power is exerted by influencing the conduct of subjects. But "[p]ower is exercised only over free subjects, and only insofar as they are free" (Foucault 1982: 221). In a relationship of constraint, where the manifold ways of behaving and (re-)acting are extremely reduced, there is no relationship of power. Thus, the analysis of power relations has to focus the complicated interplay of freedom and actions upon actions of individual or collective subjects.

Looking at the volunteer sector in general, it is obvious that not only the engagement rates between women and men over the entire lifespan differ, but also the occupations pursued are gender biased. These inequalities have to be observed in the interrelations of the distribution of all kinds of work, paid and unpaid (volunteer work, housework, care work). Although the post-professional part of life offers more opportunities for a redistribution of all kinds of work, the gender inequalities in the volunteer sector continuously exist in older generations. Based on a definition of power "as a mode of action upon the actions of others" (Foucault 1982: 221) the further question is whether such seemingly gender neutral, enabling programmes do contribute to more egalitarian gender relations in the volunteer sector of the target group, at least in part.

My considerations are mainly concentrated on discussions and programmes relevant within Germany. It is apparent, however, that these have to be reflected on in the context of international and in particular of Anglo-American debates.[3]

I will start with a short analysis of the gerontological models of an 'active' and 'productive age/ageing' which have great influence on practical programmes and which can be seen as the theoretical basics of activating and enabling strategies in the volunteer sector. To specify these strategies, I will analyze the rationale of a recently finished practice-related project. It is an interface project related to two discourses: the discourse on age/ageing and the discourse on civic engagement and voluntary work.[4] What I would like to show by this example is that the neo-liberal rationale can be found increasingly in the concepts of age and ageing. The individual is made responsible for the well-being, caretaking is a matter of private responsibility, and self-concept and self-management are prominent issues in the educational work with the elderly. At the same time it is intended to encourage people in community building and to lead the individual, without coercion, to a socially useful behaviour. Departing from the perspective on the rationality of the programme inspired by Foucault's term of governmentality, I will further ask if such programmes may contribute to a change of gender relations in a part of the volunteer sector and to a redistribution of voluntary work among the older volunteers.

3 Cf. for a Foucauldian perspective on gerontology and volunteering: Powell/Edwards (2002), Powell/Biggs (2003); cf. for governmentality and social policy on ageing: Katz/Green (2002), Powell (2006: 105 et seq.); cf. Foucault and ageing from different perspectives: Powell/Wahidin (2006).

4 In the German discussion, very often the terms 'bürgerschaftliches Engagement' and 'zivilgesellschaftliches Engagement' (civic engagement), 'neues Ehrenamt' (new honorary engagement), 'freiwilliges Engagement' (voluntary engagement), and 'Freiwilligenarbeit' (voluntary work) are used as equivalents, although these terms have different traditions. I will use the term 'voluntary work' in the sense that people work voluntarily, orientated to the public welfare, for themselves and others and without pay. Voluntary work is part of civic engagement. The rationale of voluntary work is different from that of paid and subsistence guaranteeing work, although the examples will show that political practices at the intersection of the notions of 'volunteering', 'citizenship', 'learning', and 'ageing' could lead to a reduction of civic engagement and of voluntary work to unpaid work.

1 The realization of the potentials of the elderly as an aim of an enabling and activating state

Despite similarities in the rhetorical expressions between assisting volunteers and the assist-and-demand-structure in labour market and unemployment policies, the elementary difference lies in the fact that volunteers are not subject to legal regulation of their basic social care. So what is the rationality of these programmes and how do they impact people's range of possible actions?

Firstly, these programmes are loosely connected with the gerontological theories of 'active'' and 'productive' age(ing). Both can be seen as central frames in discussions about the potentials of old age. Secondly, what both theories have in common is their reference to a 'close to healthy age(ing)' and their interest in varying strategies to maintain or to extend this situation. But it should be noted that in today's discourses the question of an individual well-being is more and more accompanied by the question of what is societally desirable or useful.

The social-gerontological *theory of activity* originated from empirical studies conducted in the USA and published in the 1950s (cf. Kolland 1996: 20).[5] But it was not until the 1970s and early 1980s that this theory was developed and implemented in professional practice concepts. A retreat from social relations and the loss of competencies is seen as a result of a loss of roles and functions in old age. The central assumption of the activity theory is that in old age achievement capacities can be preserved or even extended in some areas by continuous demands and challenges and by a new construction of the meaning of life – up to the point where the limits are defined by factual physical developments (cf. Lenz et al. 1999: 40).

In social work with older people the concept of an 'active age' is instrumental for the promotion of participation in the societal life by activation and for the realization of a positive image of old age (cf. Zeman/Schmidt 2001: 240). Educational activities regarding the individual are conceived as a value on their own. They are also perceived as necessary for the development of activities desirable for society. But it is not central that these activities are useful for others.

Meanwhile, new pilot projects of the federal government such as the re-

5 Franz Kolland (1996: 21) observes a relation between 'activism' as a cultural value in the US-American society and the development of this concept.

cent programmes *Age Creates Innovation – the Active in Old Age Programme* (2008/2009)[6] or *To Shape Demographic Change in Municipalities – Use the Expertise and Experience of Older People* (2007-2009)[7] combine the aspect of active ageing and productivity for society.

The 'active ageing' policy of the World Health Organisation (WHO) comprises more than "the ability to be physically active or to participate in the labour force". It explicitly includes those "who are frail, disabled and in need of care" (WHO 2002: 12). Nevertheless, there are programmes in which the concept of 'active age(ing)' serves to neglect the reality of life situations and of biographies and careers, e.g. under the aspects of 'gender' and 'class'. Indirectly the individuals are made responsible for success or failure in old age (cf. for a critical assessment Lenz et al. 1999: 41; Backes/Clemens 1998: 118).[8] According to Gertrud Backes and Wolfgang Clemens (1998: 117), the end of the professional situation is perceived as *the* central event, whereas the middle part of life as point of reference is seen too positively.[9] It is obvious that family and care work, which is still mostly women's work even more in older generations is not taken into consideration. This sort of work (and therefore activity) continues in old age.

Despite numerous criticisms regarding the 'active age(ing)' concept and the social-gerontological theory of activity, almost all assistance programmes for older people in the volunteer sector rely on this concept. The 'active senior' appears to be an unquestioned natural figure, *the illusio* (Bourdieu) in the field of social and educational work with older people (cf. also: Schroeter

6 The German title is: *Alter schafft Neues – Das Programm Aktiv im Alter*; cf.: www.alter-schafft-neues.de/coremedia/generator/asn/de/07__Downloads/Programminformationen.pdf (28/11/2008).

7 The German title is: *Den demographischen Wandel in Kommunen mitgestalten – Erfahrungswissen der Älteren nutzen*, cf.: www.isab-institut.de/front_content.php?idart=296 (28/11/2008).

8 In the controversial debate on the concept of 'active age' in the 1st Interim Report of the Enquête Commission on Demographic Change – challenges of our ageing society for the individual and for politics (1994) this problem and the necessity become evident, that in the context of social policy 'activity' must be related to the life situations of old age (cf. for a summary Aner 2005: 42-46).

9 The biographical interviews with female players in theatre groups of aged people reveal that some of these are glad to have overcome the high vocational and family demands and challenges especially in the phase of adult age (cf. for my interviews Karl 2005).

2002).[10] At least two reasons may be imminent for this situation: this image of older age accounts for new practice perspectives and is opposed to negative stereotypes. So it is very attractive for older people and conform to their self-perception, despite the fact that it has normative implications of a new dimension (cf. Göckenjan 2000: 25, 247).

And above that, this concept is integral to the logic and rhetoric of an 'activating state'. So the individual search for possibilities to shape one's life and those practices of government that intend to activate individuals and at the same time decompose the social state are apparently harmonized and appropriate.

'Productive age(ing)' is a theoretical framework of the late 1980s and the 1990s, although neither clearly separated from the 'active age(ing)' concept nor strictly consecutive. And it is still common, particularly in combination with active ageing and productivity for society or community productivity as shown below. The documentation of the conference *Old Age and Productive Living*, which was held at Hamburg in 1994 (Baltes/Montada 1996), presents a great variety of definitions. Hans Peter Tews, who is often cited in discussions about voluntary work, presents a sociological concept of "productivity in old age", and of social usefulness. This concept bridges the gap between the discourses on old age and on civic engagement, and it confronts the problem of "the burden the aged represent for society" with the question of a reduction of this burden by "an independent lifestyle", by "individual productivity" in old age (Tews 2000: 74). Regarding the "structural change in old age"[11] Tews asks for an understanding of "productivity in old age" which goes beyond the field of vocational and semi-vocational productivity and which should not include all fields of post- or extra-vocational activities:

> "We should define 'productive' as behaviour which creates 'value' and is socially useful. Values are dependent on exchange conditions. They can be expressed in money or [...] by payment in kind. 'Time' is a service that can also be exchanged

10 The World Health Organization has adopted the term 'Active Ageing' as "Policy Framework". In this context 'active ageing' is understood in a very broad sense: "Active ageing is the process of optimizing opportunities of health, participation and security in order to enhance quality of life as people age." (WHO 2002: 12).

11 Five aspects of the structural change in old age are mentioned: 1. The old are getting younger; 2. Lack of employment; 3. Feminization in old age; 4. Singularization; 5. Very old age is increasing (cf. Tews 2000: 81-82; cf. also Tews 1993).

> and something which the aged normally have a lot of. In principle they are marketable services which could or would have to be paid for were they not provided free of charge" (Tews 2000: 74; cf. also Tews 1996: 189).

Tews discerns "five forms of productivity in old age":

1. "retention of an independent lifestyle" in old age, which aims at individual independence and is therefore supposed to "reduce the burden the aged represent for society";
2. "inter-generational productivity";
3. "intra-generational productivity";
4. "community productivity", referring to social voluntary work, which should be retained;
5. "a further form of social productivity", which primarily relates to "self-organization in old-age and political influence" (Tews 2000: 74-76, Tews 1996: 188 et seq.).

Looking at the debates in the USA, Tews notices that the problem of usefulness and productivity is obviously accepted there in a way that it is much easier "to integrate older people in productivity-oriented programmes and initiatives", including the integration of older people as "productive elements", as "'underused active elderly'", and as societal resource into educational programmes for seniors (Tews 1996: 198)[12]. Thus the discourse on old age becomes more and more a discourse on voluntary service and civic engagement.

Tews asserts that education and educational activities are important for the development of old age and especially for the development of society and of a redefinition of "productivity in old age" (Tews 1996: 194). Education is seen as a prerequisite for productivity, useful for society.

For Tews, the concept of a "productive old age" is helpful for a renewed sociological debate on the potentials of old age (cf. Tews 1996: 208 et seq.). In this debate the question of potentials can be closely connected with the debate on the usefulness of productivity. This concept, however, is in danger of polarization. The growth of burdens and the reduction of burdens in old age are balanced (cf. for a critical position Backes 1998: 34 et seq.) and, under economic perspectives, human beings are perceived as cost-returns factors.

12 "'Underused active elderly'": Original quote from Tews (1996: 198).

And here the question arises about the negative dimension of the connection of usefulness and productivity, as the ethical problems inherent to this dichotomy are evident.

Although the final report of the Enquête-Commission *Demographic Change* (Deutscher Bundestag 2002a: 48 et seq.) strongly argues against a "re-engagement of old age" and a "social work period for elderly people", "productivity in old-age" or "of old age" (synonymous usage) is the central theme linking productivity to resources and competencies, which should be used more effectively (cf. Deutscher Bundestag 2002a: 49). So the question is which strategies are supposed to lead effectively to the designated goal: using the resources and competencies for an enhanced civic engagement? In addition to disseminating the attractive concept of active and productive ageing, there are more direct strategies to influence people's actions by educational training courses. One example of such a strategy is the model project *Experience for Initiatives (EFI)* of the German Federal Ministry for Family Affairs, Senior Citizens, Women, and Youth. The project relies on learning processes to initiate a socially useful, civic engagement. Since the project's completion in 2006, it has served as orientation for further projects.

2 "Role making" and "self-organization" of people of age as educational goals: The example of "seniorTrainers" as part of the project *Experience for Initiatives (EFI)*

Programmes of activating older people for voluntary work have to be seen not only in the context of demographic change, but also in the context of the withdrawal of the welfare state from social and educational tasks and its change to an enabling state. Although (ideational) encouragement and assisting structures are mostly based on the conviction that voluntary work does not replace paid work or reduce employment possibilities, this must be doubted especially for the social and educational sector. Opening hours of libraries, homework mentoring or additional leisure time activities at school, art projects in youth work or leisure activities with older people (in senior meeting places) are at the same time paid jobs and volunteers' activities. Looking at concrete examples, one can see that a reduction of welfare state activities is often a first, economically justified step. Later, volunteers bridge the gap to further provide the services. From a gender perspective, this situation becomes even more problematic since more women than men are employed in the social sector (between 70 percent and 80 percent are women[13]), sometimes already under precarious conditions and underpaid. So in this sector especially women's jobs are cut, and thus, women's work is again depreciated by the lack of an adequate payment, a development that might lead to a de professionalization of social work in several fields (e.g. social work with older people). Studies show that female social workers often work voluntarily in their professional field during unemployment periods to stay in the field or to engage in fund-raising for their next job (cf. Wessels 1994).

The model programme *Experience for Initiatives*, which I will analyze, was scheduled for a five year period (2002-2006).[14] The main project participants were volunteer agencies in 35 municipalities, local 'Senior citizen's offices', self-help contact points, agencies for civil involvement, and 12 educational institutions on a national scale. The 12 educational institutions were responsible for the realization of the training programmes in accord with the core curriculum. By the end of 2006, 942 persons were qualified as "senior-Trainers" and more than 3,000 projects were initiated by this group (cf. Engels et al. 2007: 53). As the model programme continues, additional seniorTrainers are being qualified in regional or communal programmes. Meanwhile some seniorTrainer or senior expertise teams are part of the nationwide model programme *Crossgenerational Voluntary Services* (2005-2008)[15], a programme that is followed by a new one called *Volunteer Services of All Generations* (2009-2011)[16]. In the project *To Shape Demographic Change in Municipalities – To Use Expertise and Experience of Older People*[17] (2007-2009), real-

13 Cf.: IAB online: www.pallas.iab.de/bisds/alphabet.asp?alpha=S (29/12/2008). Especially vocation 861, 862, and the aggregated figures under the key word "Sozialberufe" (jobs in the social sector).

14 This project is realized in 10 federal states in Germany. The Institute for Sociological Analysis and Consultancy (ISAB), Cologne, is responsible for coordination, consulting, and supervising, the University of Applied Sciences Neubrandenburg for the curriculum development, and the Institute for Social Research (ISG), Cologne, for the evaluation. There is also an advisory board.

15 The German title is: *Generationsübergreifende Freiwilligendienste.*

16 The German title is: *Freiwilligendienste aller Generationen*, cf.: www.alter-schafft-neues.de/coremedia/generator/asn/de/04__Freiweillige_20Dienste_20der_20Generationen/Ausschreibung_20Ideenwettbewerb.html (01/12/2008).

17 The German Title is: *Den demographischen Wandel in Kommunen mitgestalten – Erfahrungswissen der Älteren nutzen.*

ized at eastern German locations, the Robert-Bosch-Foundation is sponsoring the qualification of an additional 300 seniorTrainers (cf. Engels et al. 2007: 22 et seq., 187). The EFI-Project is a member of the European co-operative project *Lifelong Learning and Active Citizenship in Europe's Ageing Society* (LACE, 2005-2007).[18] The development of similar projects in other European countries is encouraged by the experiences accumulated in this project.[19] The programmatic origins of this project have to be seen in the increasing international discussions "about the part volunteering can play in the transition from paid work to retirement" (Smith/Gay 2005: 1).

The basic point of reference for the concept of the *Experience for initiative* project is demographic change with its challenges for the social, health care, and educational systems. The ability to cope with future-oriented tasks may to a great extent depend "on the active integration and participation of the citizens and in particular of the people of age to make good use of their potentials for the public good" (Braun et al. 2004: 15). So one central goal of the programme was to "assure people of age of the value of their expertise and experience and to better use this knowledge for society" (Braun et al. 2004: 15).[20] The invention and the development of the role of the seniorTrainer serves the "re-discovery of the social position of people of age and the public acceptance of their contribution to society" (Braun et al. 2004: 15).[21]

"Expertise and Experience" in the model programme is perceived as "personal resource" and as "social capital"[22]. In a process of self-reflection, it is shaped by the role of the seniorTrainer. The public promotion of this role

18 Cf.: www.lace-project.net (01/12/2008), www.efi-programm.de/dokumente/Pr%E4sentation_ISAB_23.11.05.pdf (01/12/2008), www.isab-institut.de/upload/Aktuelles/PDF/Praesentation_Zwart_Brauers.pdf (01/12/2008). Cf. for recent projects: www.isab-institut.de/front_content.php?idcat=65 (01/12/2008). Cf. for European perspectives on voluntary engagement by and for very old persons: Internationaler Rat für soziale Wohlfahrt et al. (2000).

19 For international contacts of the project cf.: Institut für sozialwissenschaftliche Analysen und Beratung (2006).

20 In a way, the well-known topic of the "wisdom of old age" (Göckenjan 2000: 413) is resumed and upgraded.

21 The working areas of the 'seniorTrainers' are quite different from those of traditional trainers, e.g. in further education.

22 For a detailed debate on "social capital" (Robert Putnam) in the context of social work cf. Kessl/Otto (2004); for the interplay of social capital, humane capital and entrepreneurial assets cf. Deutscher Bundestag (2002b); for the strategies of the World Bank: www1.worldbank.org/prem/poverty/scapital/home.htm (22/10/2006).

will help to perceive the resources and potentials of old age in society in an appropriate way, and one expects that the EFI-project will oppose the "exclusion of people of age" (Braun et al. 2004: 17). The role of the seniorTrainer is defined within the spectrum of civic engagement, which needs to be stabilized by a sustainable development, enhanced by the EFI-project.

The EFI training programme is characterized by a "three-pillar-approach". In 3x3 days, including practical and learning periods, volunteers qualify as seniorTrainers. It is important to adapt to the role of seniorTrainer and to acquire role-related competencies.

What is the essence of this new role and what is the training concept? The EFI-programme intended to win people of age for the role of seniorTrainers and to assist them in their role-finding process (cf. Braun et al. 2004: 31 et seq.). The special notion of responsibility inherent to this role concerns the engagement potentials of the elderly and the fact that these all too often have a 'roleless role' (similar to one of the assumptions of the activity theory). The concept and the core curriculum emphasize the necessity to individually develop the dimension of responsibility in the process of *role making*. But the training process also includes elements of *role taking*, as it is not intended to qualify for the vast field of civic engagement without an elaborated self-concept of one's own expertise and experience. Beyond that, the learning results should not deviate from the dimension of responsibility as the key element of the seniorTrainer role:

> "The 'seniorTrainer' role implies the emphasis on responsibility, essential for multiplying and initiating activities concerning the enhancement of civic engagement and for the transfer of experience and expertise into initiatives, societies, or organizations" (Braun et al. 2004: 32).

In the final core curriculum four different role profiles[23] are suggested, combined with a catalogue of the key competencies to be acquired in units two and three.[24] The guidelines defined for the development of an individual role

23 At the end of the project the following role profiles were suggested: 1. supporters and councellors of existing initiatives, NPOs; 2. initiators of new projects; 3. networkers in the voluntary sector; 4. coordinators and facilitators of senior expertise teams.

24 1. Communications; role of consultant, consultancy models; conflict management; group models, group dynamics. 2. initiating projects and activities. 3. rhetoric and

profile and for the educational concept may well lack the openness needed for adult learning.

In addition, the first unit of the 2004 curriculum suggests to perceive civic engagement and age(ing) "in a greater context" and to understand the "exemplary quality of the senior voluntary engagement" (Burmeister 2004: 26):

> "Whatever the practical activities of seniorTrainers are, they should do it with a professional 'civic perspective' and look beyond their own interests and expectations, taking into account the public good by stimulating others" (Burmeister et al. 2004: 16).

The training also intends to promote the capacities for the self-organization of the participants and to qualify them for "self-organized individual or collective learning processes, including local senior expertise teams and experiments with future forms of engagement, organisation, and the reflection of perspectives" (Braun et al. 2004: 162). Though the important programmatic and evaluative role of the voluntary agencies and their reduced resources are outlined, self-organization appears as an instrument to master the challenges of seniorTrainers, even with reduced personal and economic resources. In particular, self-organization is to be promoted by local "senior expertise teams" (Braun et al. 2004: 162). It is expected that these teams share the responsibility with the agencies for civil involvement in monitoring the work of the seniorTrainers (cf. Engels et al. 2007: 84).

It is clear that the EFI-project is characterized by an 'assist and demand' structure. The nurturing of participants' potentials, their assistance, is connected with the expectation to volunteer and to render useful services for the community as seniorTrainers.[25] Under conditions of reduced economic support, moral self-commitment is vital for the functioning of this interplay between 'assist and demand'.

The major difference between those who are engaged in the volunteer sector and those who are qualified for the seniorTrainer role is not so much that they are no longer working or that they are on their way from paid work

presentation; 4. networking in the volunteer sector. 5. organizational learning; public relations work in the context of local seniorTrainer teams; self-commitment and self-related communication.

25 For voluntary engagement and the activating state cf. Bußmann/Stöbe-Blossey (2003).

to retirement[26] (cf. Burmeister et al. 2004: 134), but it is the idea that those who volunteer without payment are acting self-organized, initiating, and supportive on the *basis of a role profile*, which incorporates their expertise and experience, offered to an existing or still to be created market.

The idea of *role making* is the key idea in the adult learning concept of this model programme and it represents a qualitative leap in the understanding of educating people of age: for the actively engaged seniors the aspects of self-management, self-organization, and self-formation are essential for the products they offer to potential markets and for the activation of others. The structure of honorary, volunteering, and self-help activities changes. The focus is no longer on self-help projects or tasks to be tackled by engaged people, but instead on a group of people activated and trained to expand the volunteer sector. Their qualifications and expertise are important for the creation of new projects and for stimulating active participation in society (cf. ISAB 2004). 'Active age' is still a central concept, but the concept is no longer based on the activity theory of old age(ing). This may explain why critical assessments are without influence. The promises of 'active age(ing)' seem to have reached a dynamic of their own.

The creation of a positive image of older generations is here, too, exclusively related to the usefulness of old age potentials for society. This, again, implies a depreciation of those who cannot or who do not want to comply with this norm. The dichotomy of growth and reduction of the burdens of old age is inherent to this approach, too.

The neoliberal, managerial rationale (cf. Bröckling 2000: 131) has not only found access to the field of paid work but also to the field of voluntary work and civil engagement, at least concerning the engagement of older people. Voluntarily engaged people in this programme are constituted or constitute themselves as seniorTrainers. On this basis their experience and expertise

26 In the first course, 5.3 percent of the participants were employed, 9.9 percent unemployed, and 8.6 percent partly employed (ISAB 2003: 5). The report for the first phase of the programme of 2004 (first and second course) notes an increased number of unemployed: "A significant number is unemployed; among the male participants almost every seventh". In the eastern part of Germany the unemployment rate is 18 percent, in the western part 8 percent (Braun et al. 2004: 47 et seq.). According to Martin Brussig, Matthias Knuth and Walter Weiß (2006: 39) and with reference to the micro census of 1996-2001, 40 percent of the unemployed people at the age of 50 would like to be employed again, and 80 percent of the unemployed and ready to work group at the age of 50 to 60 would prefer to be employed fulltime.

can be offered free of charge, purposefully, and controlled. Accepting the role of a seniorTrainer means seeing your potentials as resources and transforming these into a marketable product and offering this product in a self-organized way. The reduction of responsibilities of the welfare-state implies the policy options concentrated on the fields of voluntary work, self-help activities, and civic engagement. These communal forms are an ideal field for a paradigmatic change: "to transfer the steering capacity of state organs and institutions to 'responsible', 'circumspective', and 'rational' subjects" (Lemke et al. 2000: 30). The process of 'role making', realized by self-technologies, seems to be a very effective, conflict-free way of governing the individual by ways of self-formation, self-organization, self-commitment, and by the stimulation of a desirable conduct – compared to coercion or political discussions. The dimension of self-organization has always been prominent in the field of voluntary work. What is new is the idea to stimulate self-organization by programmes initiated by the state. Although the recent programme *Active in old age*[27] is based on guidelines that emphasize the participation of older people in decision making processes on the municipal level, one must assert that public interest conflicts or deeper questions of protest movements are not mentioned, a situation that often can be observed in debates on civic engagement and voluntary work (cf. Mayer 2004: 68 et seq.; for the necessity of conflict orientation Böhnisch/Schröer 2002: 203-208).[28]

So it is not surprising that the following aspects are neglected or of marginal importance in the discussion about the relation between voluntary work of older people and demographic change: though these projects are situated in a societal context, the relation between the structural changes of age(ing) and general structural changes of/in society and the responsibility of the state and of the economy in these processes of change is not discussed. What is the responsibility of the actors promoting neoliberal economic and labour-market strategies for the process of making old age 'younger' and for the shrinking numbers of younger generations? What are the contributions of the economic and political systems to the depreciation of old age and to the notion of old age as a burden to society? In particular, projects such as EFI do not deal with the relationship and the characteristic differences of paid and voluntary work. It is insufficient to proclaim that volunteer work is not a continuation

27 The German title is: *Aktiv im Alter.*

28 For a detailed presentation of this complex relationship cf. Backes (1998).

of vocational activities or even an equivalent to qualified professional work, because the differences between voluntary work and employment are – as the example shows – continually fading away. So the necessary discussion on a re-distribution of paid and unpaid work and on the question of how work should be paid for is avoided.

These projects also shed light on a more general, but nevertheless urgent question: what happens to the norms and values of a society, when the societal care work, the social and educational work is more and more situated in the field of civic engagement and thus depends increasingly on individual engagement?

3 New roles in volunteer work, new gender relations?

An analytical perspective on the rationality of such programmes is one, another can focus on the practical level and the effects that can be made visible by statistical or narrative data. A closer look at the latter might especially show which positive effects on people's lives such programmes can have and how manifold practical actions are, sometimes full of conflicts, sometimes harmonious. Although these manifold voices are not my perspective in this argumentation, one must also emphasize that voluntarily engaged people need room for exchange and ask for further education (which is for 34 percent of the volunteers older than 60 years still not enough as Gensicke et al. 2005: 341 show) – to *continuously* question their routines and their experience and to approach new dimensions of learning.

In the following explanations, I leave the perspective on governmentality to take a closer look at the statistically visible gender relations in the volunteer sector, especially those within the subsector of the elderly. I will raise the question of whether a programme that focuses on the development of a new role in the volunteer sector can contribute to more gender equality in the volunteer sector.

A qualitative analysis of civic engagement of the elderly shows that the reasons for being engaged or not are grounded in the biographies (cf. Aner 2005). Looking at statistical data on voluntary engagement of older and elderly people in general in Germany, one can see that men are more often voluntarily engaged than women (2004: 37 percent women, 42 percent men between 55-64 years; 21 percent women, 34 percent men in the age 65 and older) (Gensicke et al. 2005: 266). Although the survey of the second period of life (*Alterssurvey*) shows much lower rates due to another definition (more in the tradition of honorary work) the tendencies are similar (Künemund 2006): the gap between men and women increases with age, although the differences have decreased between 1999 and 2004 (Gensicke et al. 2005: 266). One reason can be seen in the competition between household, family and care work on the one hand, and voluntary work on the other hand in connection with the continuity of voluntary work of men throughout their lives. This continuity is also linked with the fact that women are still mostly responsible for childcare even if they have a job. Looking at the engagement profiles, in general, one still observes qualitative differences: While women are more often engaged in social and health oriented, in ecclesiastic or religious activities and in school and kindergarten, men dominate in sportive, leisure, political and vocation-oriented engagement and also in fire services (cf. Gensicke et al. 2005). For the group of people older than 60 years, the engagement rates increase.

Looking at the example of the EFI-Programme, firstly, one must assert that participants are selected at the beginning of the programme so the gender rates of the participants can be influenced with the effect that more women than men participate (57 percent to 43 percent). However, the effect declines at advanced ages, and more men than women participate in the age group from 65 to 69 (cf. Engels et al. 2007: 44).

When taking a deeper look at the occupations, three aspects should be mentioned (cf. Engels et al. 2007: 54 et seq.)

1. SeniorTrainers are more often engaged in the social sector (care work of the oldest, community welfare work, work with disadvantaged persons) as the average of the whole population, men and women. But: 59 percent of the women and only 53 percent of the men.
2. The sector of school, kindergarten and youth work even shows a stronger tendency: 35 percent of the women have chosen this sector, but only 25 percent of the men. However, these rates are much higher than the engagement rates for children and youth in the survey on volunteering (*Freiwilligensurvey*) (12 percent of persons, 60 years and older, cf. Gensicke et al. 2005: 336).
3. If one looks at politics and representation of interests, it is the other way round: Only 11 percent of women are engaged in this sector, but 21 percent of the participating men.

A first, careful interpretation of the data might reveal an opportunity to open individually new dimensions of engagement (activities, target groups), although one must consider that the different data do not summarize the same topics, and thus they cannot be compared in a one to one nature. But in tendency, it seems that the role making process offers room to develop new perspectives. Nevertheless, these changes leave the gender *gap* untouched.

The analysis of the rationale of activating programmes in the volunteer sector has shown how the field of possible action is structured and thus how power relations 'work' without coercion to shape demographic change. I have also shown that the idea of using the potentials of the aged must be seen in connection with the change of the welfare state. Although the rationale of the recent activating programmes has no explicit gender perspective, their effects must be seen in the greater context of the gendered distribution and interrelation of all types of work and the gender relations in the social sector. The discussion about activating structures for voluntary work in old age within the context of demographic change therefore must take into consideration the gender inequalities in all kinds of work. And it is also necessary to pick up the discussion about the re-distribution of paid and unpaid, voluntary work and the relations *between* the different types of work under a gender perspective.

Translated by Ute Karl/Dieter Keiner

Bibliography

Aner, Kirsten (2005): *"Ich will, dass etwas geschieht". Wie zivilgesellschaftliches Engagement entsteht – oder auch nicht.* Berlin: Ed. sigma

*Backes, Gertrud M. (1998): "Zur Vergesellschaftung des Alter(n)s im Kontext der Modernisierung." In: Backes, Gertrud M./ Clemens, Wolfgang (eds.): *Altern und Gesellschaft. Gesellschaftliche Modernisierung durch Altersstrukturwandel.* Opladen: Leske + Budrich, 23-60.

Backes, Gertrud M./ Clemens, Wolfgang (1998): *Lebensphase Alter. Eine Einführung in die sozialwissenschaftliche Alternsforschung.* Weinheim, München: Juventa

Baltes, Margret M./ Montada, Leo (eds.) (1996): *Produktives Leben im Alter.* (Schriftenreihe/ADIA-Stiftung zur Erforschung Neuer Wege für Arbeit und Soziales Leben, Bd. 3). Frankfurt/ M., New York: Campus

*BMFSFJ (Bundesministerium für Familie, Senioren, Frauen und Jugend) (ed.) (2005): *Fünfter Bericht zur Lage der älteren Generation in der Bundesrepublik Deutschland. Potenziale des Alters in Wirtschaft und Gesellschaft. Der Beitrag älterer Menschen zum Zusammenhalt der Generationen.* Bericht der Sachverständigenkommission. Berlin: BMFS-FJ, www.bmfsfj.de/RedaktionBMFSFJ/Abteilung3/Pdf-Anlagen/fuenfter-altenbericht,property=pdf,bereich=,rwb=true.pdf (01/12/2008)

Böhnisch, Lothar/ Schröer, Wolfgang (2002): *Die soziale Bürgergesellschaft. Zur Einbindung des Sozialpolitischen in den zivilgesellschaftlichen Diskurs.* Weinheim, München: Juventa

*Braun, Joachim/ Burmeister, Joachim/ Engels, Dietrich (eds.) (2004): *SeniorTrainerin: Neue Verantwortungsrolle und Engagement in Kommunen. Bundesmodellprogramm "Erfahrungswissen für Initiativen". Bericht zur ersten Programmphase.* (ISAB-Schriftenreihe: Berichte aus Forschung und Praxis, No. 84). Köln: ISAB

Bröckling, Ulrich (2000): "Totale Mobilmachung. Menschenführung im Qualitäts- und Selbstmanagement." In: Lemke, Thomas/ Krasmann, Susanne/ Bröckling, Ulrich (eds.): *Gouvernementalität der Gegenwart. Studien zur Ökonomisierung des Sozialen.* Frankfurt/ M.: Suhrkamp, 131-167

Brussig, Martin/ Knuth, Matthias/ Weiß, Walter (2006): "Arbeiten ab 50 in Deutschland. Eine Landkarte der Erwerbstätigkeit auf der Grundlage des Mikrozensus 1996 bis 2001." In: Deutsches Zentrum für Altersfragen (ed.): *Beschäftigungssituation älterer Arbeitnehmer* (Expertisen zum 5. Altenbericht, Bd. 1). Berlin: Lit, 7-51

*Burmeister, Joachim (2004): "Ergebnisse der seniorTrainerinnen-Weiterbildungskonzeption." In: *ISAB-Berichte aus Forschung und Praxis, Nr. 87 Halbzeitbilanz und Perspektiven des Modellprogramms "Erfahrungswissen für Initiativen".* 3. Zentrale EFI-Fachtagung für alle EFI-Akteure vom 21.-23. Juni 2004 in Lingen-Holthausen 2004. Köln, Leipzig: ISAB-Verlag, 20-27, www.efi-programm.de/dokumente/fachtagung/3-EFI-Fachtagung_Lingen.pdf (24/01/2009)

*Burmeister, Joachim/ Heller, Anne/ Stehr, Ilona (2004): *Weiterbildung älterer Menschen zu seniorTrainerinnen: Rahmencurriculum 2004 im Modellprogramm "Erfahrungswissen für Initiativen" des Bundesministeriums für Familie, Senioren, Frauen und Jugend.* Neubrandenburg, www.efi-programm.de/dokumente/st-weiterbildung/rahmencurriculum2004.pdf (01/12/2008)

Bußmann, Ulrike/ Stöbe-Blossey, Sybille (2003): "Aktivierung von Freiwilligenarbeit als Element eines aktivierenden Staates." In: Dahme, Hans-Jürgen/ Otto, Hans-Uwe/ Wohlfahrt, Norbert (eds.): *Soziale Arbeit für den aktivierenden Staat.* Opladen: Leske + Budrich: 127-147

Deutscher Bundestag (ed.) (1994): *Erster Zwischenbericht der Enquête-Kommission "Demographischer Wandel – Herausforderungen an den Einzelnen und an die Politik"*. Bonn: Deutscher Bundestag

*Deutscher Bundestag (ed.) (2002a): *Herausforderungen unserer älter werdenden Gesellschaft an den Einzelnen und die Politik.* Schlussbericht der Enquête-Kommission „Demographischer Wandel". Berlin: Deutscher Bundestag (Drucksache 14/8800), http://dip21.bundestag.de/dip21/btd/14/088/1408800.pdf (09/01/2009)

Deutscher Bundestag (ed.) (2002b): *Bürgerschaftliches Engagement: auf dem Weg in eine zukunftsfähige Bürgergesellschaft. Bericht der Enquête-Kommission "Zukunft des Bürgerschaftlichen Engagements"*. Berlin: Deutscher Bundestag (Drucksache 14/8900), http://dip21.bundestag.de/dip21/btd/14/089/1408900.pdf (09/01/2009)

Engels, Dietrich (2008): "Demographischer Wandel, Strukturwandel des Alters und Entwicklung des Unterstützungsbedarfs alter Menschen." In: Aner, Kirsten/ Karl, Ute (eds.): *Lebensalter und Soziale Arbeit: Ältere und alte Menschen* (Basiswissen Soziale Arbeit, Bd. 6). Baltmannsweiler: Schneider, 54-76

Engels, Dietrich/ Braun, Joachim/ Burmeister, Joachim (2007): *Senior-Trainerinnen und seniorKompetenzteams; Erfahrungswissen und Engagement älterer Menschen in einer neuen Verantwortungsrolle. Evaluationsbericht zum Bundesmodellprogramm "Erfahrungswissen für Initiativen"*. (ISAB-Schriftenreihe: Berichte aus Forschung und Praxis, No. 102). Köln: ISAB

Foucault, Michel (1982): "The Subject and Power." In: Dreyfus, Hubert L./ Rabinow, Paul: *Michel Foucault: Beyond Structuralism and Hermeneutics.* Chicago: University of Chicago Press, 208-226

Foucault, Michel (1991): "Governmentality." In: Burchell, Graham/ Gordon, Colin/ Miller, Peter (eds.) (1991): *The Foucault Effect. Studies in Governmentality.* London et al.: Harvester Wheatsheaf, 87-104

Gensicke, Thomas/ Picot, Sibylle/ Geiss, Sabine (2005): *Freiwilliges Engagement in Deutschland 1999-2004. Ergebnisse der repräsentativen Trenderhebung zu Ehrenamt, Freiwilligenarbeit und bürgerschaftlichem Engagement.* München: TNS Infratest

*Göckenjan, Gerd (2000): *Das Alter würdigen. Altersbilder und Bedeutungswandel des Alters.* Frankfurt/ M.: Suhrkamp

ISAB (Institut für sozialwissenschaftliche Analysen und Beratung) (ed.) (2003): *Informationen der wissenschaftlichen Begleitung*, No. 12: Der erste EFI-Kurs aus Sicht der seniorTrainerinnen. Ergebnisse der schriftlichen Befragungen der seniorTrainerinnen. Köln: ISAB

ISAB (Institut für sozialwissenschaftliche Analysen und Beratung) (ed.) (2004): *EFI-Newsletter*, No. 4. Köln: ISAB

ISAB (Institut für sozialwissenschaftliche Analysen und Beratung) (ed.) (2006): *Informationen der wissenschaftlichen Begleitung*, No. 34. Köln: ISAB

ISAB/ Internationaler Rat für Soziale Wohlfahrt/ Deutscher Verein für öffentliche und private Fürsorge/ Kuratorium Deutsche Altershilfe) (eds.) (2000): *Voluntary Engagement by and for Very Old Persons – a European Comparison. Documentation of the Conference of Experts of the International Council on Social Welfare*, www.forum-seniorenarbeit.de/media/custom/373_73_1.PDF (01/12/2008)

Karl, Ute (2005): *Zwischen/Räume: Eine empirisch-bildungstheoretische Studie zur ästhetischen und psychosozialen Praxis des Altentheater.* Münster: Lit

Karl, Ute (2006): "Soziale Altenarbeit und Altenbildungsarbeit – vom aktiven zum profilierten, unternehmerischen Selbst." In: Maurer, Susanne/ Weber, Susanne (eds.): *Gouvernementalität und Erziehungswissenschaft. Wissen – Macht – Transformation.* Wiesbaden: VS Verlag für Sozialwissenschaften, 301-319

Karl, Ute (2009): "Learning to Become an Entrepreneurial Self for Voluntary Work? Social Policy and Older People in the Volunteer Sector." In: Peters, Michael E./ Besley, A.C./ Olssen, Mark/ Maurer, Susanne/ Weber, Susanne (eds.): *Governmentality Studies in Education.* Rotterdam: Sense, 433-451

Katz, Stephen/ Green, Bryan (2002): "The Government of Detail: The Case of Social Policy on Aging." In: *Journal of Aging and Identity* 7 (3), 149-163

Kessl, Fabian/ Otto, Hans-Uwe (eds.) (2004): *Soziale Arbeit und Soziales Kapital. Zur Kritik lokaler Gemeinschaftlichkeit.* Wiesbaden: VS Verlag für Sozialwissenschaften

Kolland, Franz (1996): *Kulturstile älterer Menschen. Jenseits von Pflicht und Alltag.* Wien, Köln, Weimar: Böhlau

Künemund, Harald (2006): "Tätigkeiten und Engagement im Ruhestand." In: Tesch-Römer, Clemens/ Engstler, Heribert/ Wurm, Susanne (eds.): *Altwerden in Deutschland: sozialer Wandel und individuelle Entwicklung in der zweiten Lebenshälfte.* Wiesbaden: VS Verlag für Sozialwissenschaften, 289-328

*Lemke, Thomas/ Krasmann, Susanne/ Bröckling, Ulrich (2000): "Gouvernementalität, Neoliberalismus und Selbsttechnologien." In: Lemke, Thomas/ Krasmann, Susanne/ Bröckling, Ulrich (eds.): *Gouvernementalität der Gegenwart. Studien zur Ökonomisierung des Sozialen.* Frankfurt/ M.: Suhrkamp, 7-40

Lenz, Karl/ Rudolph, Martin/Sickendieck, Ursel (1999): "Alter und Altern aus sozialgerontologischer Sicht." In: Lenz, Karl/ Rudolph, Martin/ Sickendieck, Ursel (eds.): *Die alternde Gesellschaft. Problemfelder gesellschaftlichen Umgangs mit Altern und Alter.* Weinheim, München: Juventa, 7-96

Mayer, Margrit (2004): "Vom Versprechen lokaler Kohäsion. Blindstellen in der internationalen Debatte." In: Kessl, Fabian/ Otto, Hans-Uwe (eds.): *Soziale Arbeit und Soziales Kapital. Zur Kritik lokaler Gemeinschaftlichkeit.* Wiesbaden: VS Verlag für Sozialwissenschaften, 63-78

Miller, Peter/ Rose, Niklas (1992): "Political Power beyond the State: Problematics of Government." In: *British Journal of Sociology* 43 (2), 173-205

Powell, Jason L. (2006): *Social Theory and Aging.* Lanham, Boulder, New York, Toronto, Oxford: Rowman & Littlefield Publishers, Inc.

Powell, Jason L./ Biggs, Simon (2003): "Foucauldian Gerontology: A Methodology for Understanding Aging." In: *Electronic Journal of Sociology* 7 (2), http://sociology.org/content/vol7.2/03_powell_biggs.html

Powell, Jason L./ Edwards, Margret M. (2002): "Policy Narratives of Aging: The Right Way, the Third Way or the Wrong Way?" In: *Electronic Journal of Sociology* 6 (1), http://sociology.org/content/vol006.001/powell-edwards.html

Powell, Jason L./Wahidin, Azrini (eds.): *Foucault and Aging.* New York: Nova Science Publishers, Inc.

Schroeter, Klaus R. (2002): "Zur Allodoxie des 'erfolgreichen' und 'produktiven' Alterns." In: Backes, Gertrud M./ Clemens, Wolfgang (eds.): *Zukunft der Soziologie des Alter(n)s.* Opladen: Leske + Budrich, 85-107

Smith, Justin Davis/ Gay, Pat (2005): *Active Ageing in Active Communities. Volunteering and the Transition to Retirement.* Bristol: The Policy Press

Statistisches Bundesamt (2006): *11. koordinierte Bevölkerungsvorausberechnung. Annahmen und Ergebnisse.* Wiesbaden: Statistisches Bundesamt

Tews, Hans Peter (1993): "Neue und alte Aspekte des Strukturwandels des Alters." In: Naegele, Gerhard/ Tews, Hans Peter (eds.): *Lebenslagen im Strukturwandel des Alters. Alternde Gesellschaft – Folgen für die Politik.* Opladen: Westdeutscher Verlag, 15-42

*Tews, Hans Peter (1996): "Produktivität des Alters." In: Baltes, Margret/ Montada, Leo (eds.): *Produktives Leben im Alter.* (Schriftenreihe/ADIA-Stiftung zur Erforschung Neuer Wege für Arbeit und Soziales Leben; Bd. 3). Frankfurt/ M., New York: Campus, 184-210

Tews, Hans Peter (2000): "Introductory Speech on the Subject of Old Age." In: Internationaler Rat für Soziale Wohlfahrt/ Deutscher Verein für öffentliche und private Fürsorge/ Kuratorium Deutsche Altershilfe (eds.): *Voluntary Engagement by and for Very Old Persons – a European Comparison. Documentation of the Conference of Experts of the International Council on Social Welfare.* Köln: Moeker Merkur Druck, 74-83

Wessels, Christiane (1994): *Das soziale Ehrenamt im Modernisierungsprozeß. Chancen und Risiken des Einsatzes beruflich qualifizierter Frauen.* Pfaffenweiler: Centaurus

WHO (World Health Organization) (2002): *Active Ageing. A Policy Framework.* Madrid

Zeman, Peter/ Schmidt, Roland (2001): "Soziale Altenarbeit – Strukturen und Entwicklungslinien." In: Deutsches Zentrum für Altersfragen (ed.): *Lebenslagen, Soziale Ressourcen und gesellschaftliche Integration* (Expertisen zum Dritten Altenbericht der Bundesregierung, Bd. 3). Opladen: Leske + Budrich, 235-277

*All translations of quoted German texts by Dieter Keiner.

Symbolic Fields of Demographic Change

Mary Daly and Kirsten Scheiwe

Changing Gender Models in Law and Social Policy in Germany and the UK

Gender has proved a popular, and fruitful, line of analysis of contemporary welfare states. However, the bulk and the best of gender scholarship tends to look backwards – it has proved much more difficult to characterize emerging changes and trends. That is what this paper seeks to do, focusing on emerging models of gender relations in law and social policy in Germany and the UK. The paper proceeds by first engaging in a discussion and review of how the existing literature has conceptualized the gender models underpinning social policy. It then moves on to analyze relevant developments in law and social policy in the UK and Germany over the last ten years or so. In seeking to characterize and compare developments in the two countries, the paper adopts an integrated perspective and explicitly links developments in social policy with those in family law. These areas are typically treated separately by scholarship, making it difficult to identify broad patterns and connections across spheres.

The paper is organized into three parts. The first considers how gender-related developments have been framed in the literature. The second turns the spotlight on the empirical analysis of the changes underway in both national settings. The third and concluding section draws out the implications of the findings, especially with reference to expanding and updating thinking about how gender relations and structures are being manipulated by current policy and legal developments. We also devote some attention to the implications for future scholarship.

1 Theoretical/conceptual elaboration of gender models

Social policies and law relate to families and possess gender dimensions in multi-dimensional ways. They do so, for example, through assumptions about such matters as how the income situation of families should be secured or poverty prevented, how mutual financial and support obligations between different family members should be organized, how adults should cooperate and share the burden of maintaining themselves, their children or other dependants, and how income, housework, care and the socialisation of children should be distributed (Scheiwe 2007). Law and policy seek to affect both micro-level relations – the roles of women and men as earners, carers and parents – and also macro relations – the relationship between public and private actors in regard to care, education and socialisation, the appropriate role and interrelations of different policy sectors and, ultimately, the relationship between the state, market, and family.

The existing and emerging models of gender relations that underlie policy and law have been characterized in different ways by the literature (Daly/Rake 2003). The most enduring characterization is the male breadwinner model, especially as elaborated by Jane Lewis (1992). Surveying social policy provisions in Europe, Lewis suggested that states varied systematically in the degree to which they endorsed a traditional breadwinner role for men and a caring role for women. As is well known, she identified three variants of the model – strong, moderate and weak breadwinner – and pinned these variations to particular countries on the basis of their underlying social policy regime. This frame served scholarship, especially that on gender and welfare state variation, relatively well until recently. Now, the literature is more fragmented or complex (depending on how one views it) as it tries to grapple with a rapidly changing policy landscape. There are (at least) three overlapping but also quite distinct approaches in play at the present time.

First, there is work which looks at the treatment of women in particular and gender roles more broadly. Here one finds recent work by Jane Lewis which speaks now in terms of a move towards an adult worker model. While Lewis nowhere sets out explicitly the theoretical features of this model,[1] the adult worker idea appears to be a variant or descendant of the breadwinner model, especially the moderate and weak versions of it. The characterization is more empirical than theoretical, however. In a series of papers, Lewis identifies a number of empirical features of the social policy template involved in the adult worker model. If one distils all this down, it would appear that for Lewis there are three main indicators of a move to an adult worker model (especially in a UK context). Of significance first is the move to encourage employment on the part of both parents, a widespread development in Europe (and a central goal at EU level). A second relevant direction of recent policy

1 The most comprehensive outline is in Lewis (2001).

is 'defamilization', essentially facilitating care to take place outside of the family (especially the care of children). Various 'incentives' are introduced for this purpose but the use of tax allowances has been particularly significant in the UK. Commodification of care is a related process (whereby childcare increasingly acquires the features of a marketised exchange process). A third associated trend identified by Lewis as part of a move to an adult worker model is individualization – for benefit purposes the aspect of a person's status that counts above all now is one's relationship to the labour market, whereas in the past family-related status was much more dominant among the criteria governing entitlement to welfare state services and benefits.

Lewis's work has some commonalities with scholarship tracing the impact of welfare state and social provisions on women's (mothers' especially) participation in the labour market.[2] This work is mainly carried out by labour economists and has been developed especially under the auspices of some of the gender-funded activities of the EU.[3] It too is interested in the role of mothers but more for what it says about the division between 'public' and 'private' actors as regards the care of children and adults and how the details of provision affect economic behaviours of family members than for the nature of motherhood or family roles themselves. This work has contributed a fine-grained analysis of the constituent elements of policy and their implications in terms of mothers' employment and the organization of family life. To the extent that it problematizes mothers' behaviour, it sees it as a function of the incentives, explicit and implicit, contained in policy and provision and locates mothers' behaviour in the context of the family as an economic unit. This work is not overtly theoretical, although it has both rational choice and feminist affinities. Nor does it posit a particular trajectory of change.

Orloff's (2005) analysis is different again but is close in spirit to that of Lewis. Her work is theoretical – she uses the over-arching frame of economic citizenship, an approach which draws from her long-standing concern about the extent to which welfare states enable women to be autonomous (Orloff 1993). Stratification is the sociological referent concept here. Her conclusions, while generally similar to those of Lewis, shed another light on how

2 For some recent examples cf. Del Boca/Wetzels (2007), Gornick/Meyers (2003) and Bettio/Plantenga (2004).

3 In particular the network of experts on gender equality and employment, which was chaired for many years by Jill Rubery.

(liberal) welfare states are changing and how particular groups of women are affected. Orloff sees three broad axes of reform in the US. The first is the undermining of care-giving as a source of social rights, and, associated with this, an increased role for discretionary assistance within social provision. According to Orloff, this type of change has been particularly significant for women of colour and women who are poor. The second element is the extent to which reform has expanded the role of the market in the provision of income and care. This has the effect of worsening the role of market-based inequalities in structuring access to care. Thirdly, picking up on a trend underway elsewhere as well, Orloff points to a shift in patterns of stratification away from gender 'difference' and toward gender 'sameness'. In other words, institutionalized expectations about paid work for mothers no longer are distinguished from those for fathers. Despite continuing differences around the performance of 'private', unpaid care work, both partners are required to be employed, and the underlying model is of an unencumbered (implicitly masculine) worker. Her conclusion overall is of a (qualified) removal of the (few remaining) maternalist elements in the US welfare state.

The individual is at the centre of Orloff's work as it is in that of Lewis and to the extent that both are theorizing a trend it is that of individualization. This makes their work quite different from another body of work which takes as its starting point care and how the relationships associated with care are affected by state policies. In this work, the main area of interest and departure point are family-related processes (as well as structures). Family is in the foreground here whereas in the work referred to up to now family is the background or backdrop to individual functioning, roles and relationships.

The work on care looks at law, policy and programmes for how they construct care-related activities and gender relations as part of this. One of the guiding frames of analysis here is the familization/defamilization framework. This, essentially continental European in origin, scholarship starts from a more sociological perspective, and for it familization/defamilization connotes profound changes not just from a gender perspective but also from the perspective of the family's role in society. It views state entitlements in terms of how they speak to and reinforce people's familial and occupational status and relations – husbands and wives, fathers and mothers, generations, employees and so forth (Leitner et al. 2008: 177). One key axis of analysis in this perspective is the extent to which states reinforce family obligations and shape family roles. More specifically, this perspective is especially interested in how states treat children, elderly people and the many who provide care on a regular basis (especially those who provide unpaid care). The work by Leitner (2003) and Leitner et al. (2008) is perhaps the most elaborate analysis yet using this lens. There is a narrative of change in this approach. The recent reforms in Germany are analyzed in terms of whether they free families from care obligations (defamilization) or whether they add to families' care obligations (refamilization). While conceptually this perspective is quite broad, when it has been operationalized it has tended to narrow down quite a lot to focus mainly on how the provision of care is incentivised and how policy frames the rights of mothers and of mothers' relationship to their partners and to family life more broadly. In this it is revealing, but the utility of the perspective in analyzing the broad panoply of relevant changes and the connections across spheres has yet to be fully exploited.

We believe that there is insight in each approach – the adult worker model draws the attention to gender and how a change in the role envisaged for mothers gets to the heart of the reform project; the work of the labour economists sheds light on the interaction between the state, the market and women's labour; and the familization/defamilization approach is insightful about care, family relations and the place of family in society. While they are not all grounded to the same degree in an analysis of change, the different approaches offer interesting revelations about the direction of change, proffering on the one hand the thesis of individualization and on the other that of familization/defamilization. Both of these merit further investigation and we revisit them later in the paper.

However we also have serious reservations about each of the existing bodies of work (and scholarship in the field in general). Individually, each approach is quite narrow and so can capture only a portion of what is happening. Connectedness is in our view critical. We are engaging here with large institutions – care, family, economy – and so need to work on a broad canvas. In addition, and more fundamentally, we do not believe that any of the approaches alone accurately describes what is happening. Thirdly, when it comes to the analysis of change, there is an implicit qualification or hesitation in each of their examinations but none spells this qualification out. In other words, each is an incomplete account of what is happening.

We propose an encompassing framework that focuses on gender-related roles and institutions. Roles we analyze in terms of the assumptions, expectations and incentives relating to the behaviour and obligations of mothers and fathers that underpin or are to be found in social policy and family law. Institutions are the rules of the game in a society and as structures and practices shape both human interaction and change over time. The institutions that we are especially interested in are marriage, parenthood and the family since these comprise the broader frames of reference for gender and generational relationships. On the basis of this framework we will pursue an analysis of changes in the areas of social policy and family law over the last ten years. The empirical focus of our analysis are the changes in law and social policy (including childcare policy and provision, taxation law and policy, family law, pension provision, provision for parental leave and other care-giving related measures). We are interested in reforms that have been made rather than the analysis of political discourses or rhetoric. We assess the significance of the reforms in terms of how they frame key roles and institutions, rather than in terms of their direct effects on individual behaviour at the micro level (such as 'doing family' or 'doing gender' at the level of bargaining, decision-making, behaviour, attitudes, values or opinions of individuals who belong to a family).

The crux of our argument is that recent reform has had to balance gender with a host of other considerations in relation to family and hence any moves towards individualization are qualified and halting and even contradictory. We will show that while there might be some moves towards individualising people (both adults and children), what the UK and German welfare states are doing is:

1. repositioning individuals vis-à-vis the family,
2. repositioning family-related institutions vis-à-vis other institutions, especially state and market.

2 Main changes underway in Germany and the UK

In both Germany and the UK, family is a dynamic policy domain and family policy and law a site of considerable change. In Germany family-oriented policies have expanded in parallel with retrenchment in unemployment and pension support. This trend, which started in the 1980s, was accelerated by the Red-Green coalition in the late 1990s and early 2000s and has been further deepened by the comprehensive reforms enacted by the current grand coalition government (in power from 2005-2009). In the UK over the course of New Labour's ten years in government, family-related considerations have been drawn to the heart of British social policy and law. The result is a remarkably sustained (if not always consistent) programme, oriented both to family behaviour and well-being (especially of children). While there is variation cross-nationally in the nature of reforms being introduced, it is possible to identify several common trends. Here we concentrate on what we consider to be the main ones, focusing first on family law and then on social security.

There are two common cross-national trends in family law reform.

First, there is a visible trend towards upgrading child support claims over those relating to the maintenance of an ex-spouse after divorce. In England, the Child Support Act 1991 changed the claims of children living with one parent to make them non-waivable so as to restrict the formerly common practice of renouncing child support claims in 'clean-break' divorce arrangements. This reform was intended also to reverse the trend towards shifting child support costs to the tax-financed Income Support provision. In practice it represented an attempt to privatize these costs to the parents. In Germany, a reform undertaken in 2007 upgraded child support claims over an ex-wife's post-divorce maintenance. Effectively, it created a new ranking with children first, caring parents (married or not) second, and ex-wives not caring for a child third (with the exception of divorcees from a long-lasting marriage, who were moved up to the second rank). The intention was to reduce child poverty and to lower the number of poor children receiving means-tested social benefits – to the disadvantage of mothers and ex-wives (also improving the position of second families vis-à-vis the first family). Now, not only the child's claim but also the duration of a caring parent's maintenance claim tends to be equalized between divorced and never married lone parents (after serious political controversy and an intervention of the Federal Supreme Court). The underlying trend in both countries, then, is to upgrade claims based on parenthood and parenting vis-à-vis those based on marriage. This is linked to a longer-term trend (visible since the 1970s) to dissociate marriage and parenthood. Among relevant changes here were the easier dissolution of marriage through divorce law reform and the ban on discrimination against children born out of wedlock.

A second trend is towards affirming and extending the fatherhood role and status of men. In family law, the parenting role of fathers is being reframed both for fathers after divorce and for non-married fathers. Joint custody after divorce is the rule now in nearly all Western European countries. Fathers who are not married to the mother can now obtain parental responsibility, albeit that this is easier in England than in Germany. It is more difficult in Germany because a non-married mother still enjoys a strong veto position against paternity recognition and against joint custody which cannot be reversed in court proceedings (a gender connotation which is now unique). English law is more gender neutral, and parental responsibility can be granted by courts on application, even to a caring person other than the mother or father. This trend towards extending the fatherhood role and status of men is realized also by the general strengthening of parenting and the equal treatment of children born in or out of marriage.

Elements of these trends are echoed in legal and policy changes in social security. Along with these there are three other trends.

The first, very widespread, tendency in both Germany and the UK is to encourage mothers to be employed. Maternal employment is 'incentivised' by changes in employment and taxation policy as well as a strong growth in service provision substituting for mothers' services. In both countries employment and social policy places a strong emphasis on activating people to be employed. Reforms of unemployment benefits have played a central role. They affect families as well as gender roles in various, partly contradictory, ways. The reform of unemployment benefits in Germany, which came into effect in 2005, amalgamated the former second-tier of unemployment assistance with the flat-rate income support benefits at the lower level of income support. This meant lower benefits, thus income losses and stricter means-testing, for many long-term unemployed beneficiaries. Cuts in benefit levels also implied a stronger reliance upon the income of other family members or the partner.

With activation as the goal, policy focuses upon all employable household members. In Germany, although care for children is considered to be an impediment to employment until the children reach three years of age (this was already the case before 2005 – regulation did not change in this respect), employment agencies engage much more in activities to bring housewives with older children into, at the minimum, part-time jobs, which are often precarious. The reform of post-divorce maintenance regulation of 2007 points in the same direction. It has reinforced the expectation that a divorced mother should take up employment earlier than before if childcare facilities exist. In addition, the down-grading of the divorcee's maintenance claim will increase dependence on means-tested income support. The lowered level of benefits for long-time unemployed persons is another factor pushing mothers into employment. They seek to supplement household income, even though the additional earnings are low due to the low threshold of means-testing. Earlier reforms in 2003 had already promoted the expansion of so-called 'mini-jobs' (precarious part-time employment with lower social security rights) and reduced the claims of (almost exclusively female) 'returners to the job' as well as cutting down reinsertion programmes. In 2006, the possibility of moving out of the parental household was restricted for young unemployed persons below the age of 25 – they have to demonstrate to the employment agency that this is essential or else face a cut in benefits. This, on the one hand, means prolonged dependency on parents and income-sharing in a common household and, on the other, erects barriers against forming a new family or living as part of a couple, since means-testing of benefits obliges the new partner to join into maintaining the cohabiting partner. Too heavy financial burdens on financial support by the family or a new partner may be hostile to family formation or repartnering.

A second arm of policy incentivising maternal employment is taxation. Tax changes also work to promote a two-earner household, especially in the UK. The introduction of tax credits, to top up wages for those in work, has been the central element of New Labour's 'make work pay' strategy. Starting in October 1999, they were designed to make employment more feasible and attractive for families. Here too, the familial or collective orientation of the provision is noteworthy – these benefits are fundamentally premised on the combination of incomes and behaviours on the part of different family members. In Germany, tax law has been used much less to incentivise maternal employment. The possibility of deducting childcare expenses from taxable income if both parents are employed is rather limited. From 1984 to 2000 this option was open only to employed lone parents. Between 2000 and 2006 all parents – employed or not – caring at home for the child or spending on childcare could deduct a lump sum for care and educational needs. Hence, contrary to the logic of tax law, home-based care for children by a non-employed parent was deductible on the same terms as childcare expenses of both employed parents. Since 2006, the allowances for the latter are more generous. However, low-income families get little out of this tax advantage as for them and lone mothers the reduction of fees for public childcare is much more important than tax deduction of childcare expenses.

A further trend is a growth in the provision of childcare services outside of the home. These developments are in line with EU policy objectives to diminish disincentives for women's employment. They are also in line with the European Council's Barcelona targets of 2002 for childcare development in the EU: by 2010, 33 percent of children under three years of age and 90 percent of children aged three to obligatory school age should have access to a form of childcare. Both countries move towards extended provision, but on different paths – while Germany plans to extend public provision, especially for the under-threes, Britain promotes expansion through the commodification of care services.

In Germany, the (Western German) paradigm of home care for children seems to be shifting to broader provision and a changing educational partnership between parental and public provision. In this and other ways, childcare policy has moved in Germany from becoming a somewhat marginal issue to a core concern. Based on the Day Care Expansion Act, which entered into force in early 2005, municipalities are at a first stage required to provide day care for all those children under the age of three whose parents work or are enrolled in education and training. The aim is to provide 230,000 additional places for the under-threes by 2010. One-third of the extra places are to be provided by registered childminders in private households. This programme is estimated to cost € 1.5 billion and is to be financed through 'savings' for municipalities achieved by the merger of the unemployment and social assistance programmes for the unemployed. In a second stage, based on a compromise between the political parties of the grand coalition government in spring 2007, publicly financed/subsidized care for children under the age of three years will be implemented so as to fully meet the demand by 2013, at which time the government will also introduce an individual entitlement to childcare for every child. In late 2007, the Federal government allocated an additional € 2.14 billion to support the expansion of childcare facilities by the *Länder*.

In the UK there have been several initiatives to restructure public childcare. Children aged three and four have been given guaranteed access to nursery education in schools (although on a part-time basis). Employed parents of children aged zero to five years have access to nurseries outside the school system, and fees are subsidized by childcare tax credits. The latter set strong incentives to purchase services and so lead to a commodification of childcare – in other words they subject the organization of childcare to the logic of the market (Penn 2009). Opinion is split about the impact. Some argue that it is not a paradigmatic shift, since the public-private split has been upheld, and a turn towards an equitable system would require public funding and a separate and coherent system of education and care, not watered down schooling or a commercial baby park (Penn 2008). Others claim that despite separation along class lines still characterizing the childcare system in the UK, the whole range of innovations which has taken place over the last decade has moved the system away from its initial paradigm of childcare as a private matter (Bahle 2009).

A third cross-national commonality is increased emphasis on reconciliation of work and family life. This has legitimated some recognition of family-related exigencies as a counter claim to employment-based rights and responsibilities, especially in the UK where family-based claims had less legitimacy historically. 'Reconciliation' has had two major expressions in policy. On the one hand, employed parents are given more generous but also more carefully targeted incentives and supports to both not provide care personally for their children and also, on other occasions, to take time off from employment to provide such care personally. This has involved the significant extension of leave programmes in the UK and their refocusing (in terms of income replacement and shorter duration) in Germany. In both countries, both parents are targeted as potential employees and there is increased interest in encouraging fathers to take (short periods of) time off work to care for their young children.

In Germany a major reform of the parental leave policy was undertaken in 2000 (by the Social Democratic-Green coalition). In line with EU regulations the right to parental working-time reduction was extended and both parents were allowed to take leave or reduce their working hours contemporaneously. This represented a move towards a model of equal sharing of employment and parenting between both parents. A reform of 2006 under the Christian Democrat-Social Democrat grand coalition changed the parental leave policy considerably. It was changed from a means-tested flat rate benefit of € 300 monthly to a wage-related income replacement benefit of 67 percent of former net income, while – as a compromise – the minimum flat rate benefit was retained even for non-employed parents. Arguing that incentives to shorten mothers' employment interruptions should be put in place, the length of benefit payment was shortened from 24 to 12 or 14 months maximum, while the duration of the parental leave provision remained unchanged (up to 36 months). Tying the benefit to wage replacement as well as the introduction of two months reserved for the other parent (a sort of 'daddy months') were intended to increase fathers' participation in the care of a new-born child. Controversies focused on redistribution issues (cuts for low-income families and non-employed parents and gains for better-off parents), gender issues ('forced family labour for fathers'; 'devaluation of the housewife') and the issue of 'choice' around family life that policy tried to change through shifts in incentive setting.

Reform in the UK is also proceeding along the lines of putting in place more generous and extensive leaves from employment for family (actually child-related) purposes that target both mothers and fathers. The amount of paid maternity leave has been extended (to 39 weeks from 14), and it is planned to extend it further to one year by the end of the current parliament. The leave has also been made more generous (doubling in value in 10 years) and part of it is now transferable from mothers to fathers. In addition, paid paternity and adoption leave have been introduced and plans are afoot to extend both to 26 weeks. Another innovation for the UK has been the introduction of a right to request flexible working for parents of young and disabled children. While this is at the discretion of employers, the fact that workers are given a right to request the leave is far from trivial given the otherwise strong voluntarist tradition in UK industrial relations (Lewis/Campbell 2007: 374).

The UK is also in the process of intensifying the services offered to support families, especially those that are low income or at risk. In this it has gone much further than Germany. Improving and streamlining general services for families is effected in the first instance by the Sure Start programme which began in 1998. The aims of this programme lie partly in better governance and a desire for neighbourhood renewal but they relate especially to effecting improved family practices and outcomes. The idea is to ensure that families living in the 20 per cent most 'risky' areas have available to them in their locality a range of child- and family-centred services, including health, family support and outreach and early learning so as to improve childhood and parenting and promote parental employment. Conceived as a one-stop shop, Sure Start and the Children's Centre programme that has replaced it, which will oversee the establishment of a much larger network of 3,500 centres by 2010 (trebling 2006 provision), are firmly anchored in anti-poverty and social inclusion objectives. Oriented to the performance aspect of parenthood, the measures are strongly interventionist, in their own right and in comparison with developments in Germany. By 2010 all schools will offer a range of parenting support, including information sessions as well as more specialized support for parents whose children have problems with attendance or behaviour (HM Treasury 2007).

Strengthening family relationships has been a strong axis/aim of British family policy under New Labour. As well as services focusing on children, there has been investment in relationship support (delivered through the third sector) and also support services for conflict resolution for parents whose relationships have broken down. In addition, the 2006 Green Paper – *Care Matters* – outlined proposals to help local services support families to stay together, such as assessing the impact of intensive parenting support or therapy (HM Department of Skills and Pensions 2006). Social order and social control have been strong underlying currents in these and other measures. Parenting orders, for example, compel parents, where required, to attend parenting classes and fulfil other requirements deemed necessary by the court for improving their child's behaviour. In addition, there are parenting contracts, which are two-sided voluntary agreements between parents and the local authority (or other bodies) to address specific behavioural or attendance problems.

3 Interpretation and implications

In sum then, in both family law and social security in both countries there is a closer focusing of state support on parenting and parenthood as a status against that of marriage. Within this, the father's role and the obligations of fathers are being reinterpreted. While there is also a move away from a tax privileging of marriage and a tendency to grant non-married couples similar rights and responsibilities to those of married couples in the UK, benefits and advantages linked to marriage are still very strong in Germany under both tax and social security law. Access to marriage is still barred for same-sex couples, and the institution of registered partnership is interpreted as not the same as marriage by the Federal Constitutional Court.

Are these developments interpretable in terms of an individualization hypothesis? In social science (and also policy analysis), the process of individualization is understood as the continuing separation of an individual from traditional and familial dependencies, whereby the links to status groups or communities lose importance for determining one's decisions, status and life chances. Individuals' circumstances are determined not by the norms of a certain status group or parental decision-making but rather by choices on the part of the autonomous individual; personal dependencies are replaced by abstract dependencies (on the market, the state, institutions, and so forth). Taking this definition as the starting point, to what extent is there a process of individualization underway in Germany and the UK? It seems to us that social policy could be said to be correcting for the pure individualization of market forces (which pay no heed to family situation or care obligations). In a way, this is what social policy always has done – but following the decline of the 'male breadwinner model' and the ban on discrimination against children born out of wedlock, it does so on different terms. Changing social policy intervention happens mainly through four means: changing models of parenting in family law and social law, recognition of some care-related rights[4], the claim that employment and family should be compatible, and the expansion of care and educational services outside the family.

Under the male breadwinner/homemaker-model, the different spheres of employment and the family were linked in both a hierarchical and gendered fashion. The relations were hierarchical in a number of respects: women were subordinated given the husband's rights of authority; children were subordinated under paternal power and the husband's authority; non-married mothers and 'illegitimate' children were discriminated against. Within this asymmetrical and hierarchical construction, marriage as an institution was a central link – social policy provided social security benefits for the dependants of an employed married man, and exclusion of (married) women from certain labour market areas was legitimized with the argument that they were already provided for through marriage. As a consequence, unwed mothers and their children were the main losers, since social policy was very reluctant to provide them with social security benefits or claims under family law.

The weakening of marriage as a social and legal institution through divorce law fuelled the individualization process for women, although not in a unilateral direction. This together with the ban on discrimination against children born out of wedlock strengthened the dissociation of marriage and parenthood. Substituting for marriage as the coordinating institution, parenthood is increasingly the institutional link for social policies which seek to temper individualization processes. This change from marriage to parenthood as the state's preferred vehicle of support and control involves a challenge to both the gendered and hierarchicalized order. However, since roles are gender-neutral in family law and decision-making about the division of labour is left to individuals, coordination processes are more complicated than in the former

4 Cf. Daly (2001) for a comprehensive overview of care provision in Europe.

hierarchical order. Coordination of different spheres and of numerous policy objectives is a challenge for social policy-making also, and often gender issues are subordinated – women disappear within the family, and compatibility of employment and care is designed as a female programme. This resituates hierarchies in a formally gender-neutral fashion.

Conclusions about the direction in which policy is moving need to be qualified in other ways as well. Developments in different policy areas and legal subsystems are not uniform, either within or across the two countries. More than this, there are a number of contradictory trends. These result partly from gaps in coordination between social policies across different spheres along the axes of gender, family and generations (which raises the question of what could be the 'missing links' and how these should be conceptualized). One could call these policy inefficiencies. But they are also due to ambivalence on the part of the state and to the fact that change occurs on a path dependent course, in the sense that reform always begins with the existing model of provision.

One contradictory tendency is for the institution of marriage to be strengthened in some countries alongside the tendency to dissociate parenthood and marriage and to shift the basis of claims towards parenthood). There are a number of moves in this direction. For one, inheritance claims of a surviving spouse have been upgraded vis-à-vis children's claims, even in England with its individualistic inheritance law tradition (Willekens 2006). Marriage, then, continues to have the function of providing some security and resources, independent of whether the spouse spent time caring for children or not. The introduction of the sharing of pension-credits on divorce in England in 1996 (in Germany in 1977) is another example of a policy that tries to ensure that marriage continues to assume some social security functions even if it has broken down. Survivor pensions are in both countries still based on marriage; in fact Sweden is the only country where they have been decoupled from marriage; they have been substituted by an individualized means-tested pension. This is not an artefact of the past: new claims based on marriage have been introduced in the FRG, such as cost-free co-insurance of a spouse with low earnings under the *Pflegeversicherung* 1996 (the long-term care insurance). This was introduced despite the argument that cost-free insurance should be decoupled from marital status and be linked to other criteria. Germany remains distinctive for the continuing importance attributed to marriage as a status in granting access to various advantages under social security and tax law, and in drawing a strict separating line between heterosexual marriage and same-sex registered partnership. Overall, for both countries some of the marriage-related features of the 'male breadwinner model' remain in place.

There are, secondly, limits to the tendency to push mothers into employment, which was identified as another common cross-national trend. While the shift is more pronounced in the UK, where from 2010 lone mothers are expected to take up employment once their children reach the age of seven (reduced from 16 years in the New Labour reform process), policy in Germany differentiates more strongly between different groups of women. Employment is 'normalized' as an option mainly for divorced mothers or mothers cohabiting with an unemployed person who is in receipt of benefits. Policy does not prioritize the employment of married mothers to the same extent as it does for mothers in these two other situations. Certainly, there are no direct measures (in the sense of social policy or tax provisions) that incentivise employment entry on the part of married mothers. There is also another underlying factor – failed coordination in Germany (indeed in both countries but in the UK to a lesser extent): the lack of adequate reinsertion and retraining programmes for 'returners to the job' (who are mainly female). These programmes were cut off in 2003 in Germany. Further implicit contradictions reside in the inadequacy of childcare facilities and unsuitable working hours despite the claim that employment and care should be compatible. In the UK, it is probably less a case of contradiction as differentiation by social class. There, one of the main strategies for female employment is the promotion of market-based private childcare services which increases differences in quality and creates differentiations on the basis of income level. Pushing mothers into the labour market without changing the male-biased paradigm of full-time continuous employment will increase differences based on gender as well as stratification among employed women on the basis of socio-economic class. While the increase of maternal employment is seen as a central instrument to reduce child poverty, especially of lone-parent families, pension reforms and the emphasis on private supplementary pension schemes may well increase gender-based income inequalities in old age. The compatibility approach remains contradictory without accompanying social security reforms that guarantee adequate coverage to employees with care obligations.

A third notable contradictory development in the present context is the trend to extend carers' rights. This is not necessarily contradictory – it can be complementary. But it is contradictory if employed carers get little or nothing out of it as was the case when survivors' pensions were reformed in Germany in 2001. Following this reform, a non-employed parent of two children up to the age of 10 years gains up to a third of average pension credits, while personal insurance-based pension credits of an employed parent reduce this benefit possibly to zero. We see a zigzag between incentivising employed parenthood and endorsing a mother-at-home model.

One can also see contradictions in emphasizing the role of fathers as carer and provider of child support and the sharing of both employment and care among parenting couples. The German reform of leave benefits undertaken in 2007 places at a disadvantage contemporaneous part-time work of both parents through cutting the benefit length from 14 to 7 months. This is a disincentive to equal sharing of parental responsibilities and employment.

The existence of such contradictions leads us to conclude that no fully-coordinated move towards a change of paradigm has taken place either in the UK or Germany.

4 Overview

In both Germany and the UK the incentive framework that affects choices is shifting, but not in a unilateral direction. It is certainly the case that women are getting mixed messages. There is fragmentation and incoherence between different social policy areas (employment, social security, family policy, gender and generation) and subsystems of law. That said, there is a collective project underway and while gender is a part of it so too are other family-related considerations (such as, generational relations and family functioning more broadly).

The following are some preliminary conclusions about the changes underway in social policy and family law at the present time in Germany and the UK:

- There is a gender fault line in reforms, but this is not always the primary intention. That is, gender-relevant changes tend to occur not as a direct target but more in the search of other changes (such as self sufficiency, activation, redistribution of parenting responsibilities and tasks and so forth).
- While formal equality and gender neutrality are upheld as guiding

principles of social policies, which support a trend towards individualization and treating all adults as potentially self sufficient participants in the labour market, at the same time social policy measures contain contradictions and ambivalences.

In terms of the implications for future research, we can identify many insights. In the first instance, one has to look at the fine print – the details of policy and law matter greatly. Secondly, one has to actively look across policy domains. Research needs to make connections and take a broad starting point because if the focus is only on one domain the conclusions will be very different than if one focuses on several domains. The point must also be made that at the present time one cannot really talk about gender without talking about family. While this was always an implicit understanding of gender-oriented work, it cannot be forgotten today when we have a situation where instead of family being manipulated for gender purposes it is now the case that gender is being manipulated for family purposes.

Bibliography

Bahle, Thomas (2009): "Public Child Care in Europe: Historical Trajectories and New Directions." In: Scheiwe, Kirsten/ Willekens, Harry (eds.): *Child Care and Preschool Development in Europe – Institutional Perspectives.* London: Palgrave Macmillan, 23-42

Bettio, Francesca/ Plantenga, Janneke (2004): "Comparing Care Regimes in Europe." In: *Feminist Economics* 10 (1), 85-113

Daly, Mary (2001): "Care policies in Western Europe." In: Daly, Mary (ed.): *Care Work – the Quest for Security*. Geneva: ILO, 33-55

Daly, Mary/ Rake, Katherine (2003): *Gender and the Welfare State: Care, Work and Welfare in Europe and the USA*. Cambridge: Policy Press

Del Boca, Danièla/ Wetzels, Cécile (eds.) (2007): *Social Policies, Labour Markets and Motherhood: A Comparative Analysis of European Countries*. Cambridge: Cambridge University Press

Gornick, Janet C./ Meyers, Marcia K. (2003): *Families that Work: Policies for Reconciling Parenthood and Employment.* New York: Russell Sage Foundation

HM Department for Education and Skills (2006): *Care Matters: Trans-*

forming the Lives of Children and Young People in Care. London: Department for Education and Skills

HM Treasury (2007): *Aiming High for Children: Supporting Families*. London: HM Treasury

Leitner, Sigrid (2003): "Varieties of Familism." In: *European Societies* 5 (4), 353-375

Leitner, Sigrid/ Ostner, Ilona/ Schmitt, Christoph (2008): "Family Policies in Germany." In: Ostner, Ilona/ Schmitt, Christoph (eds.): *Family Policies in the Context of Family Change*. Wiesbaden: VS Verlag für Sozialwissenschaften, 175-202

Lewis, Jane (1992): "Gender and the Development of Welfare Regimes." In: *Journal of European Social Policy* 2 (3), 159-173

Lewis, Jane (2001): "The Decline of the Male Breadwinner Model: Implications for Work and Care." In: *Social Politics* 8 (2), 152-169

Lewis, Jane/ Campbell, Mary (2007): "Work/Family Balance Policies in the UK since 1997." In: *Journal of Social Policy* 36 (3), 365-381

Orloff, Ann Shola (1993): "Gender and the Social Rights of Citizenship: The Comparative Analysis of Gender Relations and Welfare States." In: *American Sociological Review* 58 (3), 303-328

Orloff, Ann Shola (2005): *Farewell to Maternalism? State Policies and Mothers' Employment*. Chicago: Northwestern University Working Paper Series, WP-05-10

Penn, Helen (2009): "Public and Private: The History of Early Education and Care Institutions in the UK." In: Scheiwe, Kirsten/ Willekens, Harry (eds.): *Child Care and Preschool Development in Europe – Institutional Perspectives*. London: Palgrave Macmillan, 105-125

Scheiwe, Kirsten (ed.) (2007): *Soziale Sicherungsmodelle revisited – Existenzsicherung durch Sozial und Familienrecht und ihre Geschlechterdimensionen*. Baden-Baden: Nomos

Willekens, Harry (2006): "The Puzzle of Inheritance Law's Resistance to Social Change." In: Swennen, Frederik/ Barbaix, Renate (eds.): *Liber Amicorum Mieken Coene-Puelinckx*. Mechelen: Kluwer, 493-517

Andrea Petö

Anti-Modernist Political Thoughts on Motherhood in Europe in a Historical Perspective[1]

After 1989, the demographic crises also reached Hungary in the form of the 'Second Demographic Transition'. At present, women generally follow the late fertility model, and in cities more children are born out of wedlock than to married parents. According to data from the Central Statistical Office in 2006, 35.6 percent of newborns, or 35,500 children, were born out of wedlock. The traditional rhetoric of domesticity, however, has received support from two unexpected places. On the one hand, there is the increase in the traditional public rhetoric of women expected to stay at home and have more children, and some aspects of the recent focus of the EU's rhetoric on demographic crises can be used to support this argument of domesticity (Kakucs/Petö 2008). According to the surveys, Hungary is one of the most family centered societies as far as values and attitudes are concerned, and one of the most individualistic ones as far as fertility practices are concerned (Tóth 1997). This change had already begun in the 1980s, in which on the rhetorical level 'family' as cohabitation and as a social unit comes with prestige while the number of marriages decreases and the number of divorces increases. The collapse of the statist feminist regime, which administratively supported the heterosexual nuclear family as a social unit, only accelerated the process. So how can we account for this contradiction: on the one hand there is the constant decrease in the birth rate (in 1989 123,304, in 2003 94,650) while on the other hand the rhetoric is more traditional than ever?

I would like to answer the question of the demographic rhetoric with reference to the normative motherhood of the Virgin Mary (see Petö 2003, 2003a, 2008). I shall use the term rhetoric as *Begriffsgeschichte* following Koselleck's term as "production and mediations of meaning" (cf. Joyce 1987: 6). I will explore how the meaning of 'motherhood' is produced in the present Hungarian political rhetoric and then expand my argument to other countries in EU.

This paper is based on my participant observations and life story inter-

1 This article was supported by European Association of Social Anthropologists.

views with 23 women activists from the conservative and extreme right wing women's movement in Hungary, where the number of women's organizations with a conservative agenda outnumbers the organizations with a feminist agenda from 1990s onwards (cf. for the results of the project Petö 2003, 2006a, 2006b, 2008). (Accession to the EU just sped up this differentiation process inside the women's movement even more.) I would like to connect the rhetoric of the women's movement underlining the common mobilizational roots of the neoconservative and extreme rightist women's movements in Hungary as far as the rhetoric of normative motherhood is concerned.

I would like to argue in this paper that the increasing right wing radicalism and anti-EU sentiments use the rhetoric of Virgin Mary forms of protest, agency and critique the heritage of the communist emancipatory project. I argue that those anti-modernist political movements in Hungary and other parts of Europe use the rhetoric of normative motherhood in order to create a space for critiquing policy measures applied by the EU. To understand this political move, it is important to know that previously, similar to this policy, measures such as work-life balance were used by the failed leftist emancipation project to create a space for the political mobilization of women (Petö 2006a, 2006b).

The phenomenon of increasing right wing populism requires special scholarly attention in Eastern Europe for at least two reasons. First, the extreme right wing radicalism and the existence of oppressed conservatism existed as subcultures: oppressed by the dominant communist political system. Second, major changes happened in the gender relations during communism which were integrated in, appropriated by the programme, rhetoric of the victorious neoconservative politics after 1989 leaving the emancipatory leftist politics in a defensive position (cf. Held 1996; Ramet 1999; Mudde 2000; Petö 2003).

The academic literature is rich on transition from communism to liberal market economy and also on the rise of anti-modernist thoughts, and I would like to build on one line of this literature (see Held 1996; Ramet 1999). This literature argues defining Eastern European 'difference' from a path dependency position. Dividing it from the standpoint of 'Old Europe' points out the changing family structures and demographic characteristics of countries with statist feminist heritage. Using the difference as a descriptive and not as an analytical category diminishes the heuristic potential of this position. Gender studies scholars and experts were quick in explaining the political apathy towards liberal feminism and the revival of traditional gender values with inherent conservatism and traditionalism of Eastern Europe using the Cold War area studies language. This argument during the enlargement process contributed to the marking process of 'New Europe' as 'the other' painfully resembling some of the characteristics of the colonial discourse inside Europe (Funk 2004).

What are the consequences of this scholarly approach? This approach first prevented the critical assessment of the statist feminist period, the period of state socialism in Soviet occupied Eastern Europe, the failed leftist experiment from assessing its results and advantages. Second, it also doomed the EU policy measures in 'New Europe'. The EU policy follows the same directions and uses the same policy tools as the statist feminist period, the failed leftist emancipatory project with promoting increase in women's employment as a measure and precondition of emancipation and progress. This discrepancy is making room for anti-European sentiments.

Rhetoric and women's movements: normative motherhood and agency

The rhetoric of the emancipatory women's movement: "New Woman" discourse was labeled by Rita Felski in her work *The Gender of Modernity* as "prisoners of progress" (Felski 1995: 11-33). In the rhetoric of the women's movement, women represent the new beginning, imagining future in a linear development as a normative project. The historical meta-narrative about women's past is hierarchical and exclusive while it aims to forge counter-identity. The discourse of the emancipatory women's movement is a strategic discourse which is emotionally charged. Its language creates collective subjectivity with shared rituals, symbols of meanings and stories. The post-1989 women's movement, born on the ruins of the failed leftist emancipation project in Eastern Europe, reached back to the symbols, rituals and stories of the pre-1945 period. This led to the emergence of research on the Feminist Association and Rosika Schwimmer as forerunners of women's emancipation as a way of establishing political legitimacy (Petö 2007). The present day right wing women's organizations are reaching back for symbols, for legitimization and for discourse to the central figure of the politics of motherhood, to the Virgin Mary, so there is an order to fill the historical continuity gap in political ideology caused by 50 years of communism. I argue together with Roger Griffin, who pointed out "fascism itself can be seen as a political variant of modernism" (Griffin 2007: 6). So the anti-modernist emancipation is a necessary consequence and parallel rival to the modernist women's movements.

Analyzing the historical continuity, we observe that the cult of the Virgin Mary served to collect the anti-communist forces both in Italy and in Hungary right after World War II. Slovakia, Poland and Croatia can be added to this list. As Blackbourn argued, symbols of the cult of the Virgin Mary "were a rival set of emblems" to the flags, anthems and monuments of the modern nation-state (Blackbourn 2001: 27). The criticism towards existing modern political Catholicism developed parallels with the social democratic movement from the second half of the 19th century. Therefore, in interwar Hungary these two political platforms were also represented in the Hungarian parliament by women. Female MPs signaled that the political parties considered women's issues and women's votes important. The two mobilizational frames constructed two different women's movements: the social democratic, leftist and the Christian movements. Victoria De Grazia underlined in the case of Italy the richness of Catholic civic organizations under fascism, against both liberalism and modernity that ironically underlay the rise of fascism itself (Grazia 1992: 243-244). Also in Hungary during the interwar Horthy regime, political Catholicism and the different women's organizations served as a site of resistance to the emerging fascist Arrow Cross women's mobilizational attempts (Petö 2003). After 1945, the social democrats found the newly emerging Communist Party supported by the Red Army in Hungary, also the revival of political Catholicism. For the opening of the Year of Our Great Lady on 17th August, 1948 the Director of *Actio Catholica*, Zsigmond Mihalovics declared the purpose of the year as "a quest for us for spiritual renewal, intellectual orientation, social forces, and the sources of national life" (Mihalovics 1947: 1). 1948 was declared the year of the Virgin Mary by Cardinal Mindszenty, head of the Catholic church in Hungary, which

> "aimed at deepening the traditional cult of Mary and strengthening the religious consciousness […] not a question which is directly related to politics was mentioned on these days of Mary" (Mindszenty 1982: 176).

The same political and rhetorical fight happened in Italy around the cult of the Virgin Mary after World War II (Ventresca 2003).

The re-emerging cult of the Virgin Mary in Hungary in the post-1989 context also served as an alternative political 'set of emblems'. The same type of *Kulturkampf* has started. I would like to illustrate this rivaling set of emblems with the political rhetoric.

The emerging cult of the Virgin Mary as a set of emblems and a political rhetoric is also interesting in the framework of resisting communism.

During communism, the stereotypical women's characteristics as intimacy, sensitivity, family centeredness were labeled as a resistance to 'state-ist feminism', because these characteristics were relativised by the 'state feminism'. The private resistance to communism was based on restoring the so-called 'female virtues' in the family, based on the cult of the Virgin Mary, which aims to preserve family values in private life against the pseudo-equality of state socialism (Petö 2003; Petö/Szapor 2004). The experiment of the social democrats to support autonomous women's political existence failed. The wives of communist functionaries were not visible, playing the part of the wife supporting the husband, so they were not able to construct alternative role models. Therefore, the untouched patriarchal framework with the normative cult of motherhood survived communist intervention into the family policy and reemerged as a victorious interpretative frame after 1989. The state-ist feminist failed to produce an alternative civic set of emblems. The previously dominant Christian iconographical patterns about women remained unchanged despite the efforts of the promoting female labourer as an independent individual. By the end of the 1990s, it also became clear that the "masculinization of Eastern Europe" (Watson 1993) did not bring the revival of feminism, nor women's movements with a feminist agenda in Eastern Europe. The number of conservative and/or religious women's organizations in former Eastern European countries outnumbers organizations with explicit feminist agendas. Therefore, the analysis of why these movements are popular is a political and academic imperative today.

The Hungarian version of the Virgin Mary, the 'Woman Dressed in Sun' as a site of resistance

I used different qualitative research methods as life story interviews, discourse analyses to explore the historical roots of extreme right wing mobilization in Hungary who explicitly support the idea of normative motherhood. First, I analyzed the publications and the striking theme of the Virgin Mary. Among the authors of books on these topics we find disproportionately more women. In 2000 I also used the participant observation method and attended several public lectures on the Far Eastern origins (Aryan, Sumer) of Hungarians analyzing the social composition of those who are very active in lectures. I also participated in events organized by the numerous right wing civil organizations aiming to recover the historical 'Truth' about the origins of the Hungarian tribes conquering the Carpathian basin in the 9th century A.C. In the case of this gender ideology, the facts related to the Far Eastern origins of the Hungarians are not as important as the belief in their interpretation of selected historical facts. They reject the Finno-Ugric origin of the Hungarians and advocate that the imagined oriental homeland of Hungarians was not in the Ural Mountain but in Persia. The legitimacy of this discourse refers to the sins committed by the communist politicians of science who did not support research on this field, which is according to them, the cause of the present ignorance. The language of Far Eastern origins of the Hungarians is a minority discourse; it was developed against the majority oppression and offers points of identification for the participants. A typical argument says: "The Sumer language is the ancestor of the Hungarian, those who are dealing with this issue without a prejudice will not question this." (Bobula 2000: 177)

The research direction of the origins of the Hungarians was decided in an unprecedented way in the history of science with a decree of Minister of Education Ágost Trefort in 1877 when he proposed to subsidize only research which would point towards the Finno-Ugric origin. After 1945, Hungary was under Soviet occupation so again that gave a special political push to prove uncritically the Finno-Ugric relationship. The anti-communist Hungarian emigration mostly in Canada, Australia and South America financed research proving the Aryan and Far Eastern roots of the Hungarians opposing internationalism. Hungarian immigrants who left Hungary in 1945 or in 1956 living in Latin America, Canada and Australia played an important role in shaping the political rhetoric.

The results of the participant observation I conducted also show an astonishing overrepresentation of women in events covering historical, linguistic and artistic aspects of the Far Eastern origins of the Hungarians. I formulated the question: why so many women got mobilized to listen to quasi-academic counter-discourse about the imagined and occult origins of the Hungarian tribes while the gender rhetoric of these talks supported the traditional hierarchical gender regimes: women should stay in the domestic sphere and produce children.

This paradox of how a woman might be active in public when the public expectation is that she has to stay passive was solved with the post-1990 revival of the cult of the Virgin Mary as a cult of maternity. This normative cult of motherhood aims not only to strengthen 'the nation' but also regulates the order in the relationship between the two sexes. It has a potential of regulating extreme forms of masculinities (e.g. violence against women) which might be considered as a possible form of agency for women. I would like to narrow further my topic to focus only on the question of whether women's agency can be found in discourses of right wing extremism as an explanation for their political mobilization.

In order to explain why the figure of the Virgin Mary is crucial both for the Hungarian political discourse and for the understanding of the different levels of women's political agency, I need to focus on the normative cult of motherhood. Motherhood is a social construct (Taylor 1996: 195) which is legitimized in three public discourses: religious (role of Mary as mother of Christ as a normative pattern for women's activity in the public sphere), military (identifying the body of the nation with the body of women) and quasi-scientific (women are the weaker sex who are the only ones to bear children) discourses. In the following, to explain why the cult of the Virgin Mary unites all right wing political forces in Hungary, I mention three discursive methods to analyze the cult of Mary in the religious discourse: the analyses of the female psyche, the feminist theology and the patchwork cult of the Virgin Mary. I use the definition of Clifford Geertz for religion as a cultural system:

> "Religious symbols formulate a basic congruence between a particular style of life and a specific (if most often implicit) metaphysical, and in so doing sustain each with the borrowed authority of the other." (Geertz 1993: 90)

From this point of view it is crucial to understand women's experience in the religious discourse and practice around the cult of the Virgin Mary in the Hungarian context. After 1998, conservative women were experimenting with the construction of a new non-party framework. Following the example of the influential pre-1945 women's institution, they formed an umbrella organization, the Alliance of Hungarian Women at the Turn of the Century (MAESZ), which aimed to unite all conservative women's NGOs. A new political party was also formed for women, the Party of Hungarian Women, which labeled the preexisting political party framework inappropriate to represent the interest of national-conservative women. The changing structural framework of Hungarian right wing women active in politics can also be traced in the different religious and spiritual movements such as the Hungarian catholic renewal movements, e.g. *Regnum Marianum.* These movements not only oppose globalization in their programme but they also fight for the revival of the Hungarian female saints of the Arpad dynasty. The renewal of the cult of the Great Lady of the Hungarians, which is not the Virgin Mary, also contributes to the spiritual revival bonding together the Catholics and the Protestants because it offers a social space for women to harmonize maternal and political duties in an approved patriarchal framework in the syncretic belief of the Virgin Mary and pagan cult of 'Woman Dressed in Sun'.

As far as the women's politics of the national right wing political parties are concerned, they all put the normative cult of motherhood in the center. In the political language these parties have no 'women's politics' but 'family politics', which covers the social role of women by models offered by the cult of Mary. The liberal-leftist criticism opposing the normative cult of motherhood offers women's individual human rights and the right to choose motherhood. This option includes the right to reject maternity, which in the conservative discourse is regarded as 'national' sabotage. During the newly emerging pro-natalist campaigns, the rhetoric of the "6 million unborn Hungarians" during the fifty years of communist rule in Hungary became a permanent part of the campaigns (Petö 2002) when reproductive practices were different. Reproductive rights in Hungary were regulated following the intervention of the Constitutional Court, which stirred public debates. The reproductive rights were regulated by a decree which was labeled as unconstitutional by the Constitutional Court in 1991. The public debates concluded in the legislation of reproductive rights in 1992 named as the law of protecting fetal life. The law neither satisfied the feminists, who considered it a violation of women's human rights to have the fetus in the centre of the legislation and not the mother, nor Christian and extreme right wing groups, who still considered the law too permissive and consequently anti-patriotic. In 1998 the Constitutional Court set a deadline of June 30, 2000 to the Parliament to define 'serious crises' which in the text of the law opened up the possibility for the pregnant woman to decide. While leftist liberal parties advocated protecting the human rights of the mother, the conservative right wing political forces demanded more state intervention in diminishing the 'serious crises' (Petö 2003: especially 187-199). During the newly emerging pro-natalist campaigns the rhetoric about the "6 million unborn Hungarians" during the fifty years of communist rule in Hungary became a permanent part of the campaigns when reproductive practices were different (Petö 2002).

Conclusions

The Hungarian right wing women's politics is characterized by the quest for spirituality after 50 years of official atheism and with a strong involvement of historical churches. The appropriation of the different layers of the cult of the Virgin Mary is a reaction to the profound social, economic and cultural changes of the transition, which opened up room for agency for ordinary people and church hierarchy. It is also a response to the collapse of communism, and a criticism towards neoliberal globalization returning to the pre-modern set of values and practices. The complex patchwork cult of the Virgin Mary offers a position of agency and victorious victim-hood of communism at the same time without the pressing moral need of examining different forms of collaboration with communism in the past fifty years. The success can be explained by the openness and flexibility of the political rhetorical frame of the Virgin Mary that it offers space for sometimes competing aspirations.

Victoria de Grazia used the term 'post political citizenship' to analyze fascist Italy, where she stated that the identity politics served as a strategy for resistance and agency (Grazia 2000: 356). In contemporary Europe it is key to question how women's identities were formed and what contents are placed there.

The question for Hungary is how the conservative (meaning non-leftist) women's unity will be implemented, where the different sometimes-contradictory right wing discourses are represented by different political parties. The symbol of the Great Lady of Hungarians offers a possible site for uniting the different elements as Catholic, Protestant, ancient Hungarian, Sumer and Indian, which could also serve as a site for questioning patriarchy from an essentialist position still having critical potential. The patchwork character of the cult of the Virgin Mary cannot resist the revolutionary reconceptualisation based on occultism. This new occult redefinition could be questioned only with order and hierarchy arguments, which means that this will diminish the potential agency of conservative women in Hungary in the near future while it forces women to accept hierarchical arguments. As Judith Butler said:

> "One thinks one is opposing Fascism, only to find that the identificatory source of one's own opposition is Fascism itself, and that Fascism depends essentially on the kind of resistance one offers." (Butler 2000: 173)

It will be very difficult to conceptualize the forms of resistance to the normative definitions of motherhood if the EU discourse on motherhood does not move away from the rhetorical and political trap described in this article.

Bibliography

Blackbourn, David (2001): *Marpingen: Apparitions of the Virgin Mary in a Nineteenth-Century German Village*. New York: Vintage Books

Bobula, Ida (2000): *A magyar nép eredete*. (Origins of Hungarian Nation) n. p.: Anahita-Ninti

Butler, Judith (2000): "Competing Universalities." In Butler, Judith/ Laclau, Ernesto/ Žižek, Slavoj (eds.): *Contingency, Hegemony, Universality. Contemporary Dialogues on the Left*. London: Verso, 136-181

Felski, Rita (1995): *The Gender of Modernity*. Cambridge/ Mass.: Harvard University Press

Funk, Nanette (2004): "Feminist Critique of Liberalism: Can They Travel East: Their Relevance in Eastern and Central Europe and the Former Soviet Union." In: *Signs* 29 (3), 695-724

Geertz, Clifford (1993 [1973]): "Religion as a Cultural System." In: Geertz, Clifford: *The Interpretation of Cultures. Selected Essays*. London: Fontana, 87-126

Grazia, Victoria de (1992): *How Fascism Ruled Women: Italy, 1922-1945*. Berkeley, Los Angeles: University of California Press

Grazia, Victoria de (2000): "Nationalising Women: The Competition between Fascist and Commercial Cultural Models in Mussolini's Italy." In: Furlough, Ellen/ Grazia, Victoria de (eds.): *The Sex of Things. Gender and Consumption in Historical Perspective*. Berkeley, Los Angeles, London: University of California Press, 337-359

Griffin, Robert (2007): *Modernism and Fascism*. London: Palgrave

Held, Joseph (ed.) (1996): *Populism in Eastern Europe. Racism, Nationalism, and Society.* Boulder: East European Monographs

Joyce, Patrick (1987): "The Historical Meanings of Work: an Introduction." In Patrick, Joyce (ed.): *The Historical Meanings of Work.* Cambridge, Cambridge University Press, 31-64

Kakucs, Noemi/ Petö, Andrea (2008): "The Impact of EU Accession on Gender Equality in Hungary." In: Roth, Silke (ed.): *Gender and Politics in the Expanding European Union. Mobilization, Inclusion, Exclusion.* New York, Oxford: Berghahn Books, 174-193

Mihalovics, Vid (1947): "A fölfelé vezető úton (On the Road Leading Up)." In: *Új Ember* 17 (August), 1

Mindszenty, József (1982): *Hirdetem az Igét* (Spreading the Word). Budapest: Mindszenty Alapítvány

Mudde, Cas (2000): *The Ideology of the Extreme Right.* Manchester: Manchester University Press

Petö, Andrea (2002): "Women's Rights in Stalinist Hungary: The Anti-Abortion in Campaign of 1952." In: *Hungarian Studies Review* 29 (1B2), 49-77

Petö, Andrea (2003): *Napasszonyok és Holdkisasszonyok. A mai magyar konzervatív női politizálás alaktana* (Women of Sun and Girls of Moon. Morphology of Contemporary Hungarian Conservative Women Doing Politics). Budapest: Balassi

Petö, Andrea (2006a): "Im-possibilities of turnovers, the moment of entering into politics by Hungarian Conservative Women in 1989." In: Profantova, Zuzana (ed.): *The Small Histories of Great Events in Czechoslovakia after 1948, 1968 and 1989.* Bratislava: Veda Publishing House of the Slovak Academy of Sciences, 142-155

Petö, Andrea (2006b): "Redefinitions of 'Statist Feminism' and Contemporary Conservative and Extreme Rightist Hungarian Female Politicians. The Case of the Hungarian 1956 Revolution." In: Sauer, Edith/ Lanzinger, Margareth/ Frysak, Elisabeth (eds.): *Women's Movements. Networks and Debates in Post Communist Countries in the 19th and 20th Centuries.* Köln, Weimar, Wien: Böhlau, 317-337

Petö, Andrea (2007): "An Untold Story about the Feminist Association." In: Gazsi, Judit/ Petö, Andrea/ Toronyi, Zsuzsanna (eds.): *Gender, Memory, and Judaism.* Budapest: Balassi Kiadó/ Herne: Gabriele Schaefer Verlag, Studien zur Geschichte Ost- und Ostmitteleuropas, Bd. 6, 107-121

Petö, Andrea (2008): "Die Marien in der Sonne. (Die Apokalyptischen Madonnen)." In: Laakso, Johanna (ed.): *Woman and Nation: Contributions to Questions of Gender, Nation, and Ethnicity. Frau und Nation: Beiträge zu Fragen von Gender, Nation und Ethnizität.* Finno-Ugrian Studies in Austria 5. Wien: Lit, 138-174

Petö, Andrea/ Szapor, Judith (2004): "Women and the Alternative Public Sphere: toward a Redefinition of Women's Activism and the Separate Spheres in East Central Europe." In: *NORA. Nordic Journal of Women's Studies* 12 (3), 172-182

Ramet, Sabrina P. (ed.) (1999): *The Radical Right in Central and Eastern Europe since 1989*, Philadelphia: The Pennsylvania University Press

Taylor, Diana (1996): "Making a Spectacle: Mothers of the Plaza de Mayo." In: Jetter, Alexis/ Orleck, Annelise/ Taylor, Diana (eds.): *The Politics of Motherhood: Activist Voices from Left to Right.* Hannover, London: Dartmouth College, 182-196

Tóth, Olga (1997): "Családformák és együttélési minták a mai magyar társadalomban." (Family and cohabitation patterns in contemporary Hungary). In: Lévai, Katalin/ Tóth, Olga/ György, István (eds.): *Szerepváltozások.* Budapest: TÁRKI-MüM, 73-85

Ventresca, Robert (2003): "The Virgin and the Bear: Religion, Society and the Cold War in Italy." In: *Journal of Social History* 37 (2), 439-456

Watson, Peggy (1993): "The Rise of Masculinism in Eastern Europe." In: *New Left Review* 198 (3-4), 71-82

Waltraud Ernst

Towards a Global Gender Democracy? Rethinking Citizenship in the Context of the Globalization of Gender Relations[1]

> "Freedom, autonomy and the right to be different – central credos of democratic citizenship – are pitched against regulating forces of modernity and the state and subverted by discourses of 'culture and tradition' – of nationalism, religiosity and the family." (Yuval-Davis/Werbner 1999: 1)

This chapter focuses on a specific aspect of the current discourse on the interconnection of demographic change, restructuring of the welfare state and gender relations in Europe[2]: on the globalization of gender relations[3] and the meaning of citizenship. Driven by the promise of efficiency, European welfare states are restructuring their government policies. These changes concern many aspects of life and have significant effects on social rights, especially re-

---

1 For comments on an earlier version thanks to Heike Kahlert, Sabrina Dittus, and Sandra Schiller.

2 Here, 'Europe' refers to a geographic construction with varying borders throughout history; it also refers to a normative construction of citizenship, as will be discussed later in the text; moreover, and relatedly, 'Europe' functions here as a marker to bring universal theoretical aspirations down to their regional and temporal situatedness. European Union (EU), by contrast, refers to a clearly defined set of countries, although the number is also subject to historic change and the countries involved are not equal to the countries involved in the contract regarding the border policies of the 'Schengen area'. Since for the different questions discussed in this paper different aspects of 'Europe' are relevant, I will employ these different terms and meanings, according to the issues discussed below. Although some aspects discussed here might be neither restricted to 'Europe' nor unique to its borders, it is for the sake of the argument (to point out some contradictions) that I focus here on this part of the world.

3 Whereas Connell (2002) means with the notion of "the globalization of gender relations" the general widening of the feminist research perspective from a rather local or national one to a more global scale, I focus here on the global interdependence and interaction of gender relations with its resulting problems and chances. He also uses "gender democracy" synonymously for gender equity, whereas I explore here problems and chances of citizenship as a democratic institution in the context of global interrelations of gender.

garding the cutback in public care services. At the same time, gender relations are changing in the sense that women, traditionally the main care providers for their relatives, now play an ever greater part in the labour market.[4] In this context, the question regarding who will care for children and the elderly becomes increasingly important, since within the debate on demographic change in Europe the prognosis of an ageing population is addressed as a serious political problem.[5] It is important to look at migration in this context because to a great extent female migrants from all over the world working as care providers under precarious conditions fill the gap left by these developments discussed so eagerly. I argue that these migrants seem to embody the globalization of gender relations, which appears as a consequence of the developments mentioned above. By contrast, they are, similar to care providers in earlier times, barely mentioned in these debates, rarely have access to social benefits and are seldom granted the rights of full citizens. Furthermore, I argue that these 'cosmobile'[6] care providers challenge traditional concepts of citizenship on an epistemic, normative and empirical level in far reaching ways.

Citizenship has been a contested element in debates of political philosophy and in struggles against oppression in Europe. From the very beginning of these debates and struggles, two questions have always existed: "Who should be granted citizenship?" and "What rights and duties come with citizenship?" Since the eighteenth century, nation-states with formally independent governments were constructed as the main political powers. Thus, it has been a crucial question to determine which people living on a nation-state's territory are understood and registered as its citizens with clearly defined formal rights and duties (Küster 2007).[7] It was during the French Revolution of 1789 when the demand for equal rights for everyone by vast numbers of women and men of all social backgrounds could no longer be ignored (Blättler 1995). However, instead of these rights being granted, this demand provoked a problematic dis-

4 Cf., for example, the chapters by Gabriele Michalitsch and Nina Berven in this book.

5 The chapters by Ute Karl and Jutta Hartmann in this book discuss a current change in the meaning of ageing from a problem of care to an economic resource for the society, which contains the danger of tabuing the fact that elderly people often lack the health conditions for 'active ageing'.

6 I borrow this term from Maria Rerrich's book title (cf. Rerrich 2006).

7 Küster argues that it was the struggle of the authorities with the migration of the poor in the context of the disintegration of the feudal estate system in Europe which gave the initiative for the codification of citizenship at the beginning of the nineteenth century (Küster 2007: 197-199).

course on sameness as the precondition for equal rights, which has remained vivid until today, even in feminist debates (Nagl-Docekal 2004).[8] As I will try to show in what follows, it is this normative dimension of homogeneity which is still problematic in striving for a pluralistic understanding of European citizens and for the struggle towards a global gender democracy in times of manifold migration processes.

During the nineteenth century and the first half of the twentieth century, Europeans migrated in large numbers to other parts of the world. By contrast, since the second half of the twentieth century, a significant number of people have migrated into Europe. This migration has been encouraged, organized, regulated and hindered since then in highly ambivalent and even contradictory ways by national and European policies (Metz-Göckel et al. 2008; Transnational Newsletter 2008).[9] In the context of globalization and a multitude of migration processes, the very idea of citizenship has been contested as patriarchal and nationalist, as will be discussed in the first part of this chapter. Especially within feminist and post-colonial discourse, it has been argued that in addition to formal rights and responsibilities, belonging and participation are also key elements of democratic citizenship (Mouffe 1993; Sevenhuijsen 1998; Yuval-Davis/Werbner 1999).[10] It has been argued that gender norms and welfare policies as well as gendered segregation of the labour market and gendered division of labour, for example, produce privileges and disadvantages when it comes to the real practise of citizenship. The question of belonging has thus been discussed less in the context of belonging to a homogeneously imagined (national or transnational) community but more in the context of whose issues are taken as relevant (by whom) to belong to a public agenda.

8 Nagl-Docekal argues that it is neither important nor necessary to be a woman or to identify with women in order to struggle for feminist goals like equal rights and opportunities for all genders, since this demand constitutes the basis of modern democracy (Nagl-Docekal 2004: 154).

9 Cf. especially Claudia Finotelli's discussion of Italian and German migration policies between restrictive purposes and structural demand (Finotelli 2008); cf. also Krystyna Slany's and Magdalena Slusarczyk's discussion of the Polish immigration policy and (almost lacking) immigrant integration policy (Slany/Slusarczyk 2008); cf. also the discussion of 'urgent measures concerning public security' enacted by the Italian parliament in July 2008 in the Transnational Newsletter 2008.

10 Mouffe argues that a democratic concept of citizenship needs to connect the ideal of rights and pluralism with ideas of the public as a lived space and ethical-political issues (Mouffe 1993: 73).

In this way, I would like to relate the discourse on citizenship to questions of the globalization of gender relations. Gender relations have changed in the following way, whether as a result of the feminist movement – where the financial independence of women has been promoted as the basis for female autonomy[11] – or as a result of economic or demographic developments. Even in western European welfare states, women increasingly participate in the economic work force while care work is not distributed more equally in a significant way between the genders (Ernst 2005). In this context, there is a growing female migration from non-European countries as well as Central and Eastern European countries to work in private households, as care workers and for erotic services in the sex industry in all parts of the EU. The legal status of these migrants is often 'undocumented,' which means that they are illegalized (Lutz 2006; Rerrich 2006). At the same time, there is a growing demand for the migration of mostly male specialists of some professions into some European countries, for example technological engineers into Germany. They are offered a special political status and social benefits. I will discuss the following questions: In what way does the globalization of gender relations challenge current nationally defined concepts of citizenship? Who is welcome under which conditions and why? How could we rethink citizenship in the context of the globalization of gender relations? Can the developments mentioned above and described in more detail in the other chapters of this book, framed as demographic change, restructuring of the welfare state and gender relations, be understood as a cause or catalyst for the globalization of gender relations? Are these processes undermining or strengthening the quest for universal human rights? Can these global interconnections of gender relations lead to a global gender democracy?

In the following, I will analyze the normative implications of the idea of citizenship and relate them to the empirical plurality of genders and cultures in Europe. I will argue for an understanding of citizenship that encompasses, but also transcends, the dimension of rights and duties to make room for an understanding of citizenship as a local, national and transnational democratic practise. I will analyze the effect of normative assumptions of citizenship on

11 Although this goal has been contested and was in no way the only one nor has been financial independence discussed as the only means for it, both have been nevertheless prevailing and taken 'seriously' for a neo-liberal strategy in national policies to recruit women for the labour market (Möhle 2005).

the practise of citizenship for formal citizens and for those with a precarious legal status and discuss examples of the struggle for a global gender democracy. In taking the UN declaration for human rights and the idea of citizenship as a democratic practise and political measure, I will argue that striving for a global gender democracy is a promising way to deal with the globalization of gender relations. Feminist networking beyond divisions of power on both theoretical and practical levels seems to be a fruitful path.

Citizenship

In Europe, the idea of citizenship goes back to Aristotle, who conceptualized citizenship as the demarcation of the 'polis' and the household. The polis was the place were free men could gather as citizens for political participation and transcendence of bodily needs, whereas the household was understood as the place where necessary life-sustaining activities were carried out by women and slaves (Spelman 1989). This means that the idea of citizenship in Greek antiquity has been developed in correspondence with a rigid gender and class order. In following the idea of citizenship promoted by Aristotle, citizenship has been conceptualized in European political philosophy until recently as a dimension of life which belongs to the public sphere without considering relations of care or other necessities and dependencies crucial for the citizen to appear as a self-sufficient individual (Tronto 1993). The philosopher Selma Sevenhuijsen describes this view of citizenship as being consistent with neoliberalism today

> "because it corresponds to the mode of regulation which guides the restructuring of many Western welfare states at this historical juncture (...) and fits into the programme of privatization of public services and the growth of market-oriented forms of regulations" (Sevenhuijsen 1998: 130).

Sevenhuijsen criticizes this view because it implies that individuals ought to

> "translate their care needs into market-oriented behaviour, thus conceiving themselves as care consumers, participating in a system of care provisions which works according to the principles of supply and demand" (Sevenhuijsen 1998: 130).

She makes clear that in such a view citizenship is deeply related to economic, social and political independence. Traditionally, this ideal of economic, social and political independence, she continues, functions as a norm of exclusion from social participation in Europe. As we will see, this ideal and its exclusive effects are highly gendered.

In contrast, democratic citizenship, as Sevenhuijsen suggests, tries to avoid this gendered ideal of economic, social and political independence as a precondition for citizenship and brings other ideals into play. Democratic citizenship assumes that people are able to judge between good and bad and can therefore be held accountable for their actions. Citizens, in this account, have to be capable of dealing with the radical alterity of human subjects by recognizing their individuality and diversity while at the same time conceiving of them as equals. In her discussion of the feminist slogan 'the personal is political,' Selma Sevenhuijsen rejects identity as a suitable basis for political action and promotes the idea of active citizenship:

> "Here the public sphere is seen as a meeting ground where people shape identities through action and interaction, through the exchange of narratives and opinion, through deliberation and debate, and where, in so doing, they can continually revise and transcend their images of 'self' and 'other'. Here identity depends more on what you do than what you are. Rather than being fixed, it remains open to change. The public sphere then enables people to act in the sense of 'starting something anew'." (Sevenhuijsen 1998: 14)

In the context of this paper, this means that citizenship is not restricted in its meaning to formal rights and duties. Democratic citizenship is understood here as active citizenship, as a practice. Formal rights and duties would be no more than the potential basis or starting point for the 'real' capacity and experience of being an active citizen. Below I will discuss if it is a necessary basis. But first it is important to investigate further the strategies of inclusion and exclusion in Europe involved in the concept of citizenship and in its practice.

Citizenship has been celebrated as a realization of human rights and the foundation of constitutional democracy in Europe. What does it mean to say that it is constructed in exclusionary ways not only in the past, but also in the present? To understand this, it is necessary to turn the focus from formal rights to real chances for social, economic and political participation and representation. In this way, we can investigate the access to citizenship in Europe and ask how it is regulated along norms of gender, class, ethnicity, sexuality, religion and education. This is the recent result of various analyses from scholars of different disciplines from all over Europe:

> "Citizenship is never only a legal status; its inclusive character depends on many contexts: it has to do with cultural diversity, recognition of difference, access to professions and hierarchies on the labour market, not least in universities with traditions in political as well as visual representation, with institutional practices of openness." (Oleksy et al. 2008: 10)

This means that the inclusive or exclusive quality of citizenship is deeply related to social hierarchies and cultural norms. This result puts into question the hope that equality on the formal level of basic rights has the programmatic power to shape reality. If formal citizens do not all have the same opportunities to experience and to practice their citizenship, we have to look more closely at the relationship between citizenship and social inequalities.

In their collaborative work *Gendering Citizenship in Western Europe. New Challenges for Citizenship Research in a Cross-National Context,* experts from different European countries address this field of study. They investigate how citizenship works in quite ambivalent ways, functioning at the same time as inclusionary promise and as exclusionary practice both for marginalized groups within nation-states and for migrants and asylum seekers moving between them. Moreover, citizenship seems to have simultaneously an emancipatory and disciplinary quality. Policies that require the search for paid work as a condition of social security rights, for example, can have emancipatory effects for some women, whereas for those who prefer to provide full-time care it has rather disciplinary qualities. In a similar way, language requirements for legal citizenship depend in their emancipatory and disciplinary dimension on the context of the educational capacities of persons addressed and the opportunities of courses (Lister et al. 2007: 11).

Therefore, the authors consider citizenship as a lived experience and believe that citizenship may be experienced by people within the same country differently, depending on factors such as age, class, ethnicity, religion, gender, sexuality and (dis)ability (cf. Lister et al. 2007: 2). They take 'regime' as a current, useful notion to compare dominant institutional patterns and policy logics of social welfare across national borders in Europe to show how different elements of citizenship are interconnected with it:

> "The lived experience of gendered citizenship in any particular country is heavily influenced by the dominant gender regime as well as by the nature of the welfare and care regimes, which govern social citizenship – the nexus of rights and responsibilities underpinning individuals' welfare, broadly understood – in particular" (Lister et al. 2007: 3).

Because these institutional patterns and policy logics define the way persons are enabled or obliged as citizens within certain national borders, the authors speak of various forms of regime, welfare, care, gender, citizenship and migration, which constitute formal citizenship (cf. Lister et al. 2007: 4).

With this diversification and contextualization of citizenship, the authors strive for a theoretical positioning within and beyond the feminist criticism of traditional philosophical approaches on citizenship as liberalism and communitarianism. In criticizing the 'false universalism' of both of these traditional approaches for perpetuating inequalities, they conceptualize citizenship as something that is not static but develops in response to individual and collective practises of persons through political and civil society associations (Lister et al. 2007: 10). Furthermore, they relate the critique on the gendered domestic division of labour and the status accorded to unpaid care work to the rights and responsibilities of citizenship. Although they consider that global care dynamics point to the notion of a global or cosmopolitan citizenship, on the conceptual level the authors do not follow this path any further (Lister et al. 2007: 8, 173).[12]

On the empirical level, however, the study provides for an in-depth analysis into the policies of the European Union that frame citizenship within and at its borders. Through the *Charter of Fundamental Rights,* which was adopted in 2000, the European Commission encouraged citizenship practice in informal cross-EU networks. This is an interesting move, since the legislation concerning the legal requirements for acquiring citizenship is still a rather national affair and varies widely throughout the countries of the EU. The length of residency necessary to gain nationality, for example, varies from five to ten years and language requirements do not exist everywhere (Lister et al. 2007: 81-84). But the logic and dynamics of migration, multiculturalism and gender also differ. Recent debates about forced and arranged marriages and the headscarf, or hijab, and the divergent 'solutions' in national policies,

12 For a discussion of cosmopolitanism see Mouffe (2005) and Nagl-Docekal (2005).

for example, bring into play contradictory attitudes about the relation between European norms of modernity and risks and rights of cultural and religious diversity as well as individual rights to express one's uniqueness or anti-normative resistance (Lister et al. 2007: 90-100). The authors show that cultural practices and their meaning are always subject to change within local and national contexts. Moreover, although migrant women live under different pressures, young women often successfully navigate between majority norms and their own family culture, between claims of gender equality and rights to cultural respect:

> "On the whole, European states' reaction has been to revert to a model of integration based on greater assimilation into the nation state and its cultural 'traditions' and less to an embrace of a multicultural, post-nationalist society [...]. However, even this shift is not quite so determined because, at the same time, the very development of supranational governance sets in motion a notion of citizenship that exists beyond the nation state, even though it is still territorialised within the walls of 'Fortress Europe'." (Lister et al. 2007: 90)

I agree with the authors that it is precisely this tension and the emerging fluid space between overdetermined national ideas of citizenship and envisioned transnational one's, whether inside or outside the 'Fortress Europe', which seems to provide for – although precarious – chances for new democratic practices of citizenship. Yet, as I will show with the following example from Slovenia, normative ideas of homogeneous European citizens combined with a lack of a positive attitude towards alterity can hinder those who are considered not to match the norm, to make use of this emerging fluid space and participate in public discourses.

The concept of 'lived citizenship' (Lister 2007) not only allows us to discuss unequal access to social rights and normative barriers to the experience of citizenship within one country and between different states in the EU. It also allows us to discuss the ambivalences and tensions of young women and men stretching from belonging to the Slovenian nation to understanding themselves as European citizens. Along these lines, Daniela Gronold aims to trace cultural inscriptions within citizenship requirements:

> "Since European nation states mainly base their imagination of identity on homogeneity, newcomers who do not fit into the 'compulsory normality' of a state have trouble obtaining citizenship." (Gronold 2008: 38)

At the same time, the European citizen is constructed not as a diverse subject with manifold cultural affiliations and various political belongings, but around so fluid but powerful values as the secular, modern, progressive, democratic and capitalist. Therefore, the self-perception of people from the new member-states is deeply influenced by these values. As a consequence, new exclusions arise and old ones are hardened in Slovenia, as Gronold delineates:

> "The interviews show how the feelings of belonging to Europe support the idea that a 'normal' Slovenian citizen is Christian, non-Roma, non-Islamic and does not belong to the Balkans" (Gronold 2008: 51).

The author argues that exclusive public discourses and practices contribute to the expectation that marginalized people live with their identities in private and individual isolation and are thus prevented from political agency with other people, and thus from 'lived citizenship'.

In the struggle for a concept of citizenship in Europe, which values diversity and plurality, it seems important to not only ascertain diversity in EU policies and regulations. Beyond that, it seems necessary to contest the production of norms of homogeneity for ideal European citizens. Yet, to decipher norms is not easy because they are not necessarily explicit like laws or rules but instead operate within social practices as implicit standards of normalization (Butler 2004: 41).[13] Thus, to overcome homogeneity as the norm for European citizens would break radically with those strands of European knowledge production that related material differences of a person's body, wealth or income and cultural differences of a person's education, religion, nationality or tradition to a strictly hierarchical value system. This holds for both public discourse and practices, since we have seen that these dimensions are deeply interrelated. This might open paths to enable everyone to live a 'lived citizenship' in Europe. To celebrate the heterogeneity and plurality of genders and cultures, which have always been an empirical reality in Europe, not only on the same legal ground but also on the basis of an equal material condition, would realize those ideas on citizenship which have thus far been classified as utopian.[14]

13 As Butler describes it: "Norms may or may not be explicit, and when they operate as the normalizing principle in social practice, they usually remain implicit, difficult to read, discernible most clearly and dramatically in the effects that they produce" (Butler 2004: 41).

14 María do Mar Castro Varela investigates the utopias of female migrants as visions of critical members of a democratic society (Castro Varela 2007).

Globalization

At the beginning of the second wave of the international women's movement in the 1970s, the universality of gender hierarchies was a main ideological point of departure in the mobilization against gender hierarchies in Europe. In arguing against the discrimination of all women and in promoting slogans as 'we all have the same (hi)story', the idea was to unify – and strengthen – the worldwide struggle against the oppression of women in all countries. Since then, it has become evident that although 'man' signified and still signifies the privileged gender position in most of the social and political settings in this world, gender privileges and gender hierarchies differ widely throughout the globe.

In terms of areas and topics relevant for discrimination, of the relations of other aspects of social hierarchies, as well as of the dimension of difference constructed between genders, many different stories are told. For example, exclusive binary and dichotomous gender orders are much more fundamental in Christian and Muslim cultures than in cultures inspired by Buddhism, Hinduism and shamanism. Moreover, it has been shown that gender relations are not only interconnected with other social privileges, but that, most importantly, gender relations are interconnected internationally through manifold histories of class struggles, of colonization, de-colonization, post- and neo-colonialism. It is because of these connections that privileges and discrimination cannot be understood in absolute terms but need to be investigated as complex relations of power. Therefore, gender hierarchies are neither universal nor constructed independently from each other on a national, regional or local level, but are highly interrelated on a global dimension and in many ways. This becomes evident when we take into account the power relations intertwined in the situation of the 'cosmobile' care providers in Europe today.

Transnational interconnections of gender relations have been articulated from the start of the movement, but have nevertheless only very slowly begun to enter dominant debates of feminist research and politics in Europe. In this sense, it is important to study how gender relations are interrelated on a global dimension in order to understand the different stakes of various actors involved in the global "politics of reality" (Frye 1983: 155). Thus, I do not use the term 'the globalization of gender relations' to mean that the worldwide interconnection of gender relations is something rather new or that it has just recently come into existence. Instead, I wish to employ this term to refer to the power relations involved in epistemic politics as a necessary process that can make visible, with a widened epistemic horizon, those who are too many and too near to be ignored any longer. To explain this, it is helpful to point out the difference between the concept of universality and the concept of globalization. Universality is of crucial importance and epistemic power in philosophy. For example, to argue for human rights on a universal basis has been very important since the Enlightenment as a power of rationality within conflicts between governments of nation-states and their citizens as well as the citizens of other nation-states. Yet, the idea of the universal human has been criticized for its orientation on a masculinist and Eurocentric ideal of the citizen. Moreover, universality has also been criticized for ignoring the historical, social and cultural situatedness of empirical realities. To counter this criticism, others have argued that to focus on the rational plausibility of the universality of human rights as the basis of citizenship represents the very aim to overcome empirical power relations on a programmatic level.

Globalization, by contrast, emphasizes the empirical dimension of a worldwide process. The concept describes mostly recent developments since the late twentieth century, sometimes even by ignoring long-term interrelations of historical processes. Since globalization stands for economic, political, social, and cultural processes, it can shed light on power relations and can show the politics of location in different contexts. For example, the lack of respect for human rights concerning the working conditions in transnational enterprises in free trade zones can be described as part of the globalization process as well as the struggle for those rights. On the other side, migration processes into Europe have been described as the danger that Europe would become 'overloaded' by too many foreigners and therefore migration ought to be restricted.[15] Nevertheless, global changes bring power relations into play, as new actors emerge in Europe and struggle for survival, for sovereignty and citizenship, as we will see in what follows. In this context, it is interesting to have a closer look at the interconnection of gender arrangements in Europe and migration from many different parts of the world to Europe. As I showed in the previous section, on a formal level, citizenship is still a privilege to be

15 It is in this context that meanwhile 25 European states (not corresponding with the members of the EU) signed the so called Schengen agreement between 1985-2007, which created an area without inner borders but spot check controls and strengthened border controls with non-member states.

entitled by a sovereign government of a nation-state. But – as I will show in the next part – on the level of social rights and opportunities for participation in the social and political settings of a state, it is an issue debated and decided more and more on a local and transnational or global level.

Global care and erotic services

As Selma Sevenhuijsen pointed out:

> " [by] defining care as domestic labour feminists made it clear that necessary care could just as well be provided on a professional basis and that it was high time that men finally fulfilled their duties in that respect" (Sevenhuijsen 1998: 5).

Yet, many European gender arrangements are emancipatory to the point that even within affluent heterosexual couples, professional women take part in the labour market to a significant degree and an increasingly small number of women struggle even successfully for career options and compete with their male colleagues. But these gender arrangements are not emancipatory to the dimension that men, male members of households or male partners do not take a significant share in care work and household labour. As Joan Tronto illustrates this ambiguity:

> "The use of nannies allows upper middle-class women and men to benefit from feminist changes without having to surrender the privilege of the traditional patriarchal family. The hired household worker is an employee, but she is mainly treated as if she were a wife. Nannies can be imposed upon as if they were members of the family, and that imposition often proves to be abusive" (Tronto 2002: 47).

Hence, it is migrants from all over the world who provide important services for these 'emancipatory' gender arrangements in Europe, often without legalized political status. Migrants without a legal status are at double risk: First, they are vulnerable to exploitation in so far as they are not protected by any law or institution that would guarantee the respect of their personhood or fair wages. Second, they risk to be caught and sent back the long way they came – often from countries where survival has become difficult and economic prosperity almost impossible, precisely because of global economic and political power relations. On the other side, the global mobility of workers has become a fundamental column of the European welfare states. For the national economies in Europe, migrants have become an important reservoir of cheap labour that is easy to mobilize through private agencies in times of need. The mobility of workers serve not only to secure the new more or less emancipatory gender arrangements of the European middle class in providing crucial services of cleaning and caring in private households mostly as illegal employments (Lutz 2005; Rerrich 2006). Moreover, migrants also feed the social security systems of European welfare states through legal employment in sectors with unattractive working conditions and meagre wages.

According to the International Labour Organization (ILO), globally almost half of all labour migrants are women. Furthermore, 80 to 90 percent of all refugees worldwide are women and children. Women migrate because of political, economic, social, and individual reasons. The gendered nature of the labour market forces most women to work only in certain jobs: Many have to sell their bodies or their reproductive capacities. These jobs are rarely recognized as professions, are poorly paid and are not socially valued. Examples include work in the informal and unregulated sectors of prostitution, domestic work, the entertainment industry, and 'marriage' (Joo-Schauen/Najafi 2002: 224).

Jae-Soon Joo-Schauen and Behshid Najafis show that in this context the importance of counselling organizations is evident. They themselves belong to a working group against international sexual and racial exploitation in Germany (AGISRA). This agency supports victims of trafficking in women and sexual and racial discrimination as well as women who have been coerced into prostitution or marriage and they advise women in asylum matters. They consider their work as successful to the extent that public awareness of the problems has increased and more support is available for victims. Yet, they emphasize that there is still no guarantee for government protection and respect of human rights:

> "To offer economic, social and work opportunities for women in the countries of origin and legal migration opportunities to the destination countries still requires our continued effort. We demand the implementation of human rights standards for migrant women." (Joo-Schauen/Najafi 2002: 234)

In this context of the globalization of gender relations in Europe, the following questions arise: What does it mean that human rights standards are not implemented for migrant women? Since the UN human rights declaration of 1949 was signed by every European country, must not every European state guarantee them for every human being living on its territory? If this is not the case, on which basis are human rights promoted by the EU vis-à-vis countries like the People's Republic of China or the Russian Federation? Is it possible that migrants, especially from outside of the EU, can be treated and conceptualized so differently from European citizens that this problem does not occur as a contradiction to the consciousness of EU authorities? Who is responsible for shaping this political reality?

Did globalization processes, changes in European gender norms and special welfare policies make it possible for 'domestic' care workers to become as affordable on a regular basis to professional European women as 'exotic' sex workers to professional European men? Maria Rerrich quotes a Swiss study in which migrant women from different parts of the world combined cleaning, babysitting and sex work to make a living (Rerrich 2006: 18).[16] It is interesting to note that, for the affluent European 'emancipatory' gender arrangement, the identities and bodies of migrant women incorporate both of these seemingly contradictory and exclusionary terms: the domestic and the exotic. As household workers, migrant women are confronted with trustful housework and care relations and even confidential aspects of the private life of their mostly female employers. As sex workers, they are confronted with the bodies, fantasies and erotic projections about insight or virtuosity, subordination or servility by their mostly male clients. This points to the curious fact that the concept of the 'domestic' interrelates here in a special way with the concept of the 'exotic' within the construction of the migrant woman as a service provider in Europe.[17]

In her programmatic article *Precarius labor et stuporum corporis. Prekarität und die bezahlte sexuelle Dienstleistung,* Luzenir Caixeta discusses paid sexual service in the context of informal care work and household labour within changing work opportunities through globalization. She points to the

16 Krystyna Slany and Magdalena Slusarczyk note in their study on migration to Poland that about 40 percent of the women involved in street sex work were migrants (Slany/Slusarczyk 2008: 293-294).

17 It would be interesting to investigate how this connection of the 'domestic' and the 'exotic' relates to the no less precarious pair of notions of colonial times 'civilization' and 'wilderness' as metaphors for the erotic (Ernst 2009).

enormous capacity of the global sex-industry to generate incomes in the context of global migration and tourism:

> "The lifestyle in developed countries creates the need for leisure time and vacation, with a tendency towards locations of amusement and the exotic where exchanges on emotional and sexual levels are sought." (Caixeta 2005: 1)

She problematizes the fact that sex work is a highly stigmatized area of work, especially when one realizes that in Austria, for example, 90 percent of sex workers are migrants with a special visa for three months to work only as a 'show dancer' at a registered establishment of the sex-industry. As they come with a short-term vision, it is often difficult to mobilize them to struggle for better work conditions in Austria or Europe. However, Caixeta shows not only in her article but also with her long-term engagement in the organization MAIZ[18] that exactly this is possible. To understand this, we must take a closer look at the relation of human rights and citizenship.

Global gender democracy?

To explore the idea of a global gender democracy, I draw on the discussion at the international women's university (*ifu*) in Germany in the year 2000. In their programmatic article *Feminist and Migrant Networking in a Globalising World. Migration, Gender and Globalization*, Ilse Lenz and Helen Schwenken define globalization as

> "an ensemble of interlinked processes with possibly open results characterized by increasing economic, political, social and ecological interdependence, increasing global communication and mobility and increasing influence of new actors – especially supranational organisations, transnational enterprises and Civil Society Organisations (CSOs) or NGOs" (Lenz/Schwenken 2002: 157).

The authors identify steps made in the direction of a global gender democracy by the UN *Fourth World Conference on Women* in Beijing, People's Republic of China in 1995:

18 MAIZ is the abbreviation for: Autonomes Zentrum von und für Migrantinnen (Autonomous Centre of and for Migrant Women), www.maiz.at.

> "The Beijing conference resulted in a declaration which established basic norms for and steps to achieve gender equality in a process of international negotiating between governments and feminists from very different regions and approaches. Its goals of empowerment and autonomy including the body and sexuality, equality in work and society, development and structural change, peace and non-violence (including in personal relationships) and political participation, can be seen as a feminist formula for global gender democracy." (Lenz/Schwenken 2002: 161)

I would like to take the plea for global gender democracy seriously and ask whether the authors envision it as something to be realized independently within each state or whether they argue that global interconnections of gender relations would transcend the present national world order in the end. Lenz and Schwenken argue that to realize a global gender democracy, political agency is important not only on the level of the United Nations or the European Union, but also locally. As they understand globalization as processes of interplay in a multilevel system, they emphasize the importance and the opportunities of the feminist migrant organizing on a local level, for example through counselling agencies. There, the authors discuss to which dimension feminist migrant networks open up transnational spaces and build bridges between the local and the global level. They describe an example where it was through networking and political mobilization on the local, national and international level that feminist migrant groups in Germany succeeded in 1997 in changing a national law which regulates the amount of years obligatory for foreign spouses to be married to their German partner before obtaining independent legal status (the number of years was cut in half). As a result, the authors illustrate their understanding of state regulations "as the outcome of social negotiations by state governments, interest groups (as enterprises and other organizations) and social movements" (Lenz/Schwenken 2002: 162).

This means that for the mostly female migrants concerned they were able to participate in a political process envisioned as an ideal of democracy, some of them maybe even before they were granted formal citizenship, some of them maybe even illegalized. For the meaning of citizenship, this example shows that formal citizenship is neither a necessary precondition nor a guarantee for citizenship experienced and practised as lived citizenship in Lister's sense or as democratic citizenship in Mouffe's and Sevenhuijsen's sense. If one considers political participation to be the struggle for one's rights in public and the feeling of belonging to be a sense of community of peers and of acknowledgement by others as a being worth being, then it seems that political participation is not limited to formal citizens.

But the authors also show difficulties on the way to global gender democracy. When migrant and women's groups aimed to lobby for a more comprehensive understanding of discrimination related to gender and race at the UN *World Conference against Racism, Racial Discrimination and Related Intolerance* in Durban, South Africa in 2001 by including undocumented migrants in the final documents in order to improve the situation of refugee and migrant women, it was strongly opposed by most migrant receiving countries. In my opinion, this shows that although feminist migrant organizations get the opportunity to raise their voice on the global level of democratic representation at the United Nations Conferences (in contrast to national institutions), power relations seem to still be played out in rather traditional ways. This means that the privileges of the ones are closely related to the discrimination of the others.

Conclusion

This exploration on the different dimensions of citizenship and human rights in the context of the globalization of gender relations leads to the following conclusions. Formal citizenship of a nation-state, especially of one of the countries pertaining to the European Union, is still an important goal to struggle for because it promises legal protection from violence and exploitation and access to many life sustaining benefits. Sometimes it even seems to be a precondition for the protection against human rights violations. This is a problem since the UN human rights declaration considers every human being – with or without citizenship of a country – worth respecting and protecting. This is a crucial point because, within the globalization of gender relations, migrants from all over the world come to Europe, some by personal choice and in hopes of a better life, some driven by wars and economic catastrophes, some under the personal pressure of their families or even by direct coercion. They often come on precarious journeys. Since the legal roads to migration are becoming more and more narrow or even being closed off by EU authorities, many migrants are illegalized once they reach the Schengen area. Migrants, especially women from throughout the world, provide crucial services in the informal economic sectors of care and erotic services. In the socio-political and psychological dimension, they sustain the fragile 'emancipatory' gender arrangements in Europe. In the economic dimension, they provide cheap labour in the context of the privatization of health and care services within the restructuring of the European welfare system.

On the normative level, however, this situation leads to enormous problems since the self-conception of Europe as a human rights advocate is deeply undermined, if at the core of its socio-political and economic system, persons who fulfil important intimate demands for domestic and exotic services for European citizens are not safe from human rights violations.

The examples and theoretical explorations of this paper, however, point to an interesting shift in the meaning of citizenship and the protagonists of this new meaning: It has become evident that beyond formal rights and duties citizenship is something that is lived, experienced and practised in public by courageous individuals who have the social capacity to organize themselves with peers and argue for their rights and freedom within and beyond national borders and thereby act towards a global gender democracy. Does this mean that the protagonists of the global gender democracy are the migrants, these mostly female care providers from all over the world? This question certainly requires further investigation. But to understand citizenship as a democratic practice, it is important to realize that we can learn from empirical realities where citizenship is practised through networking and by overcoming the local, national and transnational barriers installed in favour of an idea of European homogeneity. This democratic citizenship can be practised – and lived – beyond formalized institutional practises (as voting) and traditional institutions of power (as political parties) which might be intertwined too tightly with the interests of global financial markets, which benefit only a few.

In this way, we can see that it is possible to overcome the normative aspect of citizenship in Europe, which forces people to practise their citizenship along prescriptions of state authorities. Since democratic citizenship cannot be all about the obedience of norms and laws and rules in favour of those in power. Rather, it is in processes where hegemonic power structures are questioned and contested in order to overcome relations of oppression and domination that citizenship unfolds its democratic dimension. This means that at the core of the idea and practise of democratic citizenship the possibility exists that the public and the state are shaped by every person living on its territory in a creative and self-conscious way with equal rights and equal access but infinite alterity. Therefore, citizenship theory needs to reflect the empirical context of the globalization of gender relations in order to encourage and empower everyone to participate in discussions about how to shape global reality, not only those who are affluent enough to have wives at home and service personnel – like in Greek antiquity.

Bibliography

Blättler, Sidonia (1995): *Der Pöbel, die Frauen etc.. Die Massen in der politischen Philosophie des 19. Jahrhunderts.* Berlin: Akademie Verlag

Butler, Judith (2004): "Gender Regulations." In: Butler, Judith: *Undoing Gender.* New York, London: Routledge, 40-56

Caixeta, Luzenir (2005): "Precarius labor et stuprum corporis. Prekarität und die bezahlte sexuelle Dienstleistung." In: IG Kultur Österreich (ed.): *Kulturrisse* (2), http://igkultur.at/igkultur/kulturrisse/1114329221/11145229 28 (05/02/2009)

Castro Varela, María do Mar (2007): *Unzeitgemäße Utopien. Migrantinnen zwischen Selbsterfindung und gelehrter Hoffnung.* Bielefeld: transcript

Connell, Robert W. (2002): "The Globalization of Gender Relations and the Struggle for Gender Democracy." In: Breitenbach, Eva/ Bürmann, Ilse/ Liebsch, Katharina/ Mansfeld, Cornelia/ Micus-Loos, Christiane (eds.): *Geschlechterforschung als Kritik. Zum 60. Geburtstag von Carol Hagemann-White.* Bielefeld: Kleine, 87-98

Ernst, Waltraud (2009): "Metapher und Materie? Zur Wissenschaftsgeschichte des erotischen Körpers." In: Bidwell-Steiner, Marlen/ Zangl, Veronika (eds.): *Körperkonstruktionen und Geschlechtermetaphern. Zum Zusammenhang von Rhetorik und Embodiment.* Innsbruck, Wien, Bozen: StudienVerlag, 45-56

Ernst, Waltraud (ed.) (2005): *Leben und Wirtschaften – Geschlechterkonstruktionen durch Arbeit.* Berlin, Hamburg, London, Münster, Wien, Zürich: Lit

Finotelli, Claudia (2008): "Migration Policy between Restrictive Purposes and Structural Demand: The Case of the Domestic Sector in Germany and in Italy." In: Metz-Göckel, Sigrid/ Morokvasic, Mirjana/ Münst, A. Senganata (eds.): *Migration and Mobility in an Enlarged Europe. A Gender Perspective.* Opladen, Farmington Hills: Barbara Budrich, 52-78

Frye, Marilyn (1983): *The Politics of Reality: Essays in Feminist Theory.* Freedom: The Crossing Press

Gronold, Daniela (2008): "A European Matter: Examples of 'Lived Citizenship' in the Slovenian Nation State." In: Oleksy, Elzbieta H./ Petö, Andrea/ Waaldijk, Berteke (eds.): *Gender and Citizenship in a Multicultural Context.* Frankfurt/ M., Berlin, Bern, Bruxelles, New York, Oxford, Wien, Leipzig: Peter Lang, 37-53

Joo-Schauen, Jae-Soon/ Najafi, Behshid (2002): "Support, Lobbying and Networking in the Context of Trafficking in Women." In: Lenz, Ilse/ Lutz, Helma/ Morokvasic-Müller, Mirjana/ Schöning-Kalender, Claudia/ Schwenken, Helen (eds.): *Crossing Borders and Shifting Boundaries. Vol. II: Gender, Identities and Networks. International Women's University 2000.* Opladen: Leske + Budrich, 223-235

Küster, Sybille (2007): "Staatsangehörigkeit in Deutschland: Historische Aspekte der Nationalisierung und Ethnisierung von 'Fremdheit'." In: Klinger, Cornelia/ Knapp, Gudrun-Axeli/ Sauer, Birgit (eds.): *Achsen der Ungleichheit. Zum Verhältnis von Klasse, Geschlecht und Ethnizität.* Frankfurt/ M., New York: Campus, 193-209

Lenz, Ilse/Schwenken, Helen (2000): "Feminist and Migrant Networking in a Globalising World. Migration, Gender and Globalization." In: Lenz, Ilse/ Lutz, Helma/ Morokvasic-Müller, Mirjana/ Schöning-Kalender, Claudia/ Schwenken, Helen (eds.): *Crossing Borders and Shifting Boundaries. Vol. II: Gender, Identities and Networks. International Women's University 2000.* Opladen: Leske + Budrich, 147-178

Lister, Ruth (2007): "Inclusive Citizenship: Realizing the Potential." *Citizenship Studies* 11 (1), 49-61

Lister, Ruth/Williams, Fiona/ Anttonen, Anneli/ Bussemaker, Jet/ Gerhard, Ute/ Heinen, Jacqueline/ Johansson, Stina/ Leira, Arnlaug/ Siim, Birte/ Tobío, Constanza/ Gavanas, Anna (2007): *Gendering Citizenship in Western Europe. New Challenges for Citizenship Research in a Cross-National Context.* Bristol: The Policy Press

Lutz, Helma (2005): "Geschlecht, Migration und Qualifikation. Neue oder alte Geschlechterordnung in der globalisierten Gesellschaft?" In: Ernst, Waltraud (ed.): *Leben und Wirtschaften – Geschlechterkonstruktionen durch Arbeit.* Berlin, Hamburg, London, Münster, Wien, Zürich: Lit, 110-123

Lutz, Helma (2006): "Leben in der Twilightzone. Migration, Transnationalität und Geschlecht im Privathaushalt." In: Ernst, Waltraud/ Bohle, Ulrike (eds.): *Transformationen von Geschlechterordnungen in Wissenschaft und anderen sozialen Institutionen.* (Internationale Frauen- und Genderforschung in Niedersachsen, Teilbd. 2), Berlin, Hamburg, London, Münster, Wien, Zürich: Lit, 19-30

Metz-Göckel, Sigrid/ Morokvasic, Mirjana/ Münst, A. Senganata (eds.) (2008): *Migration and Mobility in an Enlarged Europe. A Gender Perspective.* Opladen, Farmington Hills: Barbara Budrich

Möhle, Marion (2005): "Die 'aktivierte' Frau: Hartz und 'neue' Subjektkonstitutionen." In: Ernst, Waltraud (ed.): *Leben und Wirtschaften – Geschlechterkonstruktionen durch Arbeit.* Berlin, Hamburg, London, Münster, Wien, Zürich: Lit, 65-77

Mouffe, Chantal (1993): "Democratic Citizenship and the Political Community." In: Mouffe, Chantal: *The Return of the Political.* London: Verso, 60-73

Mouffe, Chantal (2005): "Eine kosmopolitische oder eine multipolare Weltordnung?" In: *Deutsche Zeitschrift für Philosophie* 53 (1), 69-82

Nagl-Docekal, Herta (2004): "For a Nonessentialist Politics." In: Nagl-Docekal, Herta: *Feminist Philosophy.* Boulder, CO: Westview, 133-170

Nagl-Docekal, Herta (2005): "'Kosmopolitismus' – Einleitung zum Heftschwerpunkt." In: *Deutsche Zeitschrift für Philosophie* 53 (1), 46-48

Oleksy, Elzbieta H./ Petö, Andrea/ Waaldijk, Berteke (eds.) (2008): *Gender and Citizenship in a Multicultural Context.* Frankfurt/ M., Berlin, Bern, Bruxelles, New York, Oxford, Wien, Leipzig: Peter Lang

Rerrich, Maria S. (2006): *Die ganze Welt zu Hause. Cosmobile Putzfrauen in privaten Haushalten.* Hamburg: Hamburger Edition

Sevenhuijsen, Selma (1998): *Citizenship and the Ethics of Care. Feminist Considerations on Justice, Morality and Politics.* London, New York: Routledge

Slany, Krystyna/ Slusarczyk, Magdalena (2008): "Immigrants in Poland: Legal and Socio-Demographic Situation." In: Metz-Göckel, Sigrid/ Morokvasic, Mirjana/ Münst, A. Senganata (eds.): *Migration and Mobility in an Enlarged Europe. A Gender Perspective.* Opladen, Farmington Hills: Barbara Budrich, 281-301

Spelman, Elisabeth V. (1989): *Inessential Woman. Problems of Exclusion in Feminist Thought.* Boston: Beacon

Transnational Newsletter 2008: *CROSSING BORDERS. Movements and*

Struggles of Migration 6, www.noborder.org/crossing_borders/index.php (05.02.2009)

Tronto, Joan C. (2002): "The 'Nanny' Question in Feminism." In: *Hypatia. A Journal of Feminist Philosophy* 17 (2), 34-51

Tronto, Joan C. (1993): *Moral Boundaries. A Political Argument for an Ethics of Care*. London, New York: Routledge

Yuval-Davis, Nira/ Werbner, Pnina (1999): "Introduction: Women and the New Discourse of Citizenship." In: Yuval-Davis, Nira/ Werbner, Pnina (eds.): *Women, Citizenship and Difference*. London, New York: Zed Book, 1-38

The Authors

Nina Berven, born in 1972, received her doctor polit degree in comparative politics from the University of Bergen (Norway). Currently, she is employed as post-doctoral research fellow at the Department of Comparative Politics at the University of Bergen. Her major research interests are welfare and family policy within Europe and the United States, gender, voluntary organizations, power and democracy. Her dissertation is entitled *National Politics and Cross-National Ideas. Welfare, Work and Legitimacy in the United States and Norway*, Bergen: University of Bergen 2004.

Mary Daly is a professor of sociology at the School of Sociology and Social Policy at Queen's University Belfast (United Kingdom). She has published on such issues as poverty, welfare, gender, family and labour market. Much of her work is comparative, in a European and international context. She is especially interested in matters of the family and how different European countries relate to families. Among her recent books are *Care Work: The Quest for Security*, Geneva: ILO 2001, and *Gender and the Welfare State: Care, Work and Welfare in Europe and the USA*, Cambridge: Polity Press 2003 (with Katherine Rake).

Waltraud Ernst, Dr. phil., M.A., is the managing director of the Centre for Interdisciplinary Women's and Gender Studies (ZIF) at the HAWK University of Applied Sciences and Arts Hildesheim/Holzminden/Göttingen and the University of Hildesheim (Germany). She studied philosophy and comparative literature in Tübingen, Bielefeld, Bordeaux and Vienna. Since 1996, she has been a lecturer in feminist philosophy and gender studies. From 2001 to 2003, she was a research fellow of the Austrian Science Fund at the Department of Philosophy, University of Vienna (Austria). Main publication: *Diskurspiratinnen. Wie feministische Erkenntnisprozesse die Wirklichkeit verändern*, Vienna: Milena 1999. Web: www.hawk-hhg.de/zif/8_149.php.

Jutta Hartmann, Vertr.-Prof. Dr., works in the field of education for social work in the Faculty of Social Work and Health at the HAWK University of Applied Sciences and Art Hildesheim (Germany). She leads the Further Education group in the Federal Association of Professional Victim Support Organizations in Germany ('ado' Task Force on Victim Support). Between 2002 and 2005, she was guest professor at the Institute for Educational Science at the University of Innsbruck (Austria). She is a visiting lecturer in the field of Diversity Studies at the University of Vienna and at the Centre for Postgraduate Studies in Social Work Berlin.

Heike Kahlert, Dr. rer. soc., is a sociologist and currently project leader at the Institute of Sociology and Demography, University of Rostock (Germany). From 2008 to 2009, she was a Maria-Goeppert-Mayer guest professor for international women's and gender studies at the Centre for Interdisciplinary Women's and Gender Studies, HAWK University of Applied Sciences and Arts Hildesheim/Holzminden/Göttingen and University of Hildesheim (Germany). Her main research topics are transformation of knowledge in modernity, gender relations and social change in welfare states, sociology of education, change management in public-profit-organizations from a perspective of gender and diversity. Web: www.wiwi.uni-rostock.de/soziologie/makrosoziologie/kahlert/.

Ute Karl is an assistant professor of social pedagogy at the Institute for Social and Organizational Pedagogy, University of Hildesheim (Germany). She has published *Zwischen/Räume. Eine empirisch-bildungstheoretische Studie zur ästhetischen und psychosozialen Praxis des Altentheaters*, Berlin, Hamburg, London, Münster, Wien, Zürich: Lit 2005, *Lebensalter und Soziale Arbeit. Ältere und alte Menschen*, Baltmannsweiler: Schneider 2008 (edited with Kirsten Aner), *"Agency, Gouvernementalität und Soziale Arbeit"*, in: Hans Günther Homfeldt, Wolfgang Schröer and Cornelia Schweppe (eds.): *Vom Adressaten zum Akteur. Soziale Arbeit und Agency*, Leverkusen-Opladen & Farmington Hills: Barbara Budrich 2008, *"Metaphern as Traces of Discourses in Biographical Texts"*, in: Forum: Qualitative Social Research, 8 (1), Art. 3, http://nbn-resolving.de/urn:nbn:de:0114-fqs070139, 2006.

Gabriele Michalitsch, a political scientist and economist, is currently lecturer at Vienna University and at Vienna University of Economics and Business Administration (Austria). Over the past years, she was visiting professor at Corvinus University Budapest (Hungary), Graz University (Austria), and Yeditepe University Istanbul (Turkey). From 2002 to 2005, she was chair of the Council of Europe's group of experts on gender budgeting. Her main research topics are neoliberalism, political economy, feminist economics.

Andrea Petö, Prof. Dr. habil., is an associate professor at the Department of Gender Studies at the Central European University Budapest (Hungary), where she instructs courses on the social and cultural history of Europe. Her books include *Women in Hungarian Politics 1945-1951*, New York: Columbia University Press/East European Monographs 2003, and *Geschlecht, Politik und Stalinismus in Ungarn. Eine Biographie von Júlia Rajk*. Studien zur Geschichte Ungarns, Bd. 12, Herne: Gabriele Schäfer Verlag 2007. At present, she is working on gendered memory of WWII and political extremisms.

Kirsten Scheiwe is a professor of law at the Faculty of Social and Pedagogical Sciences, University of Hildesheim (Germany). She works mainly in the areas of family law, social law and comparative law and investigates law in a social context from the perspectives of interdisciplinary and comparative legal analysis and gender studies. Her latest publications include *Aktuelle Rechtsfragen der Familienpolitik aus vergleichender Sicht*, Baden-Baden: Nomos 2008 (with Margarete Schuler-Harms) *[Current Legal Problems of Family Policy from a Comparative Perspective]* and *Childcare and Preschool Development in Europe – Institutional perspectives*, London: Palgrave Macmillan 2009 (edited with Harry Willekens).

Mieke Verloo is a professor of comparative politics and inequality issues at Radboud University Nijmegen (the Netherlands) and scientific director of the *QUING* project (www.quing.eu) at the IWM, Institute for Human Sciences, Vienna (Austria). She works primarily on political dynamics of gender and other inequalities, but is also active in developing gender and equality policy, consultancy and training for policy makers. Together with Emanuela Lombardo and Petra Meier, she co-edited *The Discursive Politics of Gender Equality. Stretching, Bending and Policymaking*, Abingdon, Oxon, New York: Routledge 2009.